The Women's Annual
Number 4
1983 - 1984

G. K. Hall

WOMEN'S STUDIES

Publications

Barbara Haber
Editor

The Women's Annual
Number 4
1983-1984

Edited by Sarah M. Pritchard

G. K. HALL & CO. • BOSTON, MASSACHUSETTS

Library of Congress has cataloged this serial publication as follows:

The Women's annual, ... the year in review. — 1980-
   Boston: G.K. Hall & Co.,

   (Reference publication in women's studies)

   Annual
   Editor: Barbara Haber.
   ISSN 0276-7988 = The Women's annual, the year in review.

   ISBN 0-8161-8703-7
   ISBN 0-8161-8725-8   (pbk.)

   1.   Feminism—United States—Yearbooks.   I.   Haber,
Barbara.   II.   G.K. Hall & Company.   III.   Series.
HQ1402.W65   305.4'2'0973   82-641994
                                            AACR 2   MARC-S

This publication is printed on permanent/durable acid-free paper
MANUFACTURED IN THE UNITED STATES OF AMERICA

Contents

Introduction   1
Sarah M. Pritchard

Education   9
Susan S. Klein

Health   31
Adriane J. Fugh-Berman

Humanities Scholarship   60
Hilda L. Smith

International Issues   81
Mary O'Callaghan

Lesbians   107
Judith Schwarz

Mass Media and
Communications   124
Helen R. Wheeler

Politics and Law   145
Cynthia E. Harrison

Psychology   167
Sarah B. Watstein

Women of Color in the United
States   187
Jacquelyn Marie and Elaine Bell Kaplan

Work   202
Sara E. Rix and Anne J. Stone

CONTENTS

Appendix: Selected Bibliography of
Feminist Theory and General Social
Studies   221
Sarah M. Pritchard

Contributors   226

Index   229

Introduction

Despite impressions left by the media and by changes in government policy, the women's movement is growing and flourishing on many fronts. Scholarship, activism, and community programs reflect the continuing influence of feminist ideas. Once again, the contributors to *The Women's Annual* have tried to summarize these events and publications in a concise format, showing the trends in and reviewing the literature of their respective fields. As in past editions, we have included chapters on subjects basic to women's studies and issues: education, politics, psychology, work, health, literary and historical scholarship, and the experiences of women of color in the United States. To this core material, we have added three areas not previously treated in separate chapters: lesbians, international issues, and mass media and communications. This year's edition should be viewed as part of a continuing series, each volume with unique emphases and resources that together constitute a valuable whole.

The very nature of feminist thought cuts across traditional boundaries both in scholarship and in social institutions. Thus, the works treated in the separate chapters may have relevance to several topics. This year, we see a number of recurring issues tying the essays together. First is the concept of power, which has become a locus for insight into broad areas of political and social philosophy as well as into specific situations faced by women in their homes, schools, and workplaces. Questions about who has power and how it is used underlie all the essays, but especially those on lesbians and women of color, mass media, politics, international issues, and health. Control of our own sexuality and access to jobs and education are other struggles for power. "Strategies for Empowerment," appropriately, is the theme of the Second International Interdisciplinary Congress on Women in 1984.

Second, the impact of science and technology on our lives and the feminist critique of scientific thought are increasingly important. Home computers swept into the mass market in 1983; will young girls grow up with equal knowledge of them? As medical science develops new surgical techniques, drugs, and devices, will women be able to use them in a positive, healthful way? Women are monitoring the introduction of technology into the workplace, the media, and other countries.

Lastly, the particular demographics of our generation mandate awareness of the older woman in society. The health, educational, and psychological needs of older women are reviewed here, as is the almost invisible presence of the older lesbian. Employment practices and economic policies are also important in maintaining the vital place of older Americans.

The use of technology, the acquisition of power in institutions, and the impact of population changes are all fundamentally conditioned by government. Legislative proposals, cuts in government funding, and policy decisions are another strong thread in this year's *Annual*. These political maneuvers ultimately affect not only those of us in the United States but those in countries that receive American aid or are otherwise affected by our activities.

Power, science, aging, and political structures are some of the ideas that link these essays and that are the subject of radical theorizing. To indicate the scope of such work done over the past year, we have also appended an annotated bibliography on feminist theory and general social studies. In the absence of a chapter on feminist theory or sociology, the appendix provides an overview of major books in political theory, the philosophy of science, social institutions, and related areas.

The Women's Annual is a mode of communication, bringing together readers, writers, and resources. This year, Helen Wheeler looks at major segments of the mass media and communications enterprises, and does not find much for feminists to praise. Although partially overlapping with "Popular Culture" chapters in previous *Annuals*, Wheeler's essay explores crucial new concerns in computer use, librarianship, and access to the publishing industry. Reviewing trends in film, newspapers, the television industry, the arts, and advertising, she sees the continuing presence of negative stereotypes; the demise of many independent feminist filmmakers, publishers, and the like often leaves these false images unchallenged.

Not only are media and communications the source of certain images of women, but these fields also employ women workers. Wheeler notes the difficulties of women journalists, broadcasters, and librarians in gaining equal status. Just when we think we are making inroads, new challenges arise. Will cable television provide greater opportunities for feminist programming? Should feminists accept jobs and money from organizations like the Playboy Foundation? The proliferation of "video porn" creates another arena for confrontation and debate. Technology is exciting and offers the promise of increased communication and new ways to learn, but if women do not have access to and control of it, they will be excluded from yet another domain of society. Some new women-centered ventures may lead to future improvements but have yet to have a large-scale impact. Power, again, heightened by scientific developments, is at the heart of it: who owns the channels of distribution, who gets the money to support research, who determines what is acceptable?

As the mass media determine what we see and hear, so then visibility (in the broadest sense) becomes a central problem for groups that have traditionally been on the margins of society: lesbians, women of color, "differently abled" women (women who have physical, mental or developmental handicaps), poor women. The women's movement itself has been galvanized by the critiques originating among these groups, and the recognition of the diversity of women has changed the agenda for research and action.

The amount of scholarship, creative writing, group activism, artwork, and other endeavors from American lesbians over the past decade is testimony to the sense of community and validation currently experienced. Judith Schwarz prepares the *Annual*'s first review of this material, focusing on 1983 within the context of previous years. Too often, as Schwarz notes, lesbians have been treated only as a subset of some other category and not accorded their own status. Yet, lesbians have given the women's movement some of its most important insights and theories, especially in the politics of sexuality and oppression.

Still struggling against invisibility, lesbians have forged a chain of communication connecting local groups, publishers, and national organizations. From her position at the Lesbian Herstory Archives in New York, Schwarz analyzes the efforts toward self-definition among lesbians. Notions of identity must now integrate race, ethnicity, and class status into the lesbian community. The classic feminist question of the nature and manifestation of sexuality took a new twist in 1983 over the acceptability of such practices as lesbian sadomasochism, butch-fem roles, and the use of violent erotic imagery. Schwarz notes the ongoing fight that has brought forth publications, demonstrations, and affinity groups on several sides of the issue.

Schwarz follows lesbian lives through their many passages: young lesbians, lesbian mothers, aging lesbians. She sees more attention to the special health needs of lesbians and not enough to the violent attacks upon "out" women. Although such civil rights as protection from job and housing discrimination were some of the first areas of protest years ago, Schwarz reminds us that lesbians still face an uphill battle for a safe and equitable life. Her essay concludes with a tantalizing selection of recent lesbian fiction, poetry, and history.

In its discussion of race, class, and ethnicity within the lesbian community, Schwarz's essay fits neatly into the theme of storytelling which frames the chapter on women of color by Jacquelyn Marie and Elaine Bell Kaplan. Women of color are producing their own stories, through fact and fiction, that reveal new truths and destroy old myths. Stereotypes of passivity and ignorance and the very real obstacles of money, time, and education have too often prevented women of color from raising their voices. Marie and Kaplan show how film and literature are leading to greater power and visibility for black, Asian, Chicana, and Native American women. The fragility of these gains is underlined by recent setbacks: cuts in government funding for social services and employment programs and attacks on the Civil Rights Commission.

Again, as with lesbians and with women in general, "outsider" status has led women of color to form perceptive critical analyses. Kaplan and Marie sketch the important scholarly issues raised by women of color and the conflict about whether to ally primarily with feminist studies or with the struggles of their own ethnic or racial groups. In furthering this debate for all of us, women of color are establishing valuable role models for younger women in their communities and are pushing white, middle-class women to reevaluate their programs. Marie and Kaplan trace an exciting trend in both activism and writing and affirm our need to hear more stories from women of color.

To write about the psychology of women has too often meant to write about the illnesses, neuroses, and maladaptation of women. Sarah Watstein writes about what is good in psychology, what it has helped us learn about our identities, about the development of sex roles, and about our relationships with other people. Combining research with popular works, technical studies with film and literature, Watstein surveys recent progress and controversies over the acquisition of sex roles, the expression of sexuality, human bonding, and therapeutic approaches for problems faced by women.

There have been many changes in theories of the origin of and attitudes toward sex roles. Watstein notes the implications of this work for our understanding of such diverse areas as education psychology and sexual preference. Closely related to this are human patterns of bonding—in pairs, families, and groups. Popular plays and movies show us the variety and centrality of human bonds in our culture. As sex roles and family groups bring women into conflict with their surroundings, special needs arise for treating eating disorders, depression, and domestic violence.

Watstein summarizes recent feminist critiques of psychological theory and lauds the ability of Carol Gilligan to break through to a larger audience of practitioners and the general public. New journals and other professional activities signal the strong presence of women in psychology and continue the difficult methodological debate over how to integrate courses on the psychology of women into the curriculum.

The contribution of Carol Gilligan, *Ms.* magazine's Woman of the Year for 1983, is also seen by Susan Klein as one of the few positive steps for women and girls in education. Looking at the overall pattern of forward and backward steps over the past year, Klein reaches a rather pessimistic conclusion about the attainment of sex equity in the schools. Capped by the Supreme Court decision in early 1984 to accept the Reagan administration's very narrow interpretation of Title IX, 1983 was a year of cuts in funding, ideological attacks on education programs, and the appearance of six major reports on education in America which all ignored the problems of sex equity.

These negative trends were partially offset by winning the admission of girls to all-male schools and honor societies and by securing additional legislative support for math and science education. Klein presents the results of much new research in education, in itself a positive sign but not yet well-integrated into school practice. For example, studies are demonstrating the "chilly climate" for girls in the classroom and the differences in abilities in certain curricular areas. Girls are apparently making less use of computer learning equipment than are boys, which may leave them with a handicap when seeking employment or advanced study. More knowledge is needed about education for older women, rural girls and women, disabled and minority women. And, as we might expect in a traditionally female-dominated profession, salary discrimination and occupational segregation remain a problem for women teachers and educational personnel.

This gap in wages and the persistence of unequal access to job categories is a tired refrain that we repeat again, however unwillingly. Sara Rix and Anne Stone look specifically at the characteristics of women in the labor force and how they have been affected by the "economic recovery," by government policies, and by the taxing demands of combining work and family responsibilities. Although they suspect that much of the progress made during 1983 may be only symbolic, Rix and Stone affirm the major victory of the comparable-worth decision in Washington State, perhaps still to be contested by the Reagan Justice Department.

Women continue to enter the labor force, and they may account for as much as two-thirds of its future growth; however, little is changing in the basic structures of American business and industry to accommodate them. Both blue-collar and executive women face serious practical and psychological barriers in meeting child care and other family needs, and may be unable to take advantage of career-enhancing moves. The myth that women really don't need to work dies slowly, and Stone and Rix have found few serious studies of the impact of recession and unemployment on women workers.

While the acknowledgement of an aging work force may improve the status of older women workers, progress has been slower for women in nontraditional occupations and in scientific and technical fields. Rix and Stone note the reopening of some job categories to women in the military, but it is too early to tell about the success of some other government job-training proposals.

The "gender gap" does not seem to have helped women make substantive gains in education and employment nor, as Cynthia Harrison reports, in other areas under the Reagan administration. Harrison's chapter on politics and law features an editorial cartoon that illustrates the trivialization and misunderstanding of women's issues within the current administration.

The prelude to an election year, 1983 was marked by one public opinion poll after another purporting to show degrees of difference between men and women voters. Harrison interprets the conflicting statistics, noting the impact of budget cuts, presidential appointments, and other policy decisions affecting women. Even Republican women within the administration have not been able to effect real change: two high-level Republican women were removed from the Civil Rights Commission, and Barbara Honegger made headlines with her statement of the Justice Department's hypocrisy in identifying sex discrimination in federal laws.

Harrison writes about the positive achievements for women through judicial action, ironically the one branch of government least susceptible to voter preferences. Court decisions favoring women were handed down in regard to pension equity, comparable worth, pregnancy benefits, and the right to abortion. Women also have some bipartisan support in Congress for legislative proposals packaged as the Women's Economic Equity Act. However, Democratic politics in the House of Representatives forced the reintroduced equal rights amendment to an unsuccessful vote under a move to suspend the rules. Will this change the strategy of women's groups during the coming year? The National Organization for Women threw its collective hat into the ring with an early, unprecedented endorsement of Walter Mondale for president and pushed in 1984 for a woman vice-presidential nominee.

Women in the United States cannot afford to view politics and the rights of women as only an internal matter. The growth of multinational corporations, the interdependency of nations for food and energy, and the proliferation of nuclear weapons can only be addressed in an international arena. *The Women's Annual*, in recognition of these concerns, has commissioned its first essay on women and international issues. Mary O'Callaghan writes movingly of the situation of women in Third World countries: their basic needs for food, water, and health care, and the often biased or inappropriate responses of development agencies related to technology, employment, and education.

Growing since the early 1970s, the amount of literature on the status of women in developing countries has soared since the enactment of the UN Decade for Women, 1975–85. Worldwide conferences in 1975 and 1980 sparked international debate and further work within individual countries and agencies, and the final conference to be held in Nairobi, Kenya, in 1985 promises the same. O'Callaghan reviews these and several conferences held in the United States on similar topics that, although they provoke much argument, bring women face to face to achieve common understanding.

Violations of human rights are legion, and few effective remedies exist. Both the UN and nongovernmental organizations are working to eliminate political torture and sexual slavery and to ensure protection for refugees, but international law is often inadequate to the task. To many women and men, the ultimate violation is the threat of nuclear war under which we all live. Women have a long history of involvement in the peace movement; O'Callaghan traces this from 19th century organizing to contemporary feminist protests at missile bases in the United States and Great Britain.

The health of women is a subject that brings together many of the themes already present in the *Annual:* control of our sexuality; the introduction of new technology; the special problems of older women, minority women, and women in Third World countries; and the employment of women in health care fields. In her systematic review of women's health issues, Adriane Fugh-Berman interweaves medicine, law, ethics, science, and feminist activism. She particularly notes the fast-moving frontier of new birth and conception technologies. The ability to save younger and younger fetuses raises a difficult conflict with the right of a woman to undergo an abortion. The backlash from the Supreme Court's decision upholding that right continues, with an overall conservative attitude toward sexuality demonstrated by the uproar over AIDS and the attempt to require parental notification when teenaged girls receive contraceptives.

Fugh-Berman summarizes recent research in contraceptives, occupational health, premenstrual syndrome, breast cancer, estrogen therapy, and other medical conditions primarily affecting women. She alerts us to a disturbing discovery, the onset of "precocious puberty" stimulated by the presence of hormones in the food supply; the health of young children is disregarded to protect the food industry in one region.

Thus, women need more power to insist on adequate health care and to educate ourselves about medical alternatives. Feminist health care providers who have tried to do this have been harassed and legally restrained by the medical establishment. Health issues provide a forum that can unite women of diverse beliefs and conditions; good health, which we often take for granted, is out of the reach of many women.

For some people, "women's studies" is synonymous with women's history. Although it is but one discipline in an immense multidimensional field of study, women's history has given us our past, given us our sense of accomplishment, and given us a tool for changing the modes of academic research. Like history, literature by women authors and about women characters has been an effective and seemingly nonthreatening means of introducing new ideas about women. "Seemingly," because in fact we are learning about hidden messages and subtexts in even the most proper and conventional stories.

History, literature, and philosophy are the focus of Hilda Smith's essay on scholarship in the humanities. The sheer volume of academic research in this domain overwhelms, and Smith has tried to identify those works that challenge the traditional structures of the discipline, as opposed to those that merely fit women into existing categories. She believes that literature scholars have not moved as far in this direction as historians, although she singles out several recent works reflecting new critical trends. Anthologies, studies of individual authors, and explications of particular motifs predominate in literary criticism.

In the field of history, we are still immersed in the wave of social history: the telling of women's private lives and the delineation of changes in marriage, childbearing, family and household patterns. The history of women's paid labor is bridging the private and the public. Studies of women in countries other than the United States tend to be broader, because less research has been done. Scanning recent historical journals, Smith wonders if we may be seeing the beginning of a move away from the concentration on social and domestic history.

Smith finds the most sophisticated conceptual work in a few collections of philosophical essays. It is here that scholars are breaking down the ways men have defined knowledge and existence, the very notions of spheres, of domination and hierarchy, of objectivity. The application of feminist critiques to philosophy may ultimately restructure all intellectual inquiry.

We have reviewed the status of women in 1983, showing limited accomplishments in employment, education, and politics, and perhaps even less in the mass media. New research and technology are helping improve our physical and mental health, but we must maintain control over these technologies and over our self-definition. In the realms of writing, scholarship, and international women's movements, we have seen a genuine increase in the number of new voices, the strengthening of the foundations we have built, and the integration of more women into our sociocultural networks.

Sarah M. Pritchard

Education

Susan Shurberg Klein

The events of 1983 related to women and girls in education may be likened to a game of "Mother May I?" in which the "children" are allowed to take only baby steps forward and backward, thus slowing their progress toward their goal: sex equity, or freedom from sex discrimination and sex stereotyping in education. On the federal level, most of the steps were backward. But thanks to active advocacy group work, many fair-minded jurists, legislators, and educators, and much productive research and development, a few forward steps were taken as well, and in many areas girls and women held their position. The greatest number of baby steps forward occurred in the areas of (1) increased knowledge about the subtle nature of sex-based inequities that are harmful to females, and (2) the identification and development of solutions to some of these inequities.

Despite the continued backward steps caused by the Reagan administration backlash described in the 1981 and 1982 *Women's Annual* education chapters (Kaufman 1982 and Speizer 1983), women and girls overall have held the line by exerting a great deal of affirmative effort. It is likely that many women's gains in educational attainment of the past decade will be maintained, although progress toward the goal of total sex equity in educational activities and outcomes may be delayed by adverse governmental actions.

Governmental Policies and Programs

Policies

The executive branch of the federal government was responsible for many backward steps because of its interpretation and enforcement of civil rights

9

laws. In June, the *Washington Post* reported, "President Reagan said today that the decline in American education is directly related to twenty years of court orders requiring schools to take the lead in correcting 'long-standing injustices in our society: racial segregation, sex discrimination, lack of opportunity for the handicapped' " (Atkins 1983). Another backward step occurred when the Justice Department reversed its earlier position and tried to weaken the coverage of Title IX of the Education Amendments of 1972, which prohibits discrimination on the basis of sex in education in programs or activities that receive federal financial assistance. In *Grove City* v. *Bell*, the administration argued that Title IX should be program specific and that, in this case, such specificity would limit its coverage to the activities of the student financial aid office, since the only federal financial assistance to Grove City College was for this purpose.

In addition to the attempt to narrow Title IX's scope, the administration worked to weaken it in other ways. It requested reductions in the budget and staff of the Office for Civil Rights (OCR) in the Department of Education, which is supposed to enforce laws such as Title IX. OCR did such a poor job of enforcing these laws that in March 1983 a federal court order, *WEAL/Adams* v. *Bell*, was issued to structure OCR's timely enforcement of Title IX and other civil rights statutes. The administration also failed to appeal a case, so that now in the eastern district of Virginia, OCR is barred from investigating complaints of sex discrimination in intercollegiate athletics at almost all colleges and universities (Kohn 1983). The U.S. Commission on Civil Rights has stated that "inadequate and unduly slow enforcement of Title IX has diminished its effectiveness and that most of the progress in decreasing sex discrimination in education can be attributed to voluntary compliance and monitoring efforts of individuals and organizations" (AAUW 1983, 2).

Fortunately, the U.S. House of Representatives and the courts mitigated some of these backward steps. On 16 November, the House of Representatives by a 414–8 vote passed a resolution stating that the intent of Congress has been that Title IX should maintain comprehensive coverage, so that gender discrimination should be eliminated in the entire institution delivering educational services, not just in specific programs or activities receiving direct federal money, as the Reagan administration had argued in *Grove City* (House reaffirms . . . 1983). A similar resolution is pending in the Senate. According to a national survey of prominent issues in the 1984 elections, these resolutions are congruent with public opinion because "68% of those polled felt that federal equal education laws—like Title IX—should apply to all students in a school, even in areas like athletics that do not receive direct federal funds" (Cusick and Martin-McCormick 1983, 1).

Another baby step forward in support of comprehensive Title IX coverage occurred 11 April in the Fifth Circuit Court of Appeals decision on the Iron Arrow all-male university honorary society case. This decision upheld the Title IX regulation covering nondiscrimination in honor societies and maintained that having such a society limited to male members would have "infected [the] entire academic mission of [the] university, thus rendering each and every federal program at [the] university necessarily discriminatory as [a] result of society's relationship to [the] university" (*Iron Arrow Honor Soc.* v. *Heckler*, 11 April 1983, 16006). However, this case was declared moot by the Supreme Court in November.

The Supreme Court heard arguments on the Title IX *Grove City College* case on 29 November (Greenhouse 1983) and announced its decision on 28 February 1984. Accepting the Reagan administration's narrow interpretation, the Court has now asked women to take a giant step backward in implementing Title IX.

The Reagan administration was thwarted in some of its other attempts to decrease federal protections against discrimination. The Supreme Court ruled in the *Bob Jones University* case that racial discrimination was contrary to public policy under the Internal Revenue Code and that racially discriminatory private schools were not eligible for federal tax exemptions (Lawyers' Committee 1983).

Several state governments have taken forward steps to prohibit sex discrimination in education. As of 1983 all states except Kansas, Missouri, North Dakota, South Carolina, and Tennessee had implemented some laws or policies to prohibit sex discrimination in education (Bailey and Smith 1982; Bailey 1983). Some of these are general laws such as state equal rights amendments, whereas others are more specific, such as state laws worded like the federal Title IX. Three states—California, Maine, and Nebraska— added such laws in 1982 and were developing regulations and implementation procedures during 1983. For example, although there were about thirty separate California laws relating to sex discrimination in education, the new California "Title IX" provides comprehensive legislation and even improves on the federal Title IX by clarifying such issues as the totality of the law's coverage in educational institutions (California passes . . . 1982). A similar comprehensive Title IX bill made headway in New York State during 1983.

Another step forward for sex equity in education came from the *Newberg et al.* v. *Board of Education et al.* court decision in Pennsylvania. Approximately twenty-five girls were admitted to Central High School in Philadelphia, which had previously admitted only academically talented males, thus marking the end of this public school's 147-year male-only tradition. The judge ruled that the separate education offered at the Philadelphia High School for Girls was not equal to that provided by Central High and "that the all male admissions policy violated the equal protection clause of the Fourteenth Amendment because the school district failed to show an important governmental objective in maintaining separate single-sex schools." He also concluded that the previous opposing "Vorchheimer court failed to consider the constitutionality of the admissions policy under the Pennsylvania ERA, which mandates a higher standard of review than that applied to sex discrimination cases under the federal Constitution" (Avner 1983, 2). The Philadelphia Board of Education voted not to appeal the Newberg ruling. However, an appeal was filed by current students and alumni of both schools and is presently pending in the Superior Court of Pennsylvania.

Continual forward and backward steps have occurred during congressional attempts to pass the federal Equal Rights Amendment, which would be a comprehensive way to help women in all publicly supported institutions. Like Title IX, ERA "would not tell schools what to do, but only that whatever they do, they must do fairly" (Sandler 1983a, 3). In some instances, the ERA might allow separate programs for girls or women, but only if they are designed to compensate for past discrimination for a limited period of time. Also, programs intended to address women's concerns, such as women's studies courses, need not be sex segregated. As a form of affirmative action, like the traditionally black colleges, women's schools and programs could maintain a "female climate" while they admit the few males who would like to participate (Sandler 1983a).

Programs

In addition to civil rights laws that prohibit discrimination, the U.S. Congress enacted other laws that provide assistance and sometimes incentives to help and encourage people to decrease sex discrimination and sex stereotyping and to promote sex equity in education. Most of this legislation is administered by the Department of Education. However, compared to other areas of educational interest—such as the use of computers in education or even educational programs for bilingual or handicapped students—the Department of Education's investment in women's educational equity is infinitesimal. At its height in 1980, it was $34 million or .02 percent of the total Department of Education budget; now it is about $18 million (Klein and Dauito 1982; Klein's 1983 estimate). If the administration's budget requests had been approved by Congress, this amount would be almost zero. During the past three years, the department has proposed that the major programs supporting women's educational equity, the Women's Educational Equity Act Program (WEEAP) and the Civil Rights Act Title IV program (CRA IV), be given zero appropriations by Congress and that they be included in the Education Consolidation and Improvement Act, Chapter 2 Block Grant. Fortunately, Congress has blocked this giant step backward and has appropriated $5.76 million for WEEAP and $24 million for CRA IV annually. The CRA IV funds are split among sex, race, and national origin desegregation technical assistance activities with about $8.1 million for sex desegregation in 1983.

WEEA and CRA IV   Although the WEEA program retained its appropriation and provided 70 new grants (from 850 applications) during 1983, it suffered several baby steps backward in the process. Its director for the past four years, Leslie R. Wolfe, was forced out when the department instituted a reduction in force in the Office of Elementary and Secondary Education, where the WEEA program office had been located reporting directly to the assistant secretary. During this process, the number of people on the WEEA staff was also reduced. Moreover, the program was demoted to a much lower position in the organizational hierarchy, so that remaining staff positions were downgraded in technical responsibility, although the level of work and funding remained the same as in previous years (Wolfe 1983). Similar backward steps resulting from the reorganization affected the staff of the CRA IV program. Hanrahan and Kosterlitz (1983) have described how many of these backward steps are the result of the work of right-wing officials within the Department of Education.

Effective implementation of new and continuing WEEAP and CRA IV grants and contracts was also hampered by a court ruling that the U.S. Department of Education must provide the Chicago public schools with money to help in their race desegregation efforts. Since this money was not readily available, the judge put a hold on some other Department of Education funds, such as those of CRA IV and WEEAP. The president vetoed a bill that would have provided money for Chicago early in the process. By the time the money was released, many essential project activities had been curtailed (Chicago school desegregation . . . 1983).

Fortunately, WEEA and CRA IV also made some steps forward. The five national Demonstration Projects of Women's Educational Equity were concluded as planned after four years of WEEA support. Their evaluations revealed their effectiveness in promoting educational equity and, perhaps more important, increased knowledge about how to implement comprehensive approaches toward increasing educational equity in an entire school system (Schubert 1983).

The catalog of WEEA products, *Resources for Educational Equity* listed 216 resources in 1983 and will contain about 260 in its 1984 edition. This increase will be augmented by products that are sponsored by WEEA but produced by other publishers. The bipartisan Citizens Council on Women's Education (created when President Reagan replaced the entire bipartisan WEEA-legislated National Advisory Council on Women's Educational Programs with partisan appointees) produced an evaluation of the WEEA program that shows the value of model programs and products in promoting sex equity and suggests ways the legislation could be improved when it is considered for reauthorization by Congress in 1984 (Simonson and Menzer 1984).

The Vocational Education Act and the Job Training Partnership Act   The current Vocational Education Act, which contains many provisions to eliminate sex bias, stereotyping, and discrimination in vocational education, is being considered for substantial changes when its current authorization ends in 1984. In 1983, the major alternative to the current legislation and the administration's bill was a bill developed by the American Vocational Education Association. Both the administration and AVA bills are less attentive to equity needs than the current Vocational Education Act with its 1976 sex equity amendments, and these bills are particularly deficient in provisions for sex equity, although they do mention possible support for state vocational education sex equity coordinators. House and Senate testimony by Cusick (1983) and Wells (1983) suggest that the current Vocational Education Act provisions requiring support for sex equity are useful and should be strengthened. The Job Training Partnership Act (JTPA), which is administered by the Department of Labor and was implemented in 1983 to replace the Comprehensive Employment and Training Act (CETA), "requires that efforts be made in all programs to develop training activities which 'contribute to occupational development, upward mobility, development of new careers, and overcoming sex stereotyping in occupations traditional for the other sex' " (Boyer 1983). The advantages and disadvantages of this legislation are also discussed in more detail in the chapter on work in this volume.

The Fund for the Improvement of Postsecondary Education (FIPSE)   During 1983, FIPSE with a total appropriation of $11.71 million continued some commitment to equity and funded five projects focusing on women. They included a project to help postsecondary faculty increase sex equity in their classroom interactions, a project to integrate women's studies courses into regular curricula, two unique women's studies programs, and a program to help top-level women junior college administrators.

The National Institute of Education (NIE)   Although advancing educational equity by research is one of NIE's congressionally mandated funding priorities, no new work in the sex equity area was started in 1983, although the Institute received $55.61 million in appropriations and most of its previously supported equity work was finished. Completed work included the publication of a book, *Sex-Role Research: Measuring Social Change*, edited by Richardson and Wirtenberg (1983), which resulted from a 1981 NIE conference on the topic.

Mathematics and Science Legislation   A baby step forward occurred in this area. The National Science Foundation science education budget was increased from $15 million in 1982 to $30 million in 1983. At least one item in the foundation's announcement of grants for research on the teaching and learning of science and mathematics mentioned looking at gender, and their congressionally mandated Committee on Equal Opportunities in Science and Technology continued to provide advice on equity concerns of women, minorities, and the handicapped. The legislation proposed to improve the teaching of mathematics, science, and foreign languages also mentioned the need to include "traditionally underrepresented groups, including women and racial and ethnic minorities" in some of its titles (H.R. 1310, 11; S. 1285, 25), but did not include requirements for special programs to increase women's educational equity.

State and District-Level Programs to Institutionalize Sex Equity   Although most state resources, like those at the federal level, were reduced during 1983, many states and the Council of Chief State School Officers continued to focus attention on ways to promote educational equity. States use regulatory, administrative, and leadership activities to accomplish this (Bailey 1983). Some effective strategies include a school visitation process to monitor the achievement of sex equity and simultaneously provide technical assistance, and the designation of a full-time person with specific sex equity responsibilities, such as a state vocational education sex equity coordinator. Promising school-district-level strategies include Los Angeles County's Infusion Process and Philadelphia's Affirmative Action and Equal Educational Opportunity Plan (Schmuck et al. 1985).

Trends and Discoveries Concerning Equity

Although educational equity for women was forced to take some backward steps by the Reagan administration, a new field of inquiry and activity related to sex equity in education was identified, and many of the findings from research, evaluation, and practice have been synthesized and consolidated in a monumental twenty-five-chapter publication, *Handbook for Achieving Sex Equity through Education* (Klein 1985).

Basic Understandings and Public Impressions

Public Impressions   During 1983, the public, like our "Mother May I" players, must have been very confused because it heard quite a bit about the gender gap in politics, but nothing about the gender gap in the many national reports advocating educational reform. This occurred despite the fact that the majority of students in elementary, secondary, and postsecondary education are now female and that elementary teaching has long been a predominantly female profession. An analysis of the major 1983 reports on education reform efforts reveals a strong focus on excellence and a decrease in the traditional national concern of using public education to promote equity. If equity was mentioned at all, it was clear that the authors were not addressing sex equity (Simonson 1983; Bailey 1983). Also ignored in many of these reports were critical issues that are particularly relevant to women, but have a major impact on all education, such as the decreasing numbers of high-quality teachers stemming from the fact that many bright women now have other more attractive and remunerative career options.

Women and girls were not even mentioned in the Commission on Excellence report or by Secretary of Education Bell in his November statement on the department's fiscal year 1984 goals and priorities. It is also distressing to note that of the major 1983 studies on education reform none of the panels was chaired by a woman. Nor were women listed as principal report authors, although in at least one case in which no one was listed, a black woman, Adrienne Y. Bailey of the College Board, was in charge of the project. Feminist organizations are trying to correct these omissions by having public speak-outs, such as one in November in New York City, and by discussing how equity and excellence must be compatible (Campbell 1983). Susan Bailey (1983) has also pointed out how equity standards should be incorporated into state regulatory responsibilities relating to the new reform efforts in the areas of accreditation of education institutions and the certification of educational personnel.

The New Scholarship on Women   Continued steps forward have been made in the area of new scholarship on women. In addition to developing sex equity in education and feminist scholarship as legitimate areas of inquiry with some full-time professional workers, organizations, and postsecondary courses and programs, educators and others are validating *Ms.* magazine's Woman of the Year Carol Gilligan's (1982) findings about how women speak, perceive, and value some things differently than men (Van Gelder 1984). Sari Biklen (1983) has come to a similar conclusion in her analysis of how women elementary schoolteachers perceive their occupation in ways that differ from the previous male-centered research on definitions of occupations. This new research and related conclusions should be taken seriously in the development of plans to improve the teaching profession and to promote sex equity in education.

Two works by British authors look at the importance of gender in the educational experience. *Invisible Women: The Schooling Scandal* (Spender 1983) analyzes not only the history of the academic disciplines, but school staffing practices, classroom interactions, and girls' access to the creation of knowledge. Papers from the Westhill Sociology of Education Conference have been published in a volume that seriously considers social class, power, and work in relation to the problems of education (Walker and Barton 1983). Bibliographies in that volume cover the role of gender and class in the educational systems of Britain, Europe, Australia, and the United States. In *Learning Our Way: Essays in Feminist Education* (Bunch and Pollack 1983), American women discuss feminist education and processes both within traditional institutions, such as women's studies in universities, and in outside independent settings, such as prisons, community women's centers, and rural lecture series.

Sex Differences and Sex Stereotyping   Major research syntheses in 1983 have helped us take a long step forward in our understanding of sex differences in educational outcomes. Despite a recent book (Durden-Smith and Desimone 1983) that suggests that hormones cause male and female brains to develop differently, the bulk of the research reveals that sex differences on cognitive and psychosocial factors are explained by environment much more than by genetic factors (Linn and Petersen 1985). Contrary to common stereotypes, sex differences "in cognitive test scores and most other ability-related outcomes (excluding differences based on sex differences in body build such as upper body strength) are very small (about 5 percent) and never as large as differences in the range of abilities within the same sex group. Sex differences in some areas of achievement (such as auto repair, mathematics, typing, or child care) are somewhat larger, because enrollment in many of the courses designed to teach these skills has been unofficially, but predominantly single sex. And finally, sex differences in career choice and wages are very large, even where educational attainment and achievement are similar. On the average, females receive 40% less earned income than males. The pattern is quite clear: there are larger sex differences in outcomes in areas that are most influenced by socialization" (Klein et al. 1985).

There are also indications that as female and male students receive more similar and less sex stereotyped learning experiences, sex differences in education-related outcomes decrease. For example, a contemporary stereotyped expectation is that girls will do better than boys in elementary school—and they generally do in spite of the fact that males receive more teacher attention. However, by upper levels of high school and in colleges and universities, men are expected to outperform women—and they often do because the males continue to receive more favorable treatment than the females from faculty and peers (Klein and Bogart in press).

Trends for Sex Equity in Education

Status of Education Personnel   Sex discrimination in faculty and administrator salaries continues at all levels of education, although there is a much smaller percentage of women staff at the postsecondary level and sex discrimination in their salaries is substantially greater than that in the salaries of their female elementary and secondary colleagues. On the average, male elementary and secondary teachers (33 percent of the total) earn $1,915 more than female teachers, and male postsecondary faculty (73 percent of the total) earn $5,374 more than female faculty (Klein and Bogart in press). This means that in 1982 women college and university faculty earned 78.5 percent of the salaries of their male coworkers (Rubin 1984). At all levels of education, as the status of the faculty or administrative position increases, the number of females in the prestigious positions decreases.

Given this type of discrimination and the fact that most elementary and secondary teachers are not receiving pay comparable to that of people in other careers with similar educational backgrounds and abilities, it is not surprising that many of the highest scoring females are exercising their wider options by choosing to enter careers other than teaching (Schlechty and Vance 1982). Also encouraging the most able, creative teachers to leave the profession for a career with more autonomy and possibly a less male-dominated administrative hierarchy are such factors as a projected decrease in job growth in most educational positions during the 1990s such as − 14 percent for secondary school teachers (Rubin 1984), many 1983 proposals to pay teachers according to hard-to-define merit, increased teacher accountability procedures, and sex bias in administrator selection. This is particularly disturbing when research indicates, for example, that women elementary school principals are more knowledgeable, better instructional leaders, and responsible for higher levels of job satisfaction in their male and female teachers than are male principals (Marshall, n.d.; Shakeshaft 1985). In one baby step forward, however, in 1983 women's membership in the American Educational Research Association increased to 40 percent with a related increase on the association's governing council. Additionally, the 1982 statistics show that women received 48.8 percent of the doctorates in education (Moran 1984).

Status of Students   Female and male student enrollment is becoming more equal at all but the doctoral-degree levels where women now earn 31 percent of such degrees. Females are staying at the 51 percent level of high school graduates but now comprise 51.5 percent of college and university students. Data for 1982 reveal that for the first time women are receiving over half of all masters' degrees and are continuing a recent trend by receiving over half of bachelors' degrees (National Center for Educational Statistics 1983). "And for the first time in a decade, government statisticians are predicting a drop in female school attendance. It is projected that the 1982 enrollment figures will show that the number of women has dropped approximately 0.4 percent" (WEAL's agenda . . . 1983).

Thanks to the work of Mary Moran (1984), we now have well-documented evidence of the extent of sex bias in student financial aid. Her extensive report shows that low-income women students in 1981–82 received "$.68 for every dollar of college earnings received by men, $.72 for every dollar received by men in total grant awards, and $.84 for every dollar received by men in total loan amounts. Largest sex differences appear in aid programs where women have least input into how much money they will receive, that is, in grants and college earnings." She stated that "greater percentages of females apply for student aid at the freshman level and gradually taper downward into the senior level with a particularly sharp decrease between senior year and graduate level. For males this trend is exactly the opposite." She also found that "women are twice as likely as men to be classified as independent students (66 percent vs. 34 percent), have greater unmet need, and therefore are more likely to drop out" (Moran 1984).

A step backward was apparent when we learned from the Census Bureau that educational attainment continues to be less valuable in terms of subsequent earnings for women than for men. An eighteen-year-old male who earns a bachelor's degree will now acquire lifetime earnings of $329,000 more than if he had only a high school diploma, whereas an eighteen-year-old female with a bachelor's degree can expect to earn only $142,000 more in her lifetime than a female high school graduate. Similarly, women college graduates can expect to earn $523,000 to $1.2 million, where men college graduates can expect $861,000 to $1.87 million (Degree's earning power . . . 1983).

There has been a continued decline in numbers of single-sex schools in the United States at all educational levels, but there are more women than men in single-sex postsecondary schools and more boys than girls in single-sex private elementary and secondary schools (Klein and Bogart in press).

General Educational Practices   During 1983, there was little documented evidence of either forward or backward steps regarding the prevalence of sex equity in such general educational practices as instructional materials, tests, and classroom interactions. The assumption is that there has been gradual improvement as educators, parents, and students themselves have become more aware of women's rights and the need to be responsive to parallel decreases in sex stereotyping in society. Research has indicated that sex-biased instructional materials do have different effects on students than sex-equitable instructional materials. For example, sex-equitable materials expand sex-role attitudes and knowledge about sex roles, influence sex-role behavior, and increase both the motivation to learn and comprehension (Scott and Schau 1985). However, some conservative groups have continued to attack sex-equitable materials, such as "Freestyle," a thirteen-part television show designed to help children realize that they have non–sex stereotypic career options. Moreover, most educators continue to use sex-biased instructional materials. Forward steps have been greater in testing, where most commercial tests (unlike teacher-prepared tests) are developed so as not to contain sexist language or otherwise discriminate against students by sex (Diamond and Tittle 1985).

Substantial attention in 1983 was given to learning how to make the school climate more equitable for both females and males. *We've All Got Scars: What Boys and Girls Learn in Elementary School* by Raphaela Best (1983) documents two hidden curricula. One curriculum defines the differences in expected behavior for girls and boys based on sex stereotypes; the other describes the children's self-taught sex education activities. National Institute of Education–supported research projects by David and Myra Sadker at American University and by Marlaine Lockheed at Educational Testing Service have also documented the extent of sex segregation and differential treatment of female and male students in upper elementary school classrooms and studied ways to ameliorate these inequities (Lockheed 1985; Sadker, Thomas, and Sadker 1983). Hall and Sandler's 1982 paper, *The Classroom Climate: A Chilly One for Women?* synthesized the research on ways in which the college and university environments had negative effects on women and identified many types of subtle differences in the treatment of women and men in the classroom. The work by the Sadkers and the report by Hall and Sandler on sex inequities in interpersonal interactions were described in the widely circulated *Parade* magazine (Sexist . . . 1982; Safran 1983) and by television and public forums. Researchers and other educators have continued to give special attention to strategies to decrease sexual harassment and to increase the extent and effectiveness of mentor/mentee relationships for women in postsecondary institutions. The importance of becoming aware of biases in personal perceptions is described in an excellent booklet on *Seeing and Evaluating People* (Geis, Carter, and Butler 1982).

The Content Areas   Researchers made some steps forward in learning key issues and strategies to promote sex equity in many content areas. Most national attention, however, was given to identifying and decreasing sex inequities in mathematics, science, and computer education activities.

Although there have been continual baby steps forward in increasing the enrollment of females in *mathematics and science courses*, women still receive 12 percent or less of the Ph.D.s in mathematics, physical sciences, and engineering. Some are no longer finding sex differences in spatial visualization, and there are generally no sex differences in quantitative skills favoring boys before tenth grade when students' mathematics backgrounds are similar. Recent research and evaluations have indicated that most programs that are successful in increasing female participation in mathematics and science use multiple strategies to motivate, promote confidence and skills, and provide hands-on experiences (Stage et al. 1985). Progress in promoting sex equity in mathematics and science has been associated with effective integration of research, evaluation, and development. The National Science Foundation facilitated this integration by sponsoring a book to help educators evaluate math and science programs for women (Davis and Humphreys 1983).

The hottest topic of 1983 was that of identifying inequities in female use of *computers*. As is true in the related areas of mathematics and science, girls compared to boys seem to be less involved with and proficient in the use of computers particularly after elementary school. Some studies suggest that males have more positive attitudes toward computers and that they use computers more frequently in and outside of school (Campbell 1983a; Lockheed, Nielsen, and Stone 1983). Many of the computer games and other software and promotion activities, including the new Childrens' Television Workshop computer magazine *Enter*, seem to be biased toward boys. Out of over two hundred and seventy computer education projects during 1983, the U.S. Department of Education funded twelve that focused some attention on aspects of this important sex equity issue (Klein 1984).

In the area of *reading and verbal skills*, we learned that while girls continue to score higher than boys on many measures, the gap is narrowing. For example, there are few sex differences in verbal scores until after age ten, when females surpass males, but males perform higher on vocabulary tests and some tests of higher level verbal skills such as those measured on the verbal sections of the SAT (Scott, Dwyer and Lieb-Brilhart 1985). Results from the National Assessment of Educational Progress (1983) indicated that in reading, males at all three age levels (nine, thirteen, and seventeen) were performing closer to the level of females in 1979–80 than in 1970–71, that differences between males and females decrease as the level of parental education increases, and that the performance of females and males in reading comprehension who read the same amount of time tended to be more similar than the performance of males and females overall.

During 1983, sex equity in *social studies* moved a step forward as feminist educator Carole Hahn served as president of the National Council for Social Studies. Although many social studies textbooks retain their sexist biases and males outperform females on tests of political knowledge, researchers have found that gender differences favoring males in economic learning disappear when economics becomes a required rather than an elective course. Social studies researchers have also identified sex differences in student attitudes that are similar to those that are found to explain the gender gap between adults in the 1983 U.S. elections (Hahn and Bernard-Powers 1985).

Two publications informed artists and educators about the critical issues that hamper sex equity in *visual arts education* and the strategies to surmount these barriers (Sandell, Collins, and Sherman 1985; Collins and Sandell 1984). The latter publication is the first book on sex equity in visual arts at the elementary and secondary level. The three key issues include (1) the need to raise the status of women in art and art education; (2) sex-fair and affirmative practices in art education, such as the elimination of total dependence on the white, Western, male viewpoint in art history and criticism; and (3) increasing the importance of art in public school curricula.

In 1983, there was a step backward for girls in high school *athletics*, as survey results indicated that most cutbacks in athletic programs were made in sports favored by girls such as softball, volleyball, and track, whereas popular boys' sports such as baseball, football, and track were expanded (La Mothe 1983). The longest hops forward in sex equity in physical education and athletics occurred in the area of exploring the subtle and complicated issues that relate to equity, such as investigating if separate sex treatment is ever fair and understanding that sex discrimination may be common and detrimental in coeducational physical education classes (Geadelmann 1985). Thus, complex issues, such as socialization practices, sexuality and women's sports, and the promotion and public acceptance of women's sports as well as controversies about physiological and biomechanical factors affecting female participation, were important topics in the November 1983 National Conference to Develop a Blueprint of Action for Women's Sports organized by the Women's Sports Foundation and the U.S. Olympic Committee.

Two important findings emerged in the area of increasing sex equity in *career and vocational education*. First, mandated and funded state sex-equity coordinators are very effective agents in promoting sex equity in vocational education and should continue to be required in new federal vocational education legislation. Second, some research indicates that high school girls now have higher career aspirations than boys and that educators are now becoming aware of the necessity to give more attention to preparing both male and female students for joint family and work responsibilities (Farmer and Sidney 1985).

Specific Populations of Women Students   As in the past several years, the bulk of the attention and sex-equity activities during 1983 focused on women students in colleges and universities, but researchers also made some baby steps forward in learning about the sex-equity issues that are critical for preschool girls and minority, disabled, older, gifted, and rural women.

Within the *college and university* setting, particular emphasis has been given to creating institutional change that will benefit women and often men students as well. For example, attention has been given to the diverse needs of *older women* who make up an increasingly large part of the student population in junior colleges. Research shows, for example, that adult women learners are more effective academically than other groups of students and that they are also more likely to be part-time students and to be employed. Along with these steps forward, there has been a continual decline in the number of women's programs. There has also been lateral progress as men found that innovations such as special counseling programs for reentering students and the granting of credit based on student experiences are valuable to them (Ekstrom and Marvel 1985).

However, women's studies courses have continued to be both popular and a source of some excellent publications such as a new interdisciplinary text by the Hunter College Women's Studies Collective (1983). Moreover, special university projects have helped faculty incorporate new scholarship on women into a wide variety of courses, ranging from philosophy to science. Sandler (1983b), Bogart (1985), and Klein and Bogart (in press) review many other forward and backward steps for women in postsecondary education.

Selma Greenberg (1985) has articulated important patterns of sex inequities in *early educational environments*. Her research indicates that the popular view that these environments meet the needs of girls better than boys is incorrect. For example, she shows that girls come to a preschool environment with greater need for large-muscle experiences than boys, but that school activities like "free play" that provide these experiences are not required. However, small-muscle experiences needed most by young boys are a common mandatory part of all preschool curricula.

Although research on black women (Grant 1983) and a text *All the Women Are White, All the Blacks Are Men, But Some of Us Are Brave: Black*

Women's Studies by Hull, Scott, and Smith (1982) won two of the 1983 Women Educators first-place awards, relatively little is known about the diverse sex-equity needs of *minority women*. Most of the projects developed to help minority women have focused on the career needs of women, not on the varied needs of girls as they cope with multiple stereotypes (Lewis 1985).

The June 1983 issues of *Concerns* provided an excellent summary of the sex-equity issues that compound other equity issues facing *disabled students*. It concluded that sex bias has a negative impact on both girls and boys, and indicated that girls' special education needs are commonly ignored and that more discrimination against disabled women than disabled men occurs in female exclusion from vocational and postsecondary educational opportunities (A concern about . . . 1983).

Despite the national attention focused on achieving excellence in education, 1983 did not bring increased attention to the needs of *gifted women*. Gordon and Addison (1985) have shown that gifted girls are frequently not identified because of sex bias in screening procedures and that when they are identified, girls performed better in programs where there were female role models. They also presented data that indicate there was some increase between 1971 and 1982 in female participation in advanced placement exams in calculus, chemistry, and physics.

Rosenfeld (1985) reviewed literature that showed that some unique conditions contribute to equity or inequity for *rural women*. For example, isolation reduces women's access to traditional courses, yet the relatively small enrollments in rural schools may contribute to the greater participation of rural girls in advanced math and science courses.

Progress toward Equity

According to our analysis of the impact of governmental policies and programs on women's educational equity, by 28 February 1984 women ended up somewhat behind their starting point at the beginning of 1983, primarily because the Supreme Court followed the Reagan administration's lead in limiting the coverage of Title IX, the major law to provide sex equity in education. However, when we add what we observed from the trends and discoveries related to the achievement of sex equity in education, we can see continual progress, particularly related to increased understanding of the inequities faced by women, such as discrimination in student financial aid. Thus, we conclude that at best, women are less than halfway to the finish line in the critical game of achieving sex equity in education and that women are even farther removed from their goal of achieving equity in society, since education, one of the major strategies for advancing in our society, has not provided women with equal advantages.

Acknowledgments

I would like to thank Roberta Hall, Margaret Kohn, Mary Moran, Sarah Pritchard, Bernice Sandler, and Joy Simonson for suggestions on improving this chapter, which was written by the author in her role as private citizen.

References

American Association of University Women. 1983. Facts for activists: Title IX. *Graduate Woman* 2 (October).

ATKINS, J. 1983. Education. *WEAL Washington report* 12, no. 5 (October-November): 3, 5.

AVNER, J.I. 1983. First girls admitted to Philadelphia high school. *National Now Times* 16, no. 9 (November): 2.

BAILEY, S. 1983. Perspectives on the infusion of equity into educational programs. Paper presented at the Mid-Year Conference of the American Educational Research Association, Special Interest Group: Research on Women and Education, Tempe, Ariz., 2 November.

BAILEY, S., and R. SMITH. 1982. *Policies for the future: State policies, regulations, and resources related to the achievement of educational equity for females and males.* Washington, D.C.: Council of the Chief State School Officers.

BELL, T.H. 1983. Goals and performance priorities of the U.S. Department of Education for fiscal year 1984. Memorandum, 28 November. Washington, D.C.: U.S. Department of Education.

BERS, T.H. 1983. The promise and reality of women in community colleges. Paper presented at the Mid-year Conference of the American Educational Research Association, Special Interest Group: Research on Women and Education, Tempe, Ariz., 3–5 November.

BEST, R. 1983. *We've all got scars: What boys and girls learn in elementary school.* Bloomington: Indiana University Press.

BIKLEN, S.K. 1983. *Teaching as an occupation for women: A case study of an elementary school.* Syracuse, N.Y.: Education Designs Group.

BOGART, K. 1985. Improving sex equity in postsecondary education. In *Handbook for achieving sex equity through education*, edited by Susan S. Klein, chap. 24. Baltimore: Johns Hopkins University Press. Forthcoming.

BOYER, G. 1983. Women and the Jobs Training Partnership Act, JTPA, Memorandum to New Day Task Forces on Employment Issues, April.

BUNCH, C., and S. POLLACK. 1983. *Learning our way: Essays in feminist education.* Trumansburg, N.Y.: Crossing Press.

California passes sex equity legislation. 1982. *Concerns*, no. 6 (October). Issue VI, October.

CAMPBELL, P.B. 1983a. Computers in education: A question of access. Paper presented at the American Educational Research Association Annual Meeting, Montreal, Canada, 11–15 April.

————. 1983b. *Girls, boys and educational excellence.* Groton, Mass.: Campbell-Kibler Associates.

Chicago school desegregation case delays funding for equity programs. 1983. *Concerns,* no. 10 (November).

COLLINS, G.C., and R. SANDELL. 1984. *Women, Art and Education.* Reston, Va.: National Art Education Association.

A concern about . . . sex equitable education for disabled students. 1983. *Concerns,* no. 9 (June). Issue IX, June.

CUSICK, T. 1983. Statement of the National Coalition for Women and Girls in Education by Theresa Cusick, Project on Equal Education Rights, NOW Legal Defense and Education Fund before the Subcommittee on Elementary, Secondary and Vocational Education Committee on Education and Labor, U.S. House of Representatives, 3 November.

CUSICK, T., and L. MARTIN-McCORMICK. 1983. President Reagan's stand on education out of step with American people, PEER survey says. *Equal Education Alert,* 31 October, p. 1.

DAVIS, B.G., and S. HUMPHREYS. 1983. *Evaluation counts: A guide to evaluating math and science programs for women.* Math/Science Network. Oakland, Calif.: Mills College.

Degree's earning power greater for males. 1983. *Washington Post,* 14 March.

DIAMOND, E., and C.K. TITTLE. 1985. Sex equity in testing. In *Handbook for achieving sex equity through education,* edited by Susan S. Klein, chap. 10. Baltimore: Johns Hopkins University Press. Forthcoming.

DURDEN-SMITH, J., and D. DESIMONE. 1983. *Sex and the brain.* New York: Arbor House.

EKSTROM, R.B., and M.G. MARVEL. 1985. Educational programs for adult women. In *Handbook for achieving sex equity through education,* edited by S. Klein, chap. 22. Baltimore: Johns Hopkins University Press. Forthcoming.

FARMER, H.S., and J.S. SIDNEY. 1985. Sex equity in career and vocational education. In *Handbook for achieving sex equity through education,* edited by Susan S. Klein, chap. 18. Baltimore: Johns Hopkins University Press. Forthcoming.

GEADELMANN, P.L. 1985. Sex equity in physical education and athletics. In *Handbook for achieving sex equity through education,* edited by Susan S. Klein, chap. 17. Baltimore: Johns Hopkins University Press. Forthcoming.

GEIS, F., M. CARTER, and D. BUTLER. 1982. *Seeing and evaluating people.* Newark: Office of Women's Affairs, University of Delaware.

GILLIGAN, C. 1982. *In a different voice: Psychological theory and women's development.* Cambridge, Mass.: Harvard University Press.

GORDON, B.J.A., and L. ADDISON. 1985. Gifted girls and women in education. In *Handbook for achieving sex equity through education,* edited by Susan S. Klein, chap. 20. Baltimore: Johns Hopkins University Press. Forthcoming.

GRANT, L. 1983. Black females' "place" in desegregated classrooms. Paper presented at the American Educational Research Association Annual Meeting, Montreal, Canada, 14 April.

GREENBERG, S. 1985. Educational equity in early education environments. In

Handbook for achieving sex equity through education, edited by Susan S. Klein, chap. 23. Baltimore: Johns Hopkins University Press. Forthcoming.

GREENHOUSE, L. 1983. High court weighs case on sex bias: Government urges narrowed view of a law that bars school discrimination. *New York Times*, 30 November.

HAHN, C.L., and J. BERNARD-POWERS. 1985. Sex equity in social studies. In *Handbook for achieving sex equity through education*, edited by Susan S. Klein, chap. 15. Baltimore: Johns Hopkins University Press. Forthcoming.

HALL, R., and B.R. SANDLER. 1982. The classroom climate: A chilly one for women? Washington, D.C.: Project on the Status and Education of Women, Association of American Colleges.

HANRAHAN, J., and J. KOSTERLITZ. 1983. School for scandal: Right wing officials at the Department of Education have wreaked havoc, crippling or effectively eliminating many programs designed to help those students "most at risk." *Common Cause*, September-October, pp. 17–25.

House reaffirms its opposition to curb on sex discrimination. 1983. *Washington Post*, 18 November.

H.R. 1310, 98th Congress, 1st Sess., 8 March 1983 (Mathematics and Science Education Act).

HULL, G., P. SCOTT, and B. SMITH. 1982. *All the women are white, all the blacks are men, but some of us are brave: Black women's studies*. Old Westbury, Conn.: Feminist Press.

Hunter College Women's Studies Collective. 1983. *Women's realities, women's choices: An introduction to women's studies*. New York: Oxford University Press.

Iron Arrow Honor Soc. v. Heckler, 11 April 1983, 16006 Adm. Office U.S. Courts. Saint Paul, Minn.: West Publishing Co.

KAUFMAN, P.W. 1982. Women and education. In *The women's annual, 1981: The year in review*, edited by Barbara Haber, 24–55. Boston: G.K. Hall.

KAUFMAN, D.R., and B.L. RICHARDSON. 1982. *Achievement and women: Challenging the assumptions*. New York: Free Press.

KLEIN, S.S. 1984. *Computer education: A catalog of projects sponsored by the U.S. Department of Education, 1984*. Washington, D.C.: National Institute of Education.

KLEIN, S.S., and K. BOGART. In press. Achieving sex equity in education: A comparison at the pre- and postsecondary levels. *Journal of Social Issues*. Special issue on "Sex equity in academe—A decade of struggle."

KLEIN, S.S., and K. DAUITO. 1982. What's left of federal funding for sex equity in education? Washington, D.C.: National Advisory Council on Women's Educational Programs, with 1983 estimates by Klein.

KLEIN, S.S., L.N. RUSSO, C.K. TITTLE, P.A. SCHMUCK, P.B. CAMPBELL, P.J. BLACKWELL, S.R. MURRAY, C.A. DWYER, M.E. LOCKHEED, B. LANDERS, and J.R. SIMONSON. 1985. Summary and recommendations for the continued achievement of sex equity in and through education. In *Handbook for achieving sex equity through education*, edited by Susan S. Klein, chap. 25. Baltimore: Johns Hopkins University Press. Forthcoming.

KLEIN, S.S., ed. 1985. *Handbook for achieving sex equity through education*. Baltimore: Johns Hopkins University Press. Forthcoming.

KOHN, M.A. 1983. Testimony of Margaret A. Kohn of the National Women's Law Center before the House Subcommittee on Postsecondary Education of the Education and Labor Committee and the Subcommittee on Civil and Constitutional Rights of the Judiciary Committee on Title IX Enforcement, 19 May 1983.

LA MOTHE, M.K. 1983. Keeping tabs: Educational equity. *Tabs: Aids for Ending Sexism in School* 6, no. 2: 14.

Lawyers' Committee for Civil Rights under Law. 1983. Supreme Court rejects Reagan administration position and holds racially discriminatory private schools ineligible for federal tax exemption. *Committee Report* 1 (September): 8–9.

LEWIS, S. 1985. Achieving sex equity for minority women. In *Handbook for achieving sex equity through education*, edited by Susan S. Klein, chap. 19. Baltimore: Johns Hopkins University Press. Forthcoming.

LINN, M.C., and A.C. PETERSEN. 1985. Facts and assumptions about the nature of sex differences. In *Handbook for achieving sex equity through education*, edited by Susan S. Klein, chap. 5. Baltimore: Johns Hopkins University Press. Forthcoming.

LOCKHEED, M.E. 1985. Sex equity in classroom organization and climate. In *Handbook for achieving sex equity through education*, edited by Susan S. Klein, chap. 11. Baltimore: Johns Hopkins University Press. Forthcoming.

LOCKHEED, M.E., A. NIELSEN, and M. STONE. 1983. Sex differences in microcomputer literacy. Paper presented at the National Educational Computer Conference, Baltimore, 6–8 June.

MARSHALL, C. unpublished manuscript. Sex equity and school effectiveness. Philadelphia: Graduate School of Education, University of Pennsylvania.

MORAN, M. 1984. Student financial assistance: Next steps to improving education and economic opportunity for women. Washington, D.C.: American Council on Education.

National Assessment of Educational Progress Information Retrieval System. 1983. Washington, D.C.: National Institute of Education, U.S. Department of Education.

National Center for Educational Statistics. 1983. *Surveys and estimates of the National Center for Educational Statistics*. Washington, D.C.: U.S. Department of Education.

Resources for Educational Equity. 1983. Newton, Mass.: WEEA Publishing Center at the Education Development Center.

RICHARDSON, B.L., and J. WIRTENBERG. 1983. *Sex role research: Measuring social change*. New York: Praeger Publishers.

ROSENFELD, S.A. 1985. Rural women and girls. In *Handbook for achieving sex equity through education*, edited by Susan S. Klein, chap. 21. Baltimore: Johns Hopkins University Press. Forthcoming.

RUBIN, D.K. 1984. Fifth annual survey. *Working Woman*, January, pp. 59–63.

S. 1285. 16 May 1983. 98th Congress, 1st Sess. (Education for Economic Security Act).

SADKER, M., D. THOMAS, and D. SADKER. 1983. *Non-sexist teaching: Over-

coming sex bias in teacher-student interaction. Training packet. Washington, D.C.: Mid-Atlantic Center for Sex Equity.

SAFRAN, C. 1983. Hidden lessons: Do little boys get a better education than little girls? *Parade*, 9 October, p. 12.

SANDELL, R., G.C. COLLINS, and A. SHERMAN. 1985. Sex equity in visual arts education. In *Handbook for achieving sex equity through education*, edited by Susan S. Klein, chap. 16. Baltimore: Johns Hopkins University Press. Forthcoming.

SANDLER, B.R. 1983a. Testimony on the Equal Rights Amendment and education, Subcommittee on Civil and Constitutional Rights of the Committee on the Judiciary, House of Representatives. 14 September.

————. 1983b. Women in higher education, where we have been and where we are going; These are the times that try men's souls. Washington, D.C.: Project on the Status and Education of Women, Association of American Colleges.

SCHLECHTY, P., and V.S. VANCE. 1982. Recruitment, selection and retention: The shape of the teaching force. Paper presented at the NIE Research on Teaching: Implications for Practice, National Invitational Conference. Warrenton, Va., February.

SCHMUCK, P.A., J.A. ADKISON, B. PETERSON, S. BAILEY, G.S. GLICK, S.S. KLEIN, S. McDONALD, J. SCHUBERT, and S.L. TARASON. 1985. Administrative strategies institutionalizing sex equity in education and the role of government. In *Handbook for achieving sex equity through education*, edited by Susan S. Klein, chap. 7. Baltimore: Johns Hopkins University Press. Forthcoming.

SCHUBERT, J.G. 1983. *Five national demonstrations of educational equity: Evaluation summary.* Palo Alto, Calif.: American Institutes for Research.

SCOTT, K.P., and C.G. SCHAU. 1985. Sex equity and sex bias in instructional materials. In *Handbook for achieving sex equity through education*, edited by Susan S. Klein, chap. 12. Baltimore: Johns Hopkins University Press. Forthcoming.

SCOTT, K.P., C.A. DWYER, and B. LIEB-BRILHART. 1985. Sex equity in reading and communication skills. In *Handbook for achieving sex equity through education*, edited by Susan S. Klein, chap. 14. Baltimore: Johns Hopkins University Press. Forthcoming.

Sexist classroom climate. 1982. *Parade*. 24 October, p. 17.

SHAKESHAFT, C. 1985. Strategies for overcoming barriers to women in educational administration. In *Handbook for achieving sex equity through education*, edited by Susan S. Klein, chap. 8. Baltimore: Johns Hopkins University Press. Forthcoming.

SIMONSON, J.R. 1983. Statement of the Citizens Council on Women's Education for House Budget Committee, Task Force on Education and Employment, Hearings on education quality and federal policy on the twin goals of equality and quality in education, 28 June.

SIMONSON, J.R., and J. MENZER. 1984. *Catching up: A review of the Women's Educational Equity Act Program.* Washington, D.C.: Citizens Council on Women's Education, a Project of the National Coalition for Women and Girls in Education.

SPEIZER, J.J. 1983. Education. In *The women's annual, 1982: The year in review*, edited by Barbara Haber, 54–62. Boston: G.K. Hall.

SPENDER, D. 1983. *Invisible women: The schooling scandal*. New York: Norton, 1983.

STAGE, E.K., N. KREINBERG, J. ECCLES (PARSONS), and J.R. BECKER. 1985. Increasing the participation and achievement of girls and women in mathematics, science, and engineering. In *Handbook for achieving sex equity through education* edited by Sue Klein. Baltimore: Johns Hopkins University Press. Forthcoming.

VAN GELDER, L. 1984. Carol Gilligan: Leader for a different kind of future. *Ms.*, January, pp. 37–40, 101.

WALKER, S., and L. BARTON, eds. 1983. *Gender, class, and education*. New York: Falmer Press.

WEAL's agenda for women's economic equity. 1983. WEAL Washington Report. June-July, p. 2.

WELLS, J. 1983. Statement of the National Coalition for Women and Girls in Education by Janet Wells, Federal Education Project, Lawyers' Committee for Civil Rights under Law, before the Subcommittee on Education, Arts and Humanities, Committee on Labor and Human Resources, U.S. Senate, 3 March.

WOLFE, L.R. 1983, Statement of Dr. Leslie R. Wolfe, former director, Women's Educational Equity Act Program, Department of Education before the Committee on Education and Labor, Subcommittee on Elementary, Secondary and Vocational Education, and the Committee on Post Office and Civil Service, Subcommittee on Investigations, U.S. House of Representatives, 27 September.

Resources

American Educational Research Association Special Interest Group: Research on Women and Education (AERA SIG:RWE). This group of educational researchers through its newsletter, annual conference, and sessions at the annual AERA meeting encourages scholarly research on equity issues relating to women and education. Chair, Ruth Ekstrom, Educational Testing Service, Princeton, NJ 08540

Citizens Council on Women's Education. A bipartisan group of women and men with experience in education and public affairs established in September 1982 by the National Coalition for Women and Girls in Education to protect the guarantees of educational equity and opportunity established by federal legislation, to monitor the activities of the Reagan-appointed National Advisory Council on Women's Educational Programs, and to inform the public of the status of educational equity and attempts made by the Reagan administration to impede equity. Leslie Wolfe, National Coalition for Women and Girls in Education, 1413 K St., N. W., Washington, DC 20005

Federation of Organization for Professional Women (FOPW). Composed of representatives of professional organizations and individual members. Publishes a *A Woman's Yellow Book*, a directory of organizations concerned with women's issues, and a newsletter, conducts training and policy seminars, holds an annual meeting, and influences public policy on behalf of women. President, Gerry Cox, FOPW, 1825 Connecticut Ave. NW, Suite 403 Washington, DC 20009.

National Advisory Council on Women's Educational Programs (NACWEP). Created by the 1974 Women's Educational Equity Act to advise federal officials and the public about educational equity and the needs of women and girls. The current seventeen members appointed by President Reagan are all Republican women. Patricia Jensen, Executive Director, 425 13th St. NW, Suite 416, Washington, DC 20004.

National Coalition for Sex Equity in Education (NCSEE). A coalition of professionals who have responsibility for ensuring sex equity in education. Members receive a newsletter and attend the annual conference to exchange information. Jacqueline L. Cullen, Chair, NCSEE Steering Committee, Dept. of Vocational Education, Pennsylvania Department of Education, 333 Market St., Harrisburg, PA 17108.

National Coalition for Women and Girls in Education (NCWGE). A coalition of fifty national organizations working to promote equal educational opportunity for girls and women in education with particular emphasis on federal policy and practices. Barbara Stein, Chair, National Education Association, Human and Civil Rights, 1201 16th St. NW, Washington, DC 20036.

National Education Association. *Celebrate People: A Manual to Help State and Local Education Associations Observe National Women's History Week.* Washington, D.C.: NEA Human and Civil Rights, 1984. Contains suggestions for association and classroom activities, topics for meetings and exhibits, statistics, and organizational resources, such as Sex Desegregation Assistance Centers, Commissions on the Status of Women, and other organizations.

National Women's Conference Committee, Education Task Force. Representatives of national groups concerned with implementing the 1977 Houston Conference National Plan of Action work to achieve educational equity for women and men of all ages and at all levels of education by promoting public understanding and support of educational equity through legislation, implementation, and funding of equity programs. Contact Joy Simonson, American Association of University Women, 2401 Virginia Ave. NW, Washington, DC 20037.

National Women's Law Center (NWLC). Along with a wide range of legal work on women's equity issues, NWLC sponsored conferences on sex equity in education and developed a text, *Sex Discrimination in Education: Legal Rights and Remedies* by Nancy Duff Campbell, Marcia D. Greenberger, Margaret A. Kohn, and Shirley J. Wilcher. Contact NWLC, 1751 N St. NW, Washington, DC 20036.

Spencer, M.L., M. Kehoe, and K. Speece. *Handbook for Women Scholars: Strategies for Success.* San Francisco: American Behavioral Research Corporation, 1982. A resource book that examines key issues facing women scholars and lists advocacy organizations, professional caucuses for women scholars, and information on career/financial/legal resources.

Women Educators. A membership group that monitors sex equity in the federal arena and sponsors annual awards for research, curriculum, and activism. Coordinator, Patricia Ruzicka, North West Regional Educational Laboratory, 300 S.W. Sixth Ave., Portland, OR 97204.

Health

Adriane J. Fugh-Berman

The year 1983 was marked by boundary fights in the fields of law, medicine, and ethics. Advances in fetal treatment, including surgery, raised questions about fetal versus maternal rights, and parental rights were also pitted against the rights of handicapped newborns. Women and children felt the effects of federal budget cuts this year; the number of children living in poverty has more than tripled in the last four years, and the gap between the rates of black and white infant deaths is widening. A task force on food assistance, however, concluded early in 1984 that "rampant" hunger could not be documented (Stunted expectations 1984), and the fiscal year 1984 budget proposes to cut nearly $2 billion from Medicaid in the next three years, as well as freezing funding for community health centers (Vieth 1984).

Attitudes toward sexuality reached new depths of conservatism last year. Acquired immune deficiency syndrome (AIDS) replaced herpes as the disease its victims deserve; even the liberal press took the opportunity to try to scare people into monogamy.

Women continued to work toward changes in the medical care system. Births in hospitals showed a more humane trend, and cesarean sections are performed less automatically. Pregnancy, however, seems to be becoming more complicated. A great deal of information about the fetus can now be ascertained before birth, and doctors, fearful of not knowing enough to avoid being sued, are subjecting women to more and more tests. A significant number of ob-gyns simply dropped the obstetrics portion of their practice because of high malpractice insurance (Shearer 1983). Interest in self help and alternative health care continued to grow, but nonphysician health practitioners faced much legal opposition last year.

Sex and Childbearing

New research on the physiology of female sexual response shows general agreement that structures other than the glans and shaft of the clitoris are involved in orgasm. At the 6th World Conference of Sexology, Shere Hite spoke on the role of the vestibular bulbs (internal tubes analagous to the male tubes that fill with blood during an erection). The swelling of these bulbs cause the vulva to swell during arousal, and orgasm occurs as the tubes empty in waves, causing "vaginal" contractions (Henry 1983b).

While women learn more about their sexual functioning, they are also moving towards delaying that once-inevitable consequence of sex—motherhood. Between 1970 and 1980, the rate of first births to women in their thirties climbed 66 percent (Substantial rise . . . 1983). Childlessness is also becoming an option for many women; articles in *Family Planning Perspectives* found that from 12 to 25 percent of women may remain childless (Young American . . . 1983; Women having . . . 1983). They may not find their decision socially acceptable, though; a spate of articles, some by feminists, accused Americans of hating children. An article in *Ms.* gave examples of child-hating behavior such as ignoring children at the dinner table and poisoning their Hallowe'en candy (Pogrebin 1983). Hardly a fit comparison. Pogrebin weakens her good points with a worship-the-child philosophy that crept into many articles last year.

Reproductive Technologies

Prenatal genetic screening is rapidly becoming a common procedure. New screening methods will enable earlier testing and overnight results. The implications of prenatal screening have been the subject of furious debate, and a workshop on this subject at the 14th Women and the Law conference was well attended. Barbara Katz Rothman wondered whether genetic screening is really quality control; Ruth Hubbard warned against "eugenic-type thinking"; Deborah Kaplan stated that neither doctors nor women are given enough information to make truly informed decisions about the quality of life for a disabled person (Dejanikus 1983).

Many women under thirty-five (at least educated, upper-middle-class women) are pressuring the medical profession to provide them with access to amniocentesis. They are succeeding, although perhaps at a cost. Prior to age thirty-five, the risk of aborting because of amniocentesis is greater than the chance of carrying a genetically abnormal fetus (Pollner 1983).

Chorionic villi sampling arrived in 1983 and may well replace amniocentesis in a few years. There are several advantages to this technique, in which a tiny amount of a membrane around the fetus is removed through the cervix; it can be done as early as the eighth week of pregnancy, and preliminary results may be obtained in twenty-four hours.

Alpha fetoprotein (AFP) test kits will soon be available to ob-gyns. Elevated levels of AFP can indicate brain or spinal cord defects, including spina bifida (open spine). Unfortunately, elevated AFP can also mean twins, threatened miscarriage, or miscalculation of fetal age (maternal AFP rises with every week of pregnancy). Sid Wolfe of the Health Research Group calls it "valuable only as a first step"; he also expressed a well-founded concern over the rate of false positives given by the test (Wilke 1983).

In vitro fertilization clinics proliferated last year, and the pregnancy rate for the procedure has risen. It is estimated that the process costs about $50,000 for each child born. Embryo transfer, wherein an egg is fertilized in one woman and then transferred to another, became the first obstetric procedure for which a patent application was filed (Ismach 1983).

The Littlest Patients

Surgery on fetuses continues to be an area of experimentation; medicine's youngest patients now can have brain shunts for water on the brain (hydrocephaly) or be catheterized for urinary tract obstruction. The concept of fetus-as-patient has thrown a new wrench into the issue of women's medical rights. Juvenile courts in Georgia and Colorado ordered women to undergo cesarean sections which they had refused but which were deemed necessary to save the life of the child (Pollner 1983). It may be a small step from this to ordering a mother to undergo other types of surgery in the best interests of the fetus she carries.

Perinatal technology enables younger and smaller babies to survive than ever before. Babies as young as twenty-six weeks, some weighing only a pound or two, now have a decent chance for survival, and most who receive intensive care are free from disabilities; babies who cannot breathe without mechanical assistance, however, have a high level of handicaps (Disability studied . . . 1983). Also, some problems, such as learning disabilities, may not show up for years.

Advances in preemie technology have made possible the latest contest among doctors—to see who can deliver a live baby from a mother who has been dead the longest. Doctors at San Francisco's Moffitt Hospital made news in March 1983 by maintaining a brain-dead woman on life support systems for sixty-four days (No time limit . . . 1983). The newest entry in this gruesome race was the delivery of a 3 lb., 11 oz. girl at Roanoke Memorial Hospital, twelve weeks after her mother died from a massive brain hemorrhage (New record . . . 1983).

The Pill

A CDC study published early in 1983 reassured women on the pill that they had no increased risk of breast cancer and had a rate of ovarian cancer only half that of the general population. The pill's newly benign status turned benighted, however, when researchers reported in *Lancet* that certain pills, used by a particular group of women, showed a significant association with breast cancer. Women who had used high-progesterone pills for more than six years (and had started the pill while under twenty-five) had a rate of breast cancer five times that of the rest of the population. Another report from England found the incidence of cervical cancer higher in pill users than in IUD users; the incidence of the cancer increased with duration of oral contraceptive use (Silberner 1983).

The good news about the pill last year came from Sweden, where it was found that pill users may have some protection from infertility caused by salpingitis (tubal inflammation). The scarring caused by this infection is a common cause of infertility; women on the pill have a lower rate of salpingitis and, when they do contract it, less severe cases (Oral contraceptives . . . 1983).

Low-dose pills are now widely available. The adverse effects of estrogens (higher incidence of stroke, high blood pressure, heart attack) are well documented, and progesterone has emerged as another, albeit lesser, danger. The safest pills to use are the ones low in both estrogen and progesterone, not just low in one or the other.

Biphasic, or two-phase, pills are now available, and the triphasic (three-phase) pills were tested in the United States in 1983. Both are low-dose pills; their special advantage is that they have a graduated dose of hormones that should minimize the midcycle bleeding common with low estrogen pills. As with all low-dose pills, users must be especially careful to take the pills on time and should use a concurrent method when taking antibiotics (Sarrel and Sarrel 1983).

Spermicides and IUDs

A study published in *Family Planning Perspectives* refuted former studies that linked spermicide use with birth defects (Cordero and Layde 1983). A separate study also noted no connection with birth defects but did note a higher rate of miscarriage and a higher proportion of female births in women who had used spermicides around the time of conception (Scholl et al. 1983).

Dalkon shield suits continued, and the first large study relating types of IUDs to pelvic inflammatory disease (PID) found that the rate of infection was 8.3 times higher in women who used the shield than in women who used no contraception. Other IUDs caused a rate of PID 1.6 times that of noncontraceptors (Mintz 1983). The National Women's Health Network called for an international recall of the Dalkon shield (Davis 1983). The FDA has issued a warning to users to have the device removed, but attempts for a more substantive effort continue (Dalkon shield . . . 1983).

New Contraceptives

A newcomer in over-the-counter contraception is the vaginal sponge, which rests under the cervix like a diaphragm and works by absorbing sperm as well as by providing a chemical barrier. Each sponge is good for about twenty-four hours, and studies done by the manufacturer show that it is about 90 percent effective. At a dollar a sponge, it is expensive as a regular birth control method, but should be a boon to teenagers, as it can be purchased without a prescription and can be inserted well before intercourse. Concern has been expressed about the sponge and toxic shock syndrome. It bears noting, however, that no item worn inside the vagina has been proven free of risk of toxic shock syndrome.

Condoms lubricated with spermicides are now available in drugstores, although prophylactic manufacturers continue to ignore the need for different sizes of condoms.

The custom-fitted cervical cap reentered clinical trials last year. The plastic cap has a one-way valve system; menstrual blood and cervical mucus can flow out from the cervix, but sperm cannot swim through it from the other direction. Improvements were made in the molding material, but it is unclear whether dislodgement will remain a problem for many women (Prupes 1983).

An early sign of pregnancy is the rise in the hormone HCG. This hormone causes progesterone to be produced and is essential to continuation of the pregnancy. Canadian scientists are working on an altered version of the HCG molecule that would bind to the receptor site but would not trigger the production of progesterone. At this stage, experimentation has been only on rats; it will be some time before we know its effects on humans (Placental hormone . . . 1983).

A hormone-releasing vaginal ring is being tested in Brazil and the Dominican Republic (User's perception . . . 1983). Elsewhere, tiny hormone-releasing capsules implanted under the skin are being tested as contraceptives (Klitsch 1983).

The news in unisex contraception is luteinizing hormone-releasing hormone (LHRH) agonist. LHRH shifts a woman's hormonal cycle to a phase incompatible with egg implantation. In men, the substance reduces the production of three sex hormones, thus reducing sperm density and motility. Because this agonist acts only on the reproductive system rather than on the entire body, it is expected to have fewer adverse effects than the birth control pill. Women in one study have reported no adverse side effects; men, however, reported some hot flashes (Stephenson 1983).

Male Contraception

Men who persuaded their partners that vasectomies cause atherosclerosis or kidney disease now have a case only if they can also convince their partners that they are monkeys. An extensive study of twenty thousand men found that the vasectomized group was, if anything, healthier than the unvasectomized group. NIH concluded that animal studies showing an association between vasectomy and circulatory or immune system ailments do not apply to humans (Vasectomy, disease link . . . 1983).

A Johns Hopkins scientist applied to the FDA for permission to begin human trials on a hormone salve that men would rub onto their abdomens to suppress sperm production. Although dosage may be difficult to control with a salve, hormones absorbed through the skin are more effective than those taken orally (Steinberg 1983). Note that men are spared high-dosage orals. Where was that concern for women when the birth control pill was being developed and refined?

Pregnancy Perils

Bendectin, the only prescription medicine approved for use in nausea of pregnancy, was withdrawn from the market in 1983, following three hundred lawsuits against Merrell-Dow Pharmaceuticals, manufacturers of the drug. The suits charged that Bendectin was responsible for birth defects, particularly limb reductions and gastrointestinal defects. Substitutes will soon hit the market, but no drug has been proven absolutely safe for use in nausea of pregnancy. Bendectin has been the most thoroughly tested; the next drug on the market for this condition could be much worse.

Heavy alcohol consumption is known to cause fetal abnormalities, but it is news that relatively light drinking may cause problems as well. As little as one ounce of alcohol a day is enough to reduce infant birth weight, and there is an increased risk of miscarriage in women who consume as little as an ounce a week. Preliminary animal studies indicate that paternal alcohol consumption prior to conception may also have an adverse influence (Council on Scientific Affairs 1983).

In December, New York passed a bill requiring bars, restaurants, and liquor stores to post notices stating that alcohol can damage unborn children (New York requires . . . 1983). Women's groups expressed concern over the general trend toward protecting the unborn at the expense of women's freedom.

Cesareans

The rate of cesareans has stabilized, although it is still very high. In 1980 the rate was 18 percent, more than triple the rate of a decade before. In New York City, one out of four children are born by C-section. Several books came out in 1983 blasting the once-a-C-section-always-a-C-section line as medically unfounded. The vaginal birth after cesarean (VBAC) movement has grown and now has as its Bible *Silent Knife*, a new book as full of useful information as it is of fanaticism about doing a birth "right" (Cohen and Estner 1983). *Silent Knife* states that the incidence of fetal death is less with VBAC than with repeat cesareans and that the risk of death to the mother is from two to twenty-six times greater with C-section than with vaginal delivery. This is important information. If only the authors wouldn't consider vaginal birth ("purebirth") a necessity for becoming a totally fulfilled woman; the book leaves the impression that women become pregnant less to have a child than to experience the joyful pangs of childbirth.

Abortion Rights Upheld

The tenth anniversary of the Supreme Court decision legalizing abortion occurred on 22 January 1983. *Roe* v. *Wade* was reaffirmed in June when the Supreme Court struck down as unconstitutional laws intended to limit access to abortion—including twenty-four-hour waiting periods, hospitalization for second-trimester procedures, and parental consent laws (Supreme Court . . . 1983). Weeks later, the Senate rejected Hatch's Senate Joint Resolution 3, which would have held that a right to abortion is not constitutionally guaranteed (With legality . . . 1983).

The only major setback in abortion legislation this year was the passage of an antiabortion provision to a funding resolution; Federal employee health insurance will no longer cover abortions unless done to save the woman's life.

The safety record for legal abortion held up in 1983. A review in *Family Planning Perspectives* looked at the effect of vacuum aspiration abortion on future childbearing. Women who had induced abortions did not have a greater risk of low birth weight, prematurity, or spontaneous abortion. No definite conclusions were drawn about the effect of multiple induced abortions (Hogue, Cates, and Tietze 1983).

In *Our Right to Choose*, Beverly Harrison criticizes the romanticized and unexamined theological and political arguments against abortion, and develops a powerful ethical stance supporting women's reproductive freedom (Harrison 1983).

The Squeal Rule and Baby Doe

In January 1983, the Department of Health and Human Services published a regulation that would have required family planning clinics receiving federal funds to notify parents of minors who received prescription contraceptives. The Planned Parenthood Federation of North America and the National Family Planning and Reproductive Health Association filed suit against the squeal rule in Washington, D.C., while another suit was filed in New York. The rule was barred, and the Justice Department decided not to appeal the case.

The "Baby Doe" rule was released last year, requiring that hospitals post notices warning that medical care or food could not be withheld from handicapped newborns. The notices included a hotline phone number to report violations. This ruling was struck down in a federal district court in April; revised rules were submitted, but by the end of the year, there was no accord on Baby Doe (With legality . . . 1983).

Harassment of Health Care Providers

The Midwives Alliance of North America (a coalition of nurse and lay midwives) held their first annual conference in Milwaukee this year; the focus was necessarily on legislative strategies. Lay midwives, particularly, have been arrested all over the country; 1983 also saw the formation of the Midwifery Litigators Network, a volunteer-run legal service for the women arrested in what amounts to a witchhunt.

Nurse practitioners were also under siege; several were sued for providing services such as pelvic exams or breast exams. Observers believe that medical boards consider nurse practitioners to be a serious economic threat (Donovan 1983). Undoubtedly the same could be said of midwives.

Pleasing Patients

Health care may be becoming more consumer oriented. In Minnesota, doctors "voluntarily" decided to post their prices just before a law went into effect that would have resulted in state-controlled price disclosure (Minnesota doctors . . . 1983). Some doctors have set up house-call services, and free-standing emergency centers (alternatives to hospital emergency rooms) doubled to over one thousand this year (Doc in the . . . 1983).

London's College of Health, opened in the fall of 1983, may become a model for patient education. Directed at medical consumers rather than at doctors, the school offers correspondence courses, health care advice, a magazine called *Self Health* and access to 1,200 self-help groups (Britain's newest . . . 1983).

Occupational Health

A nationwide campaign to encourage research and action on health risks to women working with VDTs was announced by 9 to 5, the National Association of Working Women (9 to 5 starts . . . 1983). The National Research Council found no evidence that VDTs cause long-range damage to vision, but critics found the studies poorly designed (Office workers assail . . . 1983).

A conference on working conditions and women's health found that in five continents the majority of women's jobs require the maintenance of one position for long periods of time, and many jobs require high speed and precision (Delegates from . . . 1983).

Columbia University did a study that found that the most job-related stress is suffered by women who work on assembly lines. Other stressful jobs include waitressing, operating a sewing machine, and being a nurse's aide or office worker. One researcher found that boredom is extremely stressful and can actually cause the brain processes to slow down (The stress of . . . 1983).

Courts ruling on three cases early in 1983 decided that excluding women but not men from jobs hazardous to reproductive health constitutes sex discrimination. Since most substances harmful to the reproductive tract of women also can harm the reproductive tract of men, employers must justify discrimination policies and prove that no harm results to the children of exposed males (Victories won . . . 1983).

The Occupational Safety and Health Administration (OSHA) proposed to lower its standards for exposure to ethylene oxide, a gas used to sterilize instruments. Although ethylene oxide has been shown to cause leukemia, circulatory disease, upper respiratory complaints and changes in DNA (OSHA proposes . . . 1983), the director of health standards at OSHA blocked agency efforts to limit exposure, a move made soon after a meeting with a major manufacturer of the chemical (Kurtz 1983).

Breast Cancer

Treatment of breast cancer showed conservative trends in 1983. Diagnostic tools have become less invasive, and breast X-rays have been improved so that radiation exposure is cut by as much as two-thirds from several years ago. Breast cancer patients are also better able to give informed consent; four states passed laws requiring that patients be given complete information on all medically viable alternative treatments (Will Virginia . . . 1983).

Thermography creates a heat map of the breast; "hot" areas may warn of cancer. A new foil bra was introduced in 1983 to help women examine themselves at home. A doctor provides a color photo of the original thermal pattern, and the patient compares her heat map with the photo every month (Home device . . . 1983). At $175, this device is medical frippery, especially since researchers do not agree that thermography is a useful tool in breast cancer detection. Thermography detects large lumps but is not necessarily adequate for detection of small early masses (Radiologists adopt . . . 1983).

A new method of training women to do breast self-examination was introduced in 1983. A training center employs silicone-filled breast models with fixed and movable lumps; there are different models and a woman takes home the model that most closely resembles her own breast. The program claims that its graduates can detect lumps as small as .25–.5 cm in diameter (less than a quarter of an inch across). All women should be trained in breast self-examination; if these techniques were more widespread (and affordable), extensive surgery for breast cancer could become a rarity.

Conservative surgery (such as lumpectomy) is becoming more the norm anyway, as the medical establishment learns that radical treatments do little to extend life. An Italian study published this year showed that breast cancer patients who receive short courses of chemotherapy or have conservative surgery to remove small tumors live as long as those given more radical treatment (Italian trials . . . 1983). And a French study found that even at a late stage, conservative treatment for breast cancer can be as effective as radical surgery (French study . . . 1983).

Cervical and Ovarian Cancer

Cigarette smoking was found to be a significant factor in cervical cancer, according to a study published in *JAMA;* women who smoked had a 3.6 times greater risk of getting cervical cancer as women who didn't smoke. A cumulative effect was noted, and there was some evidence that the risk was greatest for women who began smoking at a young age (Trevathan et al. 1983). A researcher at Albert Einstein College of Medicine reported findings that cervical cancer patients reported much lower intakes of vitamin C on food records than a control group. Vitamin C may exert some protective influence, but rather than researchers depending on food records a study must be constructed that will measure physiological levels of vitamin C (Treichel 1983).

The use of talcum powder around the genital area may be linked to the development of ovarian cancer. Talc is chemically similar to asbestos and is often mined with it; asbestos has already been shown to increase the risk of cancer in those exposed to it (Ovarian cancer . . . 1983).

Estrogen Replacement Therapy

Estrogen replacement therapy (ERT) is making something of a comeback. The combining of progesterone with estrogen is thought to prevent the risk of estrogen-induced endometrial cancer, and some doctors wax enthusiastic over the role of estrogen in preventing osteoporosis (brittle bones), hot flashes, and vaginal dryness (Postmenopausal estrogen . . . 1983). Two studies presented at an ACOG meeting refute links between estrogen replacement therapy and breast cancer, and a new claim has been made that ERT can reduce the risk of coronary heart disease (Workshop findings . . . 1983). The evidence is not completely convincing, however, and it seems clear only that estrogen with progesterone offers benefits over estrogen alone.

An article in *Science News* pointed out that there are safer ways than estrogen to deal with osteoporosis. French researchers gave sodium fluoride with calcium and vitamin D to patients and found that the combination increases bone mass and reduces subsequent spinal fractures. A study at the University of North Carolina at Chapel Hill showed that exercise that stresses bones, such as jogging or tennis, slows bone loss in healthy postmenopausal women (Arehart-Treichel 1983).

Premenstrual Syndrome

Premenstrual syndrome became a recognized medical condition in 1983. Progesterone suppositories are a popular treatment, although placebos have been found to work as well (Blume 1983), and blood progesterone levels have not been shown to be different in PMS sufferers than in non-PMS sufferers (Eagan 1983). There is no standardized dose of progesterone, so patients may receive from 50 to 2,400 mg. a day. Some women find that they need higher and higher doses to achieve the same effect, and others report that symptoms reappear as soon as they stop the drug—no matter where they are in their cycles (Eagan 1983).

Very few women experience symptoms severe enough to warrant treatment of any kind; and women who experience mild to moderate discomfort may find relief with dietary changes or nutritional supplementation. The claim that from 20 to 80 percent of women suffer from PMS is discomfiting; does that include those of us who simply know when our periods are due? Women may find a proliferation of both popular and technical work on this subject (Laversen 1983; Norris 1983; Witt 1983).

Precocious Puberty

An outbreak of premature sexual development in Puerto Rico has not yet been definitely traced, although hormone-contaminated chicken is suspected. (By feeding estrogens to cattle or poultry, farmers may cut down on food but still maintain fast weight gain in stock.) Dr. Carmen Saenz de Rodriguez found that in 85 percent of her prematurely developing patients (mainly girls), symptoms regressed when they stopped eating chicken (or when their breast-feeding mothers stopped consuming local poultry). No one knows the long-term effects of estrogen exposure on children other than stunted growth (Zamichow 1983).

Sexually Transmitted Diseases

Herpes research last year concentrated on vaccines; research also continued on drugs such as Ara-A, ABPP, and Interferon (Garmon 1983; McKinstry 1983). A very new lab test can detect the presence of herpes viruses in 4½ hours. This is days faster than current tests (Pollner 1983). FDA approval is being sought for oral acyclovir; this drug speeds healing and could help a pregnant woman with active herpes recover in time to avoid a cesarean section (Gunby 1983).

Reports of herpes contracted from hot tubs prompted an investigation, which found that the virus is killed quickly in spa water but can survive on nearby plastic surfaces for several hours (Nerurkar et al. 1983).

Chlamydia trachomatis causes most of the sexually transmitted disease in the United States, but it has been largely ignored because there were no easy tests to determine its presence. Two new tests for its presence were reported in *JAMA*. Chlamydia is the single most important cause of PID (pelvic inflammatory disease) and affects 3 to 4 million people a year (Wingerson 1983).

Nonspecific vaginitis (nonspecific simply means that doctors do not know what causes it) may or may not be a sexually transmitted disease. Formerly considered a bothersome but minor problem, NSV is no longer considered a completely benign infection. Several researchers linked it with premature labor, inflammation of the uterine lining after delivery, and a type of cervicitis (NSV no longer . . . 1983).

Although AIDS affects mainly gay men, the number of women affected has become significant—about 7 percent of AIDS patients as of 1983 (Update . . . 1983). Half of these women were intravenous drug abusers, and most of the other women seem to have contracted the disease through a sexual partner who is in one of the recognized high-risk groups. It may be possible, rarely, for someone to be a carrier without actually manifesting the disease (Pitchenik, Fischl, and Spira 1983).

AIDS patients have been discriminated against in all areas of their lives, and this homophobia has also affected lesbians. Fear of AIDS patients (or even of all gays on the grounds that they may harbor the disease) must be considered a civil rights issue and thus of concern to all of us.

In general, the disease is spread only through very intimate contact, but several AIDS cases were reported this year of children born into high-risk households (where a parent is a drug user or has slept with gay men). The children have been under one year of age, and their susceptibility may be due to their immature immune systems. Some researchers theorize that *only* people with impaired immune systems are susceptible to the disease and then only when exposed intimately to someone with the disease (West 1983).

A forum on women and AIDS was held in San Francisco in September. It was stressed that AIDS cannot be passed through skin-to-skin contact, and it was cautioned that there may be a risk of contracting AIDS from donor insemination. There has been little research about the transmission of AIDS from one woman to another, but so far it appears that lesbians are at less risk than heterosexual women for contracting AIDS (Helquist 1983).

Depo for American Women?

In January, the Food and Drug Administration heard testimony about Depo-Provera, an injectable contraceptive that Upjohn, the manufacturer of the product, would like to see approved for U.S. women. Gisela Dallenbach-Hellweg shed new light on previous findings that linked Depo to endometrial cancer in monkeys. Dallenbach-Hellweg's work indicates that the target organ in women may be different than in monkeys; Depo may be linked with cervical rather than endometrial cancer (Henry 1983a).

Family planning groups testified that for women in many countries, the lives saved by Depo (because of reduced maternal and infant mortality) outweigh the possible number of deaths from the drug's unproven carcinogenicity (Skurnik 1983).

Judy Norsigian, in *Health and Medicine News*, writes that although current research shows that Depo is probably safer than the pill, the pill was approved very prematurely and we should wait for more data this time around. She also points out that if a woman has problems on Depo, she cannot simply stop using it like the pill or an IUD (Norsigian 1983).

A particularly bizarre use of Depo is as a means of chemically castrating rapists; 1983 marked the first year that judges have ordered rapists and child molesters to submit to injections of Depo (along with short or probated sentences) as alternatives to maximum prison sentences (Mills 1983).

Urinary Tract Infection and Diaphragms

A woman urologist has found diaphragms implicated in urinary tract infections. Dr. Larrian Gillespie suggests that doctors are trained to fit diaphragms too large, resulting in compression of the bladder neck which can restrict urine flow by as much as 40 percent (urine left in the bladder provides a breeding ground for bacteria that migrate there). Gillespie also criticizes the expensive urological workup typically given women with recurrent UTI; many such women are "treated" by having their urethras repeatedly dilated. The traditional theory behind this is that the woman's urethra is too narrow and must be periodically stretched. Gillespie states that new technologies show us that any normal urethra will constrict around a catheter or probe; the "narrowness" is simply a response to the measuring instrument (Gillespie and Margolis 1983). Gillespie's work shows that urology may be as exploitative of women as obstetrics-gynecology has been.

Tampons

A blood test was introduced in 1983 that may help to identify people at risk for toxic shock. In addition, Proctor and Gamble (makers of Rely tampons) was accused during the year of covering up data from a study completed two years ago, which strongly implicated Rely-brand tampons in toxic shock syndrome. Interestingly, *S. aureus* (the bacteria implicated in toxic shock) grew equally well on different kinds of tampons, but the amount of toxin produced by the bacteria raised on Rely tampons was about four times the amount on other brands (Marwick 1983).

Tampons were also linked to vaginal ulcerations. Super-absorbent tampons are most commonly implicated in this problem as well as in toxic shock (Vaginal/cervical lesions . . . 1983).

The Boston Women's Health Book Collective called for uniform tests and regulations to determine the safety and effectiveness of tampons.

Women of Color

The first Black Women's Health Conference was held at Spellman College in Atlanta, Georgia, with over 1,500 women attending. Workshop topics included patient's rights, the health status of women in prison, birthing alternatives, the myth of mental illness, lupus, and black women as healers. The conference had the ambitious goals of educating women about self-care, presenting a cultural and historical perspective on health from a black view, increasing awareness of policies that affect access to health care, and acting as a network for black women (Johnson 1983).

The Black Women's Health Project has become a fast-growing network of self-help groups; it tries to reach low-income black women who have little access to health care. Twenty-six groups across the nation are now working on a broad range of issues (Youngblood 1983).

The difference in life expectancies between blacks and whites decreased slightly in the last decade, but the infant mortality rate for black infants is still twice that of white infants—this figure has not changed in twenty years. The biggest differences in death rates between black and white women, according to the latest statistics from the *Monthly Vital Statistics Report* (National Center for Health Statistics), occur in cases of diabetes, complications of pregnancy and childbirth, high blood pressure, and cerebrovascular disease. All these rates are more than twice as high for black women than white. Blacks also lead whites in cancer rates and cardiovascular disease (Advance report . . . 1983).

Hispanic populations are also at increased risk of health problems, particularly those related to pregnancy. The populations in this group tend to be young (and therefore at higher risk of pregnancy) and poor, and often their lack of English skills complicates access to health care.

Infant formula abuse is not just an overseas problem; breast feeding is discouraged in some U.S. hospitals, especially those that serve minorities. In general, only about a fourth of black women breast feed, and these tend to be well-educated women who know of the health advantages. At one hospital in Washington, D.C., a primarily black and Hispanic population is served; 95 percent of the women use infant formula rather than breast feed (Fugh-Berman 1983).

The health benefits of breast feeding are also of importance to Native American women. A very successful program on a Papago reservation in Arizona educated women about breast feeding and subsequently reduced rates of infant diarrhea, infection susceptibility, and dental problems. Native American women continue to suffer from a high rate of alcoholism; women in their reproductive years have a cirrhosis death rate thirty-seven times that of white women and three times that of other non-American Indian women (K. Cook 1983).

Mid-Life and Older Women

Older women are organizing in growing numbers in order to fight budget cuts, abuse of the elderly, and negative stereotypes. The elderly poor, 75 percent of whom are women, will be seriously affected by the proposed budget cuts in Medicare, the Older Americans Act Nutrition Program, and the food stamp program. Older women already spend a third of their median income on health care. Overmedication of the elderly is also an issue that should be addressed; older patients may take as many as fourteen to eighteen different drugs a year and nursing home patients may take from twenty to thirty drugs annually (Hecht 1983).

The First Conference on Midlife and Older Women was convened in October in New York City. Workshop topics included sexuality, abuse of the elderly, mental health, and independent living. A fifty-point action agenda was adopted to help influence future legislation. Recommendations included the creation of a national health plan, elimination of gender as a factor in setting insurance rates and pension benefits, and the elimination of negative sexual images of older women (Klemesrud 1983). The Second National Conference on Lesbian and Gay Aging included discussions of health workers' prejudices against sexually active elders (especially gays) and the lengths that lesbians and gay men have to go to in order to secure legal rights for their lovers (L. Cook 1983).

Disabled Women

Disabled women were actively involved in the debates on genetic screening and the rights of handicapped newborns last year. Some women maintained that abled people make no distinctions among types and degrees of disabilities (Dejanikus 1983). Anne Finger pointed out, however, that the rights of handicapped women and men must not become secondary to the issue of disabled children. Also noted was a lack of portrayals of disabled people as sexual beings (Finger 1983). An article in *Gay Community News* discussed sexual issues that especially affect disabled gays and lesbians (Langer 1983).

Sports

Women's fitness is a continuing trend; feminists, however, emphasize strength over figure control. A very thorough book published last year was *The Outdoor Woman's Guide to Sports, Fitness, and Nutrition* (Maughan and Collins, 1983).

Mona Shangold, writing about athletes and reproductive health, states that although many women worry about the effects of strenuous exercise on the reproductive system, few athletes suffer from menstrual dysfunctions. Those who do usually had preexisting problems (Shangold 1983).

Dieting

Concerns about the Cambridge diet were expressed during the year. Ads for this low-calorie, "balanced" powder (brought to us by the same people who sell the Mark Eden bust developer) imply that Cambridge dieters lose no body protein; in fact, that is untrue. More than 138 complaints of illness (including 6 deaths) from people using the diet have been reported to the Food and Drug Administration (Wadden et al. 1983).

Most reducing diets are unhealthy, according to Terre Poppe, who wrote in *off our backs* that fat women rarely eat more than their thin counterparts; but dieters suffer a slowing of metabolism that makes it very easy to gain lost weight back (Poppe 1983).

The ideal-weight concept was criticized on methodological grounds in *JAMA* (Knapp 1983). Knapp pointed out that some studies found that very underweight people also have high mortality rates. He suggests that the "outlier" (the very heavy and the very light) be studied with care and that the focus be switched from ideal weights to dangerous weights.

Even children have been caught up in the dieting obsession. A significant number of children referred to a New York hospital because of short stature or delayed puberty failed to develop because of self-imposed starvation. Fear of fat caused these children to skip meals or reduce caloric intake (Pugliese et al. 1983).

Anorexia and bulimia remained problems in 1983. Too few women consider themselves "normal" eaters. Whether self-starvers, obsessive eaters, or binge/purgers, many women are uncomfortable about their weight or their sense of control of it (Squire 1983).

The National Women's Health Network and the Center for Science in the Public Interest are trying to ban pills containing phenylpropanolamine (PPA). These pills are related to amphetamines; they can raise blood pressure and aggravate other health problems. The FTC has warned advertisers that safety and efficacy claims must be proven and that disclosures stating that one must eat less in order to show weight loss must be included in future ads (Diet pill ads . . . 1983). According to a *New York Times* article, PPA can cause tremor, agitation, and hallucinations. It is used in nasal decongestants as well as diet pills, and a dieter with a head cold could end up consuming three times the daily dose allowed by the FDA (Brody 1983).

Conclusion

There is still a great deal of work to be done on improving health care for all women, especially women of color and poor women. Medicine is becoming more and more technological. In the midst of the wizardry, we must maintain control over the decisions made about our bodies. We cannot do this unless we educate ourselves on all the alternatives.

48 ——— ADRIANE J. FUGH-BERMAN ———

References

Advance report of final mortality statistics, 1980. 1983. *Monthly Vital Statistics Report* 32, no. 4, supplement.

AREHART-TREICHEL, J. 1983. Boning up on osteoporosis. *Science News* 124, no. 9:140–41.

BLUME, E. 1983. Premenstrual syndromes, depression linked. *Journal of the American Medical Association* 249, no. 21:2864–66.

Britain's newest "medical college" will educate patients, not doctors. 1983. *Medical World News* 24, no. 24:50.

BRODY, J.E. 1983. Pills to aid the dieter: How safe are they? *New York Times*, 9 November.

Cancer-risk drop for pill-taking women confirmed. 1983. *Medical World News* 24, no. 6:88–89.

COHEN, NANCY WAINER, and LOIS J. ESTNER. 1983. *Silent knife: Cesarean prevention and vaginal birth after cesarean.* South Hadley, Mass.: Bergin and Garvey Publishers.

COOK, K. 1983. Native women work on reproductive rights, education in their communities. *Big Mama Rag*, January.

COOK, L. 1983. Lesbians and gays discuss aging. *off our backs*, October.

Council on Scientific Affairs. 1983. Fetal effects of maternal alcohol use. *Journal of the American Medical Association* 249, no. 18:2517–21.

CORDERO, J.F., and P.M. LAYDE. 1983. Vaginal spermicides, chromosomal abnormalities and limb reduction defects. *Family Planning Perspectives* 15, no. 1:16–18.

Dalkon shield IUD. 1983. *Network News*, July-August.

DAVIS, H. 1983. Health group wants Dalkon shield recall. *Washington Post*, 26 April.

DEJANIKUS, T. 1983. Genetic screening. *off our backs*, May.

Delegates from five continents discuss health problems arising from women's work. 1983. *Women's Occupational Health and Resource Center (WOHRC) News*, July.

Diet pill ads halted. 1983. *Network News*, September-October.

Disability studied in premature infants. 1983. *Research Resources Reporter* 7, no. 5:5–6.

Doc in the box. 1983. *Medical World News* 24, no. 16:36.

Doctor at door, helping homebound, not just nostalgic figure. 1983. *Medical World News* 24, no. 17:131–32.

DONOVAN, P. 1983. Medical societies vs. nurse practitioners. *Family Planning Perspectives* 15, no. 4:166–71.

DOUDNA, C. 1983. American couples: Surprising new finds. *Ms.*, November, pp. 116–19.

EAGAN, A. 1983. The selling of pre-menstrual syndrome. *Ms.*, October, pp. 26–31.

Fertility rate slows in 1980, but large increases continue among older mothers, unmarried women. 1983. *Family Planning Perspectives* 15, no. 1:38–39.

FINGER, A. 1983. Disability and reproductive rights. *off our backs*, October.

French study lends support to conservative breast cancer therapy. 1983. *Medical World News* 24, no. 21:99–100.

FUGH-BERMAN, A.J. 1983. Maternal and child health: Issues for women of color. *off our backs*, May.

GARMON, L. 1983. Advances reported in the design of drugs to battle herpes. *Science News* 123, no. 14:213.

GILLESPIE, L., and Z. MARGOLIS. 1983. Cystitis can be cured. *Ms.*, June, pp. 98–101.

GUNBY, P. 1983. Genital herpes research: Many aim to tame maverick virus. *Journal of the American Medical Association* 250, no. 18:2417–27.

HARRISON, B.W. 1983. Our right to choose: Toward a new ethic of abortion. Boston: Beacon Press.

HECHT, A. 1983. Medicine and the elderly. *FDA Consumer* 17, no. 7:20–21.

HELQUIST, M. 1983. Women and AIDS. *Washington Blade*, 9 September.

HENRY, A. 1983a. Evaluating DMPA. *off our backs*, February.

HENRY, A. 1983b. Discovering the vagina. *off our backs*, July.

HOGUE, C.J.R., W. CATES, JR., and C. TIETZE. 1983. Impact of vacuum aspiration abortion on future childbearing: A review. *Family Planning Perspectives* 15, no. 3:119–26.

Home device shows suspicious breast spots. 1983. *Medical World News* 24, no. 3:60.

Inequality of sacrifice: Older women. 1983. *Owl Observer*, May. Available from 3800 Harrison St., Oakland, CA 44611.

ISMACH, J. 1983. Infertility. *Medical World News* 24, no. 23:55–78.

Italian trials suggest women have less to fear in breast cancer therapy. 1983. *Medical World News* 24, no. 23:85.

JACOBS, P. 1982. Premature sex growth in children examined. *Los Angeles Times*, 9 June.

JOHNSON, L.A. 1983. Black women's health issues. *off our backs*, August-September.

KLITSCH, M. 1983. Hormonal implants: The next wave of contraceptives. *Family Planning Perspectives* 15, no. 5:239–43.

KLEMESRUD, J. 1983. Problems of older women focus of parley. *New York Times*, 26 October.

KNAPP, T.R. 1983. A methodological critique of the "ideal weight" concept. *Journal of the American Medical Association* 250, no. 4:506–10.

KURTZ, H. 1983. OSHA official blocked efforts to restrict chemical. *Washington Post*, 1 November.

LANGER, N.A.F. 1983. Different abilities, the same queer pleasures. *Gay Community News*, 10 December.

LAVERSEN, N. 1983. PMS, premenstrual syndrome and you. New York: Simon & Schuster.

MARWICK, C. 1983. Holdup of toxic shock data ends during trial in Texas. *Journal of the American Medical Association* 250, no. 4:3267–69.

MAUGHAN, J.J., with K. COLLINS. 1983. *The outdoor women's guide to sports, fitness, and nutrition.* Harrisburg, Penn.: Stackpole Books.

McKINSTRY, D.W. 1983. Herpes research: Developing vaccines and drugs. *Research Resources Reporter* 7, no. 1:1–5.

MILLS, K. 1983. Chemical "castration" poses moral, legal dilemmas. *Washington Post*, 24 December.

MINTZ, M. 1983. Study says contraceptive device carried high risk of infection. *Washington Post*, 17 March.

Minnesota doctors "voluntarily" make fee lists available. 1983. *Medical World News* 24, no. 1:61–62.

NERURKAR, L.S., et al. 1983. Survival of herpes simplex virus in water specimens collected from hot tubs in spa facilities and on plastic surfaces. *Journal of the American Medical Association* 250, no. 22:3081–83.

New breast models used for self-examination training. 1983. *Medical World News* 24, no. 17:20–21.

New record birth of baby after mother's brain death. 1983. *Medical World News* 24, no. 15:28.

New York requires warning to pregnant women. 1983. *Washington Post*, 9 December.

9 to 5 starts nationwide drive for VDT research and action. 1983. *Women's Occupational Health and Resource Center News*, July.

No time limit on maintaining "dead" mother to save fetus? 1983. *Medical World News* 24, no. 9:20–21.

NORRIS, R.V., with C. SULLIVAN. 1983. PMS/Premenstrual syndrome. New York: Rawson Associates.

NORSIGIAN, JUDY. 1983. Depo-Provera: A new offensive. *Health and Medicine*, Winter-Spring, pp. 3–5.

NSV no longer thought benign. 1983. *Medical World News* 24, no. 17:92.

Office workers assail NRC report on safety of VDTs. 1983. *Women's Occupational Health and Resource Center News*, September.

Oral contraceptives may help preserve fertility after salpingitis. 1983. *Medical World News* 24, no. 18:29.

OSHA proposes new ethylene oxide standard. 1983. *Women's Occupational Health and Resource Center News*, April-May.

Ovarian cancer and talc: Is there a connection? 1983. *Network News*, January-February.

PITCHENIK, A.E., M.A. FISCHL, and T.J. SPIRA. 1983. Acquired immune deficiency syndrome in low risk patients. *Journal of the American Medical Association* 250, no. 10:1310–12.

Placental hormone for birth control. 1983. *Science News* 124, no. 5:74.

POGREBIN, L.C. 1983. Do Americans hate children? *Ms.*, November, pp. 47–127.

POLLNER, F. 1983. The revolution in fetal health care. *Medical World News* 24, no. 17:65–91.

POPPE, 1983. The fats of life. *off our backs*, March.

Postmenopausal estrogen therapy appears to be making a comeback. 1983. *Medical World News* 24, no. 12:27.

PRUPES, K. 1983. Custom cervical cap reentering clinical trials. 1983. *Journal of the American Medical Association* 250, no. 15:1946–51.

PUGLIESE, M.T., et al. 1983. Fear of obesity: A cause of short stature and delayed puberty. *New England Journal of Medicine* 309, no. 9:513–18.

Radiologists adopt antithermography policy for breast cancer screening. 1983. *Medical World News* 24, no. 23:10.

RIA spots toxic shock susceptibility. 1983. *Medical World News* 24, no. 12:7.

SARREL, L., and P. SARREL. 1983. The new contraceptives. *Redbook*, August, p. 20.

SCHOLL, T.O., et al. 1983. Effects of vaginal spermicides on pregnancy outcome. *Family Planning Perspectives* 15, no. 5:244–50.

SHANGOLD, M.M. 1983. Concerns of athletic women about reproductive function. *Medical Aspects of Human Sexuality* 17, no. 12:66–74.

SHEARER, L. High risk baby deliveries. *Parade*, 13 November, p. 8.

SILBERNER, J. 1983. The pill revisited: New cancer link? *Science News* 124, no. 18:279.

Skirmishes on teen reg, office transfer shape Title X renewal debate. 1983. *Washington Memo*, 27 December. Available from the Alan Guttmacher Institute.

SKURNIK, J. 1983. Depo-Provera: FDA hearings raise questions. *off our backs*, February.

SQUIRE, S. 1983. Where are you on the eating arc? *Ms.*, October, p. 45.

STEINBERG, S. 1983. Male contraceptive in stomach salve. *Science News* 124, no. 8:117.

STEPHENSON, G. 1983. New contraceptives tested for women and men. *Research Resources Reporter* 7, no. 5:1–4.

The stress of women's work. 1983. *Women's Occupational Health and Resource Center Factsheet*, September.

Stunted expectations. 1984. *Village Voice*, 17 January.

Substantial rise seen during 1970s in first births to women over 30. 1983. *Family Planning Perspectives* 15, no. 3:140–41.

Supreme Court reaffirms right to abortion, strikes down local restrictions. 1983. *Washington Memo*, 22 June.

TREICHEL, J.A. 1983. Vitamin C for the cervix. *Science News* 123, no. 2:23.

TREVATHON, E., et al. 1983. Cigarette smoking and dysplasia and carcinoma in situ of the cervix. *Journal of the American Medical Association* 250, no. 4:499–502.

Update: Acquired immunodeficiency syndrome. 1983. *Morbidity and Mortality Weekly Report* 32, no. 35:465–67.

User's perception of contraceptive vaginal ring: A field study in Brazil and the Dominican Republic. 1983. *Studies in Family Planning* 14, no. 11:284–90.

Vaginal/cervical lesions linked to tampon use. 1983. *Medical World News* 24, no. 21:65.

Vasectomy, disease link refuted. 1983. *Science News* 124, no. 24:377.

VENTURA, S.J. 1983. Births of Hispanic parentage, 1980. *Monthly Vital Statistics Report* 32, no. 6, supplement.

Victories won in discrimination cases. 1983. *Women's Occupational Health and Resource Center News*, February-March.

VIETH, B. 1984. Effects of the Reagan administration on maternal and child health. *Network News*, January-February.

WADDEN, T.A., et al. 1983. The Cambridge diet. *Journal of the American/Medical Association* 250, no. 20:2833–34.

WEST, S. 1983. AIDS update. *Science 83* 4, no. 8:16–17.

WILKE, J. 1983. Prenatal test kit wins FDA approval. *Washington Post*, 18 June.

Will Virginia become fourth state to enact breast cancer consent law? 1983. *Medical World News* 24, no. 19:24–25.

WINGERSON, L. 1983. Two new tests for chlamydia get quick results without culture. *Journal of the American Medical Association* 250, no. 17:2257–59.

With legality of abortion secured for now, battles shift to issues of access. 1983. *Washington Memo*, 27 December.

WITT, R.L. 1983. PMS: What every woman should know about premenstrual syndrome. New York: Stein and Day.

Women having fewer children before age 25, more after the age of 30. 1983. *Family Planning Perspectives* 15, no. 4:193–94.

Workshop findings inconclusive on estrogen, CHD link. 1983. *Medical World News* 24, no. 21:22–23.

Young American women delaying motherhood; 25 percent may remain permanently childless. 1983. *Family Planning Perspectives* 15, no. 5:224–25.

YOUNGBLOOD, S. 1983. Self-help groups: "Taking charge and taking care." *Network News*, May-June.

ZAMICHOW, N. 1983. Is it something in the food? *Ms.*, October, pp. 93–98.

Bibliography

ALLEN, PATRICIA, and DENISE FORTINO. *Cycles: Every Woman's Guide to Menstruation*. New York: Pinnacle Books, 1983. Covers PMS, menstrual problems, menopause; includes information on diet and nutritional supplementation.

AMMER, CHRISTINE. *The A-Z of Women's Health*. New York: Everest House Publishers, 1983. A mini-encyclopedia; readable and incorporates feminist and alternative medical perspectives.

ANDREWS, LORI B. *New Conceptions, A Consumer's Guide to the Newest Infertility Treatments*. New York: St. Martin's Press, 1983. Covers legal, medical, and emotional aspects of infertility.

ASHFORD, JANET ISAACS. *The Whole Birth Catalog*. New York: Crossing Press, 1983. Consumer's guide includes book and magazine reviews as well as extensive lists of resources.

Boston Women's Health Book Collective. *Our Bodies, Ourselves*. New York: Simon and Schuster, 1979. No book list would be complete without this one.

Boston Women's Health Book Collective and the Massachusetts Coalition for Occupational Safety and Health. *Our Jobs, Our Health: A Woman's Guide to Occupational Health and Safety*. Boston, 1983. Available from Dept. OH, Box 192, W. Somerville, MA 02144. Another valuable contribution from the BWHBC.

Center for Early Adolescence. *Early Adolescent Sexuality: Resources for Parents, Professionals, and Young People*. Carrboro, N.C., 1983. Available from Center for Early Adolescence, Suite 223, Carr Mill Mall, Carrboro, NC 27510. Listings of reading materials, films, training materials, fiction and nonfiction books.

Concern for Health Options: Information, Care, and Education. *Childbirth Choices*. Philadelphia, Pa.: CHOICES, 1982. Presents alternatives on where to birth and under whose care. Discusses obstetric procedures; also contains reading list and glossary.

DES Action National. *Fertility and Pregnancy Guide for DES Daughters and Sons*. San Francisco, 1983. Available from DES Action, 1638-B Haight St., San Francisco, CA 94117. Medical information on infertility and pregnancy problems in people exposed to DES.

Federation of Feminist Women's Health Centers. *How to Stay Out of the Gynecologist's Office*. Culver City, Calif.: Peace Press, 1981. A very good guide to self-help. Includes home remedies for minor problems and a good section on "taking the mystery out of a medical visit."

FREEMAN, ROGER K., and SUSAN C. PESCAR. *Safe Delivery: Protecting Your Baby during High-Risk Pregnancy*. New York: McGraw-Hill, 1982. Problems and treatments for pregnant women with medical problems.

HATCHER, ROBERT A., NANCY JOSEPHS, FELICIA H. STEWART, FELICIA J. GUEST, GARY K. STEWART, and DEBORAH KOWAL. *It's Your Choice*. New York: Irvington Publishers, 1982. Quick reference book on birth control. Cautions, tips, common causes of accidental pregnancy, and when to call a doctor.

JIMENEZ, SHERRY LYNN MIMS. *The Other Side of Pregnancy*. Englewood Cliffs, N.J.: Prentice-Hall, 1982. For health professionals or friends of someone who has lost a child through miscarriage or stillbirth.

———. *The Pregnant Woman's Comfort Guide*. Englewood Cliffs, N.J.: Prentice-Hall, 1982. Holistic ways of dealing with discomforts of pregnancy and the postpartum period.

KAUFMAN, JOEL, LINDA RABINOWITZ-DAGI, JOAN LEVIN, PHYLLIS McCARTHY, SIDNEY WOLFE, EVE BARGMANN, and Public Citizen

Health Research Group. *Over the Counter Pills That Don't Work*. New York: Pantheon Books, 1983. What not to use; what to substitute for what; treating without drugs; and when to see a doctor. A companion to the also excellent *Pills That Don't Work*. Together they are far superior to the pharmacy books published this year that were aimed at women.

LANGSTON, DEBORAH P. *Living with Herpes*. New York: Doubleday and Co., 1983. Comprehensive; defines its terms, covers all types of herpes, and has excellent diagrams and photographs.

MATTHEW, GWYNETH FERGUSON. *Voices from the Shadows*. Toronto, Canada: Women's Educational Press, 1983. Available from 16 Baldwin St., Toronto, Ontario, Canada. Disabled women speak out on sexuality, motherhood, education, and so on.

MELROSE, DIANNA. *Bitter Pills: Medicines and the Third World Poor*. England: Oxfam Public Affairs Unit, 1982. Available from 274 Banbury Rd., Oxford, England 0X27DZ. Drug use and promotion in the Third World. Includes positive responses and suggestions. Extensively referenced.

Microwave News. *VDTs: Health and Safety*. New York, 1983. Available from Microwave News, P.O. Box 1799, Grand Central Station, New York, NY 10163. All the 1981 and 1982 coverage on VDTs from Microwave News; includes index.

NAPOLI, MARYANN. *Health Facts*. New York: Overlook Press, 1982. Updated articles from the newsletter. Well-referenced chapters include mammography, depression, nonmedical therapies, and cancer.

PINCKNEY, CATHEY, and EDWARD R. PINCKNEY. *Do-it-Yourself Medical Testing*. New York: Facts on File, 1983. Medical monitoring of health at home.

PORCINO, JANE. *Growing Older, Growing Better*. Reading, Mass.: Addison-Wesley Publishers, 1983. Excellent handbook for women "in the second half of life." Covers sexuality, menopause, politics, life transitions, common afflictions, and so on. Resources given for each chapter.

PRICE, ANNE, and NANCY BAMFORD. *The Breastfeeding Guide for the Working Woman*. New York: Wallaby Books, 1983. Includes handling and storage of breast milk; comparison of breast pumps; directions for manual expression of milk; and breast-feeding difficulties. Contains many helpful photographs.

RUMSEY, TIMOTHY, and ORLO OTTESON. *A Physician's Complete Guide to Medical Self-Care*. New York: Rutledge Press, 1981. Covers home lab tests and when to see a doctor. Thorough, with resources.

Sex and Disability Project. *Who Cares? A Handbook on Sex Education and Counselling Services for Disabled People*. Baltimore, Md.: University Park Press, 1982. Available from 300 N. Charles St., Baltimore, MD 21201. Comprehensive listing of available services and materials.

SHAPIRO, HOWARD I. *The Birth Control Book*. New York: St. Martin's Press, 1982. Very good book. Includes research on new methods and postcoital contraception.

SHOENFIELDER, LISA, and BARB WEISER. *Shadow on a Tightrope*. Iowa City: Aunt Lute Book Co., 1983. Available from P.O. Box 2723, Iowa City, IA 52244. Writings on "fat oppression"; includes sections on medical crimes, harassment, and myths about fat.

STELLMAN, JEANNE, and MARY SUE HENIFIN. *Office Work Can Be Dangerous to Your Health*. New York: Pantheon Books, 1983. Discusses VDTs, lighting, indoor air pollution, and fire safety. Good section on the biology of office work. Includes resources.

STEWART, LEE. *NAPSAC Directory of Alternative Birth Services and Consumer Guide*. Marble Hills, Mo.: NAPSAC Reproductions, 1982. Finding an attendant and location for birth; covers both the United States and Canada.

WAITZKIN, HOWARD. *The Second Sickness: Contradictions of Capitalistic Health Care*. New York: Free Press, 1983. An MD/sociologist examines deficiencies in our health care system and their connection to social structure.

WATSON, RITA ESPOSITO, and ROBERT C. WALLACH. *New Choices, New Chances: A Woman's Guide to Conquering Cancer*. Rev. ed. New York: St. Martin's Press, 1983. Readable presentation of treatments (including holistic approaches) for cancers specific to women. Includes lists of cancer centers and programs.

WEG, RUTH B. *Sexuality in the Later Years*. New York: Academic Press, 1983. A number of different perspectives; generally holistic approach.

WEIL, ANDREW. *Health and Healing: Understanding Conventional and Alternative Medicine*. Boston, Mass.: Houghton Mifflin Co., 1983. Fascinating analysis of mind cures, homeopathy, osteopathy, Chinese medicine, and so on. Includes section on "medical treatments as active placebos."

YOUNG, DIONY. *Changing Childbirth*. New York: Childbirth Graphics, 1982. Strategy book for those who support family-centered birth.

Resources

Films

An excellent *Annotated Guide to Films on Reproductive Rights* can be obtained for $3.00 from Media Network, 208 West 13th St., New York, NY 10011. Topics include abortion, health care, sterilization, women and children, and birth control.

Also a good listing is *Audiovisuals for Sexuality Professionals: A Selected Bibliography*, available for $1.50 (and stamped, self-addressed business envelope) from SIECUS, 80 Fifth Ave., Suite 801–2, New York, NY 10011.

Health Education Films: An Annotated Guide is available from Mt. Auburn Hospital, Community Health Education Dept., 330 Mt. Auburn St., Cambridge, MA 02138.

A resource catalog that includes films is available from Planned Parenthood of Metropolitan Washington, 1108 16th St., Washington, DC 20036.

Some films produced in 1983 include:

DES: The Time Bomb Drug, by Stephanie Palewski. A history of DES. Available for rental or purchase from Limelight Productions, 11 W. 18 St., New York, N.Y. 10011. (212) 581-4895.

Choices: In Sexuality with Physical Disability, by Arlen Tarlofsky. Disabled people and their partners relate their experiences. Made in two parts so that it can be shown with or without the sexually explicit portion. Available for rental or purchase from Mercury Productions, 17 W. 45 St., New York, NY 10036. (212) 869-4073.

Sterilization Abuse and Population Control, by Reproductive Rights National Network. Slide show; covers issues of sexism and racism in population control policies. Available for rental or purchase from Reproductive Rights National Network, 40 Karen Star, New Hampshire Feminist Health Center, 38 South Main St., Concord, NH 03301. (603) 224-3521.

Matters So Fundamental, by Fran Hereth and Ilana Bar-Din. Slide show; a historical overview of abortion. Updated 1983. Available for rental or purchase from Committee to Defend Reproductive Rights, 1638-B Haight St., San Francisco, CA 94117. (415) 552-2000.

Organizations

Alan Guttmacher Institute, 360 Park Ave. S., New York, NY 10010. (212) 685-5858. Family planning research, policy analysis, and education. Publishes *Family Planning Perspectives*, *Washington Memo* (legislative update), and *Family Planning/Population Reporter*.

American College of Nurse-Midwives, 1522 K St. NW, Suite 1120 Washington, DC 20005. (202) 347-5445. National registry of nurse-midwives; list of schools; publications.

American Public Health Association, 1015 18th St. NW, Washington, DC 20036. (202) 789-5600. Various publications; list available.

American Social Health Organization, 260 Sheridan Ave., Palo Alto, CA 94306. (415) 321-5134. Pamphlets on sexually transmitted diseases. Herpes Resource Center supplies information by phone and mail. Publishes the *Helper* (newsletter on herpes) quarterly; includes list of support groups.

Black Women's Health Project, Martin Luther King, Jr., Health Center, 450 Auburn Ave., Suite 157, Atlanta, GA 30312. (404) 659-3854. Resource and referral. Quarterly newsletter. May join through National Women's Health Network. Slide show on the health of black women available for sale or free rental.

Boston Women's Health Book Collective, (mailing address) P.O. Box 192, West Somerville, MA 02144. (resource center) 465 Mt. Auburn St., Watertown, Mass. (617) 924-0271. Responds to written requests for information on women's health issues. Library open to the public.

Center for Medical Consumers, 237 Thompson St., New York, NY 10012. (212) 674-7105. Extensive medical/health library open to the public; phone-in tape service (list of health topics available with SASE). Publishes *Healthfacts*, a monthly consumer newsletter, and *Health-PAC*, a bimonthly bulletin analyzing the health care system.

Center for Occupational Hazards, 5 Beekman St., New York, NY 10038. (212) 227-6220. Answers questions by phone and mail about hazards in the arts. Publishes *Art Hazards News*, also books and pamphlets (publications list available).

Center for Population Options, 2031 Florida Ave. NW, Washington, DC 20009. (202) 387-5091. Publishes *Issues and Actions Update*, a quarterly concerned with the prevention of adolescent pregnancy.

Coalition for the Medical Rights of Women, 1638 B Haight St., San Francisco, CA 94117. (415) 621-8030. Files open to the public, list of publications available. Publications include *Second Opinion* and *Committee to Defend Reproductive Rights News*.

Center for Science in the Public Interest, 1755 S St. NW, Washington, DC 20009. (202) 332-9110. Consumer organization focused on health and nutrition. Publications list available. Publishes *Nutrition Action*.

DES Action National, Long Island Jewish Hospital, New Hyde Park, NY 11040. (516) 775-3450. Consumer group that educates on the effects of DES exposure. Publishes *DES Action Voice* quarterly; other publications available.

Do It Now (DIN) Publications, P.O. Box 5115, Phoenix, AZ 85010. (602) 257-0797. Drug, alcohol, and health information; includes material directed at children, adolescents, and the elderly. *DIN Newsservice* (bimonthly) available; also other publications.

Disability Rights Education and Defense Fund, Inc. (DREDF), 2032 San Pablo Ave., Berkeley, CA 94702. (415) 664-2555 (voice) or (415) 664-2629 (TDD). Education; legal support; research and policy analysis; technical assistance; publications. Packet available on disability policies.

Emma Goldman Clinic for Women, Women's Health Project, 715 N. Dodge, Iowa City, IA 52240. (319) 337-2111. Library open to the public; publications available, including bibliographies on sexuality and abortion.

Endometriosis Association, P.O. Box 92187, Milwaukee, WI 53202. No phone. Self-help organization. Send SASE for information and brochure. Bimonthly newsletter available to members.

Feminist Women's Health Center, 6411 Hollywood Blvd., Los Angeles, CA 90028. (213) 469-4844. Literature and audiovisual materials available.

Food and Drug Administration, Office of Consumer and Professional Affairs, HFN-5, Advisory Committee Branch, National Center for Drugs and Biologics, 5600 Fisher's Lane, Rockville, MD 20857. (301) 443-1016. Answers questions about drugs and their side effects.

Food and Drug Administration, Office of Consumer Affairs HFE-88, 5600 Fisher's Lane, Rockville, MD 20857. (301) 443-3170. Answers questions about the safety of food or cosmetics.

Health Research Group, 2000 P St. NW, Washington, DC 20036. (202) 872-0320. Research and legislative monitoring. Publications list available; includes information on Depo, the pill, cervical cancer, and breast cancer.

Healthsharing, Box 230, Station M, Toronto, Ontario, Canada M6S4T3. (416) 598-2658. Quarterly journal on women's health issues.

Hot Flash, c/o Dr. Jane Porcino, School of Allied Health Professions, Health Sciences Center, SUNY at Stony Brook, Stony Brook, NY 11794. (516) 246-3305. Quarterly publication for mid-life and older women; treats health issues from a holistic perspective.

Infant Formula Action Coalition (INFACT), 310 E. 38th St., Suite 301, Minneapolis, MN 55409. (612) 331-2333. Coalition against promotion of infant formula by multinational corporations. Literature, audiovisuals, petitions, and so on.

International Association of Parents and Professionals for Safe Alternatives in Childbirth (NAPSAC), P.O. Box 267, Marble Hill, MO 63764. (314) 238-2010. Information on family-centered childbirth programs. Publications list available.

International Childbirth Education Association (ICEA), P.O. Box 20048, Minneapolis, MN 55420. (612) 854-8660. Supports family-centered maternal care. Extensive list of books and pamphlets available. Publishes *ICEA News, ICEA Sharing* (for childbirth educators), *ICEA Review* (commentary on research and literature), and *ICEA Forum* (administrative information for groups).

Midwives Alliance of North America, c/o Concord Midwivery Service, 30 S. Main St., Concord, NH 03301. Referrals to lay and nurse-midwives. Publishes *MANA Newsletter* bimonthly.

National Association of Anorexia Nervosa and Associated Disorders, Inc. (NAANAD), Box 271, Highland Park, IL 60035. Hotline (312) 831-3438. Education and self-help organization. Free counseling, referrals, information. Send SASE (with two stamps) for brochures.

National Family Planning and Reproductive Health Association, Inc. (NFPRHA), Suite 1210, 1110 Vermont Ave. NW, Washington, DC 20005. (202) 467-6767. Concerned with changes in federal legislation. Publishes *NFPRHA News*.

National Women's Health Network, 224 Seventh St. SE, Washington, DC 20003. (202) 543-9222. Consumer group works on a variety of health issues. Publishes *Network News;* other publications available.

Network Against Psychiatric Assault, 2054 University Ave., Room 406, Berkeley, CA 94704. (415) 548-2980. Organization working against forced psychiatric treatment and involuntary commitment. Publishes *Madness Network News*.

New Hampshire Feminist Health Center, 38 South Main St., Concord, NH 03301. (603) 225-2739. Packets of information on PMS and other health care topics. Publishes *Womenwise* quarterly.

off our backs, 1841 Columbia Rd. NW, #212, Washington, DC 20009. (202) 234-8072. Monthly women's news journal covers health, labor, prisons, and legislation affecting women.

Older Women's League, 1325 G St. NW, Washington, DC 20005. (202) 783-6686. Advocacy for mid-life and older women. Provides educational materials on health care, pensions, welfare, Social Security, divorce. Publishes the *OWL Observer*.

Reproductive Rights National Network (R2N2), 17 Murray St., New York, NY 10007. (212) 267-8891. Files open to the public. Publishes reproductive rights newsletter; packets of information available.

Resolve, Inc., P.O. Box 474, Belmont, MA 02178. (617) 484-2424. National infertility organization; offers counseling, medical information, and referrals.

Sex Information and Education Council of the United States (SIECUS), 80 Fifth Ave., New York, NY 10011. (212) 673-3850. Information service, library open to the public (fee for usage); publications list available; bibliographies on sexuality, disability, family life, audiovisuals. Publishes *SIECUS Report*.

VDT News, P.O. Box 1799, Grand Central Station, New York, NY 10163. (212) 725-5252. Publishes bimonthly newsletter on office automation; includes technological issues, research, and legislation.

Women and Health Roundtable, Federation of Organizations for Professional Women, 1825 Connecticut Ave. NW, Suite 403, Washington, DC 20009. (202) 328-1415. Coalition to improve federal health policies and programs. Publishes *A Woman's Yellow Book* and *Roundtable Report*, a monthly update on women's health policy issues.

Women for Sobriety, P.O. Box 618, Quakertown, PA. 18951. (215) 536-8026. Information on self-help groups. Publishes booklets and *Sobering Thoughts*, a monthly newsletter.

Women's Health Information Center, Ufton Center, 12 Ufton Rd., London, England N1 5BY. Quarterly newsletter includes book reviews, news on international women's health.

Women's Occupational Health and Resource Center, Columbia University, School of Public Health, 21 Audubon Ave., 3rd Floor, New York, NY 10032. (212) 694-3927. Publishes *WOHRC News* bimonthly, and other publications available. Library open to the public; workshops; literature searches.

Humanities Scholarship

Hilda L. Smith

The year 1983 saw a continuation of the increasing scholarship on women in humanities fields, with especially large numbers of works appearing in literature and history. Although there were fewer publications in the field of philosophy, some of the most important collections were written by philosophers. There was much less scholarship concerning women in music and art than among the other humanities disciplines.

Each discipline, over the last decade, has identified a number of issues crucial to understanding women's place in the field's research and theoretical constructs. Few generalizations can be made about women's studies across humanities disciplines. However, there does appear to be one overall dichotomy: those works that include women in a field's preestablished questions and categories and those that question traditional categorization. The first includes reference works that compile letters and diaries as well as "women in" studies, such as women in reform movements, in labor unions, or in eighteenth-century literature. The second group tends to comprise broader studies, utilizing a more overt and systematic feminist analysis and reviewing the direction of the field generally. These works embrace questions about how women's omission from particular fields affects the area's scholarship as a whole, in addition to clarifying the important role women played.

The more broadly based works tend to raise questions within the scholarly tradition of their disciplines and to question the theories and research of historians and literary critics, rather than humanists generally. There are similar assumptions, though, made across disciplines by those concentrating on women's scholarship. These assumptions include a suspicion that their discipline will ignore or distort women's contributions if feminist scholars do not maintain a vigilant watch; that different standards for significance, excellence, and attention are applied to men and women; and that an overt or subtle assumption of lowered intellectual or scholarly standards apply to work done on women.

The most populated fields—history and literature—have begun to raise issues about how fair consideration of women might change their basic structure. Others have only begun to raise questions concerning women's contribution to their areas, and work in these areas by necessity concentrates more on collection of materials and the inclusion of women into traditional categories. Because specialists in women's history have been working for a long time to incorporate women into general treatments of the past, that field has probably advanced furthest beyond compensatory efforts. Yet philosophical works—partly by the very nature of the discipline—have developed some of the most sophisticated theories explaining women's essential social and intellectual characteristics. Writings about women's literature are often strongly feminist, but through focusing on a single individual or a close reading of a single text (or group of texts), hold less interest for scholars outside the discipline than does much historical scholarship. The works of feminist criticism that focus on the discipline as a whole are a smaller percentage than those that treat an individual author or literary theme.

Literature

Studies in literature on women divide themselves among a number of approaches: collections of lesser known authors; collected essays on groups of female writers or on the treatment of women by male authors; and collected works or individual studies of a single author. There continue to be greater numbers of collected essays than book-length studies. Of those works that collected feminist essays, two of the most important were *Virginia Woolf: A Feminist Slant*, edited by Jane Marcus, and Suzanne Juhasz's *Feminist Critics Read Emily Dickinson*. An impressive study of the literary treatment of women is Lisa Jardine's *Still Harping on Daughters: Women and Drama in the Age of Shakespeare*.

Jane Marcus, who has studied Virginia Woolf for a number of years, follows her earlier collection, *New Feminist Essays on Virginia Woolf* (London: Macmillan & Co., 1981) by placing Woolf into a general feminist and political context. In the introductory essay for her 1983 collection, Marcus discusses the historical and personal origins of Woolf's feminism, linking it to the Quaker background of her aunt, Caroline Emelia Stephen, and emphasizing the importance of celibacy in protecting women from male domination. A theme central to her aunt's *The Service of the Poor*, on clerical and secular sisterhoods serving those in need, it reappears in *A Room of One's Own*, which noted the possibilities for scholarship inherent in the single life free from incursions by the patriarchy.

The essays collected on Woolf include discussions of her relationships with other women authors and scholars of the time, including Dorothy Richardson and Katherine Mansfield; her youthful interests in women's issues; and a number of studies of her work in progress, including Susan Squier's "A Track of Our Own: Typescript Drafts of *The Years*." Although Marcus's work is a useful addition to the scholarship on Virginia Woolf, the topics are essentially unrelated and many of the essays are too brief to allow fully developed analyses.

Suzanne Juhasz's volume on Emily Dickinson includes a large number of valuable essays, and her introduction is most useful in summarizing and evaluating the feminist scholarship on the poet to date. Although these essays deal with divergent topics in Dickinson's work, they achieve a scholarly unity by concentrating on the interaction between language and thought. The last three essays by Margaret Homans, Christine Miller, and Joanne Feit Diehl all handle Dickinson's treatment and structure of love and death. Some of the most significant contributions are those dealing broadly with the connection between Dickinson's sense of womanhood and her artistic work. Especially interesting is Sandra M. Gilbert's "The Wayward Nun beneath the Hill: Emily Dickinson and the Mysteries of Womanhood." In this essay, Gilbert focuses on Dickinson as a reclusive mystery, as "a process of self-mythologizing" which created "herself-and-her-life" as emblematic or even religious text—"the ironic hagiography, say, of a New England nun." Dickinson built this myth out of the characteristics and constraints of nineteenth-century womanhood "to transform and transcend them." Such an analysis allows Gilbert to discover feminist statements in Dickinson overlooked by other scholars. In addition, the essays by Karl Keller, Joanne A. Dobson, and Adalaide Morris provide able discussions of her treatment of sexuality and male-female relationships based on close linguistic and textual analyses.

Lisa Jardine, in *Still Harping on Daughters: Women and Drama in the Age of Shakespeare*, argues that earlier feminist work on Shakespeare accepted the "conventions of orthodox criticism" and merely concentrated on female characters. Jardine grounds her understanding of Shakespeare's treatment of women in the social and intellectual setting of his age, especially Joan Kelly's questioning of the Renaissance as a period of advancement for women. Shakespeare's women, according to Jardine, reflected the differing views of male and female talents and proper life-styles widespread during the late 1500s and early 1600s. The dramatist neither "transcends the limits of his time and sex" as earlier critics have contended, nor does his "maleness" necessarily deny his ability to portray female characters sensitively. Rejecting both extremes, Jardine contends "that Shakespeare's plays neither mirror the social scene, nor articulate explicitly any of the varied contemporary views on 'the woman question.' " Rather, Shakespeare's heroines reflect his and contemporary views, and his "weeping woman as female hero" possesses "precisely those qualities [which] *negate* the possibility for heroism in the male." Their essential femininity, as Jardine shows, reveals that Shakespeare, as might be expected, did not deviate from current social norms when describing his aristocratic heroines.

A more general treatment of women authors, past and present, is feminist critic and science fiction writer Joanna Russ's *How to Suppress Women's Writing*. Her chapters are organized around the techniques used by men to deny women the opportunity to write, to publish, to claim their own work, and to receive equitable judgment of its quality. Her first three chapters, "Prohibitions," "Bad Faith," and "Denial of Agency," focus on the discouragement of women from expressing their real thoughts.

To support what she views as a systematic and perpetual denial of women's talent and accomplishments, she quotes from numerous experiences of individual authors. A typical example is the reaction of Robert Southey, poet laureate, to a request of Charlotte Brontë's to evaluate her verse. He advised that even though her work "showed talent" that "literature cannot be the business of a woman's life. . . . the more she is engaged in her proper duties, the less leisure will she have for it." Bronte, responding to him, revealed the struggle of so many women authors concerning their profession:

I carefully avoid any appearance of pre-occupation and eccentricity. . . . I have endeavored . . . to observe the duties a woman ought to fulfill. . . . I don't always succeed, for sometimes when I'm teaching or sewing I would rather be reading or writing: but I try to deny myself.

The book is rich in examples of the limitations imposed on women, such as Ellen Glasgow having to fend off sexual advances when meeting with publishers. Both Anne Sexton and Adrienne Rich speak of the destructive tension in trying to lead conventional lives while desperately wanting to write. Linda Huf in *A Portrait of the Artist as a Young Woman* notes similar doubts and limitations in the careers of Kate Chopin, Willa Cather, and others, arising from personal questioning and outside charges about the egotism and familial irresponsibility of the writer. Male critics, according to Russ, consistently noted the intellectual debts women authors owed to men or stressed the author's "masculine" abilities. One concentrated on George Eliot's debt to George Henry Lewes, and another praised Mary McCarthy for her "masculine mind." Compliments often involved the desexing of the artist, such as Robert Lowell's noting that Sylvia Plath "becomes . . . something imaginary, newly, wildly created—hardly a person at all or a woman, certainly not a 'poetess.' "

Russ describes the daily difficulties women authors face with publishers, with critics, with the press, and with those disseminating their works. The continual linking of their writing to their sex is at the heart of the matter. Although sometimes given to anecdotal material, Russ's *How to Suppress Women's Writing* traces a pervasive and convincing scenario of women's being denied significant accomplishments in literature—either in producing them or in getting credit for them.

Numerous collections of letters and source materials focus less on a feminist critique of women's literature. Included among these works are *American Women Writers: Bibliographical Essays*, edited by Maurice Duke, Jackson R. Bryer, and M. Thomas Inge; *We Shall Be Heard: Women Speakers in America*, edited by Patricia Scileppi Kennedy and Gloria Hartmann O'Shields; and *The Letters of Margaret Fuller* edited by Robert N. Hudspeth. The first volume is a useful summary of the literature currently available on some women authors, though it lacks any but arbitrary criteria for selection. Kate Chopin, Edith Wharton, Gertrude Stein, and Ellen Glasgow are included, whereas Willa Cather, Harriet Beecher Stowe, Emily Dickinson, and Louisa May Alcott are not. Descriptive bibliographical materials are more valuable than the introductions. *We Shall Be Heard*, the first anthology of women speakers in the United States, concentrates as much on the rhetorical abilities of individual speakers as on the contents of their speeches. It begins with Frances Wright and Lucretia Mott and includes contemporary speeches by Betty Friedan and Barbara Jordan. A brief biography precedes each selection.

A first volume of Margaret Fuller's *Letters, 1817–38*, unfortunately contains little about her personal life or sentiments. Concentrating on her student days and on her early correspondence with other New England thinkers, it suggests little about the motivation of one of the country's earliest women recognized as a serious intellectual.

A popular variety of literary study focuses on a type of writer or theme found in a series of works. Among this group of works are *Writing Like a Woman* by Alicia Ostriker; Josephine Donovan's *New England Local Color Literature: A Woman's Tradition; Women and Utopia: Critical Interpretations*, edited by Marleen Barr and Nicholas D. Smith; Kristin Herzog's *Women, Ethnics, and Exotics: Images of Power in Mid-Nineteenth-Century American Fiction;* Judy Little's *Comedy and the Woman Writer: Woolf, Spark, and Feminism; The Voyage In: Fictions of Female Development*, edited by Elizabeth Abel, Marianne Hirsch, and Elizabeth Langland; and Diane Bornstein's *The Lady in the Tower: Medieval Courtesy Literature for Women*.

Alicia Ostriker's work is a poet's analysis of the writing of sister poets. Accepting a female culture perspective of feminist criticism, Ostriker uses the ideas of Susan Griffin in *Woman and Nature: The Roaring Inside Her* to argue that women's writings allow them to overcome an interior voice which is "rational, authoritative, male." The work includes discussions of H.D., Anne Sexton, and May Swenson, among others. In a theoretical article on female creativity, Ostriker stresses the importance of motherhood in providing inspiration for poetic expression. The work's major flaw lies in the underlying sexism of the argument that women can write powerfully only in distinctly female, irrational, and natural forms. Josephine Donovan's small volume on New England local colorists discusses this variety of American fiction as a women's field but develops few generalizations and includes no conclusion.

The Voyage In is a collection of feminist criticism on "the female novel of development." Psychoanalytic and sociological approaches are used in this volume, which includes essays on lesbian works, black fiction, books like *Little Women* and *Jane Eyre*, and authors like Virginia Woolf, Doris Lessing, and Jean Stafford, who are portrayed as moving beyond the nineteenth-century beginnings of a literature of sisterhood. Judy Little's study of *Comedy and the Woman Writer* is a discussion of "renegade comedy" in the writings of Virginia Woolf and Muriel Spark. The author states that comedy can have either a revolutionizing or a stabilizing effect. Using psychoanalytical and sociological theory, the author links comedy and feminist themes. The work tends to be jargonistic and abstract, possibly making too much out of an account of two authors as proof of a link between feminism and comedy.

Kristin Herzog's study, *Women, Ethnics and Exotics*, includes black and Native American authors to demonstrate the masculinism and ethnocentrism of nineteenth-century American literature. Chapters include sections on primitive strength in Hawthorne's women, women and savages in Melville, Harriet Beecher Stowe's *Uncle Tom's Cabin*, and early novels by black novelists William Wells Brown and Martin R. Delany. The author notes that writers like Hawthorne and Melville grouped women with Indians and savages because of their perceived natural and primitive character. Diane Bornstein's *The Lady in the Tower* summarizes the images of women in medieval courtesy books from 500 to 1500. These images range from women as virgins, wives, and mothers to coquettes, rulers, and workers. They seldom, however, reflected the growing importance of women's economic role in medieval society. In outlining the thesis of her work, Bornstein contends that "although medieval women needed to exercise the active virtues in leading their lives, the passive ones were emphasized in the courtesy books." In ways similar to the Victorians, "femininity was equated with modesty, humility, chastity and obedience."

Taken as a whole, there is little to tie together these works on women in literature and essays and books of feminist criticism. Although each work attempts to provide first-time information and analyses of women authors or female characters, their quality and novelty vary widely, as do their levels of generalization. It is not easy to see a single direction among works on women's literature, although a larger division between feminist and theoretical works and those primarily providing "women in" information does exist.

The most promising structure for future literary criticism is presented in Elissa D. Gelfand's *Imagination in Confinement: Women's Writings from French Prisons*. The author, while using and altering Foucault's literary theories, provides an in-depth analysis of the writings of French women prisoners. Building upon his *Discipline and Punishment: The Birth of the Prison*, Gelfand shows that, although Foucault ignores women, his argument that penal policy evolved from punishing the criminal act to punishing the criminal especially pertains to women's experience in prison: women were there for "status offenses" rather than overt criminal activities and thus inherently suffered more for their person than for their crime. In addition, the control exerted over their imagination was even stronger than over male prisoners, while their personal identity, sexuality, and creativity were intertwined with their incarceration more intensely and destructively. Although Gelfand lacks the sweep of Russ's work, her combined effort to theorize, to appraise earlier analyses from a feminist viewpoint, and to study thoroughly one type of writing is what makes this one of the more impressive volumes of literary criticism focusing on women during 1983.

History

Over the last decade, women's history has produced the most varied, and in many ways, the most impressive body of writings about women. Large numbers of publications concerned women in the family, sexuality, and the definition and enforcement of proper feminine roles.

Articles especially pursued these topics, whereas monographs were more likely to concentrate on women's public activities or feminist efforts, reflecting primarily dissertation research in these areas. The focus on the average woman and on her private life has characterized the direction of women's history since the mid-1970s. This focus reflects the important influence of social history on the field and the skepticism of women's historians concerning the utility of prescriptive literature as evidence for their actual lives. During this period, evidence from demographic and quantitative sources has been applied increasingly to the study of women's past. In addition, diaries, letters, and personal accounts by women have tended to replace prescriptive and descriptive materials written by men and evaluative materials produced by governmental and other official bodies. Historians are apt now to rely on official records for statistical and descriptive materials and less on the judgments of government officials concerning the nature and scope of women's lives.

As a part of this trend, articles dealing with marriage customs, childbearing, and child rearing have proliferated over the last several years. During June 1983, the *Journal of American History* published " 'Best for Babies' or 'Preventable Infanticide'? The Controversy over Artificial Feeding of Infants in America, 1880–1920" (Levenstein 1983), and in September printed " 'Science' Enters the Birthing Room: Obstetrics in America since the Eighteenth Century" (Leavitt 1983). The *Journal of Social History* in the fall of this year included the following: "Sentiment and Science: The Late Nineteenth-Century Pediatrician as Mother's Advisor" (Jones 1983), "Maternal Health in the English Aristocracy: Myths and Realities, 1790–1840" (Lewis 1983), and "Widowed Mothers and Mutual Aid in Early Victorian Britain" (Winter 1983).

Each of these attests to the continuing interest in the history of women's sexuality, childbearing, and child rearing. The discussions of science in the birthing room and the controversy over artificial feeding are historical accounts of broad issues current in the women's movement. Judith Walzer Leavitt, in describing the displacement of midwives by male obstetricians in eighteenth-century America, raises questions about whether "scientific" medicine was preferable to the efforts of midwives who allowed natural progression rather than employing drugs or forceps during childbirth. Harvey Levenstein makes clear that the use of infant formula was controversial at the turn of the twentieth century and involved many of the same issues raised in the debate today: the importance of breast feeding in establishing early bonds between mother and child and the greater health benefits of mother's milk versus the convenience of bottle feeding and its enabling women to enter the labor force in greater numbers. The *Journal of Social History* articles focus more broadly on women's role in the family, but continue the attention on women's private lives and utilize documents that provide evidence about the nature of women's socialization toward femininity and the ties between women's health and their sexual functions.

In the preface to the Summer 1983 issue of *Feminist Studies*, the journal's editors note the continuing focus on motherhood: "Five years ago *Feminist Studies* designed an issue on the theme of motherhood, a topic that has appeared in some form or another in almost every issue before or since." They contend, though, that this issue witnesses "a subtle but consequential shift" in reassessing motherhood and in feminists' "consciousness of gender relations." Shirley Glubka's "Out of the Stream: An Essay on Unconventional Motherhood," although a discussion of contemporary mothers' questioning of maternal commitments, is clearly linked to the earlier discussions of Charlotte Perkins Gilman and Margaret Sanger. Her analysis is also tied to historical assessments of how society, institutional structures, and women's personal needs interact—often in conflicting ways—to define and control maternal practices. Essays by Michael Grossberg and Nancy Folbre present historical accounts of women's struggle for guardianship over their children and of the need for a feminist demography that evaluates how numbers of children "directly affect the division of labor or the balance of power in the household." Folbre contends there is currently little concern with the effects on women's status (especially where that status was tied directly to the production and care of children) of significant reductions in family size in Western Europe and the United States over the last two centuries. Her essay has wide-ranging implications for feminist assessments of family history and demography generally.

Historical monographs appearing in 1983 continued to reveal the variety of periods, topics, and countries covered and to demonstrate the difficulty in pinpointing a single theme or even a series of themes among those studying women's past. At best, these works demonstrate the more advanced analyses within those fields where most research has occurred over the last decade and the continuing effort to gather materials in fields where less has been accomplished. As could be expected, the largest number of works have appeared in American history for the post-1800 period; thus historians working in these areas are better able to build upon and test the theses of those preceding them. They are apt, as well, to deal closely with more specialized topics rather than employing the wide sweep of works focusing on less-populated and less-researched areas. These monographs demonstrate the field's continued interest in women's private lives and their experience as workers (both within and beyond the home), but they also include numerous treatments of women's public efforts and institutions.

Among the monographs appearing this year were Barbara M. Brenzel's *Daughters of the State: A Social Portrait of the First Reform School for Girls in North America, 1856–1905;* Sharon L. Siever's *Flowers in Salt: The Beginnings of Feminist Consciouness in Modern Japan;* Mary Chamberlain's *Fenwomen: A Portrait of Women in an English Village;* Faye E. Dudden's *Serving Women: Household Service in Nineteenth-Century America; Presbyterian Women in America: Two Centuries of a Quest for Status* by Lois A. Boyd and R. Douglas Brackenridge; Abby Wettan Kleinbaum's *The War against the Amazons; Queens, Concubines, and Dowagers: The King's Wife in the Early Middle Ages* by Pauline Stafford; Harvey Green's *The Light of the Home: An Intimate View of the Lives of Women in Victorian America; Women of the English Renaissance and Reformation* by Retha M. Warnicke; Rosalind K. Marshall's *Virgins and Viragos: A History of Women in Scotland from 1080 to 1980;* and *More Work for Mother: The Ironies of Household Technology from the Open Hearth to the Microwave* by Ruth Schwartz Cowan.

The works by Dudden, Green, Brenzel, Boyd and Brackenridge, and Cowan all focus on the experience of women in the United States. Dudden's study follows a series of books on servants in Europe and the United States, including most recently for this country, Michael Katzman's *Seven Days a Week.* Dudden's work focuses more on definitional questions than did those that preceded it and analyzes how the movement from the "hired girl" of the pre-1850 period to the "domestic" led to altered working conditions and relationships between employers and employees in the home. She contends that the transition from more flexible to more rigid work and social roles for servants accompanied "pervasive changes in the relations between home and production and between worker and workplace, even in types of work that were not industrialized." The home increasingly imitated the working conditions and relationships of industrial society. Ruth Cowan's volume, the culmination of long-term research, provides scholars and the public with a readable and convincing elaboration of her thesis that improved household technology has created more complex and numerous tasks to be completed and has thus increased the time women devote to housework. A less ambitious study, Green's book also focuses on women's work within the home and uses the materials of the Rochester Museum to demonstrate domestic tools and activities of Victorian housewives and servants.

Although the home and family would appear to hold little relevance to Brenzel's study of an early reform school, such is not the case. Rather, the school's organizers saw as their primary goal the re-creation of the structure and values of a proper Christian home within this public refuge for wayward girls. The study of Presbyterian women by Boyd and Brackenridge, despite incorporating recent scholarship in women's history and utilizing the theories of Mary Ryan concerning women's reforming tendencies, is essentially a conventional institutional history, which traces the efforts of women seeking status and power within local congregations and through church policy.

Biographies appeared in 1983 focusing on the lives of two important nineteenth-century American feminists, Elizabeth Cazden's life of Antoinette Brown Blackwell and Ruth Barnes Moynihan's study of Abigail Scott Duniway. Both are admirable biographies, weaving the facts of their subjects' individual lives into the important public activities with which they were associated. The Moynihan work adds greatly to our understanding of women's suffrage in the West, and Cazden's volume employs the Blackwell papers to provide a solid biography of a woman who combined the interests of many nineteenth-century causes. However, neither work devotes much effort to placing its account into a broad theoretical framework. They are essentially good traditional biographies of leading figures in the women's movement.

Perhaps the most interesting work among historical studies on non-American subjects is Abby Kleinbaum's account of the evolving place of the Amazon in literary, philosophical, and historical writings. She traces the imagery surrounding the Amazon from its classical origins through its use by contemporary feminists. The image of Amazons, normally as powerful, exciting, but ultimately vanquished opponents, has been painted almost exclusively by men. Amazons have proven suitable enemies for the Greeks and Romans, church fathers, the founders of anthropology, and contemporary social scientists. Feminists, on the other hand, have often turned to them as possessing characteristics and a society desirable for women generally. Kleinbaum describes it thus: "Its core is the image of a free and autonomous community of women, women functioning without the aid, direction, instruction, or authority of men." This book collects and analyzes descriptions of Amazons, concentrating on works written through the seventeenth century. Later chapters include their place in drama and popular culture and the links between feminist theory and men's age-old need both to believe in and to defeat Amazons. It is an interesting, well-written work, if sometimes repetitious. Mary Chamberlain's *Fenwomen* is a very different kind of study, but contains a similar interest, tying interviews with contemporary women living in the village of Gislea in East Anglia to a complex historical background. Although the study is current, her comments and the interviews themselves often read like timeless discussions of women's work and lives in agricultural communities. In opposing drainage of the fens to protect local fisheries, the fenwomen resist modernization that would destroy a traditional society where they have clearly defined functions. While obviously possessing little feminist consciousness, those interviewed speak directly as women about the nature of their lives.

Sharon Siever's study of the origins of the women's movement in Japan is a thorough discussion of the history of women's public activities in Japan, with separate chapters on textile workers and on Japanese bluestockings. She also includes chapters on the Women's Reform Society of the 1890s, on women socialists, and on women in the popular rights movement. One chapter reviews the early Meiji debate on women and another examines the life of Kanno Suga, an early twentieth-century anarchist who was executed by the Japanese government. Although the work often seems broad and unfocused by the standards of European and American women's history, it provides a wealth of information for those unfamiliar with the history of Japanese women.

Of similar scope, Rosalind Marshall's sweeping account of Scottish women for nine hundred years deals with the lives of many individuals while incorporating statistical data on the general status of women in Scotland. It is a ground-breaking study that furnishes historians with considerable knowledge about Scottish women. Stafford's work on medieval queens is less interesting; it lacks footnotes, although she includes general bibliographical notes for each chapter. The author outlines the opportunities and limitations among those women associated with early medieval kings. Her work reveals the degree to which their power rested on the sufferance of the monarch. Retha Warnicke's study of English Renaissance and Reformation notables has similar difficulties. Although it provides useful materials about court figures from the early 1500s through the Jacobean period, it includes slight analysis, merely summarizing their lives and humanist ideas, topics that have received considerable attention previously.

Collected materials and discussions of historiographical interest continued to appear during 1983 providing useful sources for future research. *Women, The Family and Freedom: The Debate in Documents*, edited by Susan Groag Bell and Karen M. Offen, is a broad-ranging and thoroughly annotated two-volume work of original sources on European and American women's history from 1750 through 1950. *The Woman Question: Society and Literature in Britain and America, 1837–1883* in three volumes, edited by Elizabeth K. Helsinger, Robin Lauterbach Sheets, and William Veeder, is a less useful collection of Victorian literary and journalistic sources defining women's roles during the mid-1800s. Deirdre Beddoe's *Discovering Women's History*, limited to the history of English women, is more a popular guide than a scholarly resource. Mari Jo Buhle's *Women and the American Left: A Guide to Sources* includes materials for those interested particularly in women's involvement in labor and socialist activities, and *Restoring Women to History: Materials for Western Civilization I*, edited by Elizabeth Fox-Genovese and Susan Mosher Stuard, provides helpful guidance and sources for teachers integrating women's experience into Western civilization courses. Two articles to aid scholars in their own research are Darlene R. Roth's "Growing Like Topsy: Research Guides to Women's History" in the *Journal of American History* (June) and Joyce Duncan Falk's "The New Technology for Research in European Women's History: 'Online' Bibliographies" in the autumn issue of *Signs*.

Group biographies and source collections on more limited topics include Dale Spender's *There's Always Been a Women's Movement This Century*, which combines her feminist analysis with interviews, biographies, and ideas of early twentieth-century feminists; a rather careless edition of *Covered Wagon Women: Diaries and Letters from the Western Trails, 1840–1850* by Kenneth L. Holms; *Between Ourselves: Letters between Mothers and Daughters 1750–1982* (Payne 1983), a collection of letters of feminist scholars, women writers, and leaders including Harriet Martineau, Calamity Jane, Sylvia Plath, and Jessie Bernard; *Women and the British Empire: An Annotated Guide to Sources*, compiled by Susan F. Bailey, which includes chapters on settlers, missionaries, native women, and wives of administrators and has a good and wide-ranging introduction and extensive annotations; and *Her Immaculate Hand: Selected Works by and about the Women Humanists of Quattrocento Italy*, edited by Margery C. King and Albert Rabil, Jr., which provides materials on women in the public area, women discussing women and learning, and men's letters to women. It is, however, less sweeping than the divisions would indicate, for each section focuses almost exclusively on learned women.

Lois Scharf and Joan M. Jensen's collection, *Decades of Discontent: The Women's Movement, 1920–1940*, carries a somewhat misleading title, for it includes articles on almost all aspects of women's lives between the wars. A number of the selections have been published previously, but it is a valuable addition to the few works available on women's lives during the interwar period. Its scope is useful for those who want a reader for the 1920s and 1930s that will cover women's work and political organizing and will offer discussions of black, Chicana, and Jewish women as well as the image of women in popular culture. A significant contribution to the current discussions on working-class culture is Sarah Eisenstein's *Give Us Bread But Give Us Roses*, a posthumous edition of essays on working women's consciousness in the United States from 1890 to World War I. Eisenstein emphasizes the integrated effects of working-class women's exposure to middle-class domesticity and femininity and the economic and class boundaries of their own lives. It is a thoughtful, well-written collection, which provides scholars a framework to understand the range of influences on working-class women at the turn of the twentieth century.

Historical journals during 1983 divided their treatment of women rather evenly between the "women in" studies of women's involvement in various reforms and public activities, and discussions of their sexual and marriage customs. Two essays representing the former approach were the *Journal of American History*'s "School Reform in the New South: The

Woman's Association for the Betterment of Public School Houses in North Carolina, 1902–1919" (Leloudis 1983) in which the author demonstrates that this type of reforming activity led to little alteration in sex roles but rather reinforced traditional status as wives and mothers, and "Labor's True Woman: Domesticity and Equal Rights in the Knights of Labor" (Levine 1983), which reveals that labor leaders sounded very much like middle-class male sympathizers of women's reforming activities, encouraging women's efforts so long as they did not threaten traditional sex roles. The *Journal of Family History* included the following studies: "Making Village Women into 'Good Wives and Wise Mothers' in Prewar Japan" (Smith 1983); "Marriage Formation and Domestic Industry: Occupational Endogamy in Kilmarnock, Ayrshire, 1697–1764" (Houston 1983); and "Baby Bust and Baby Boom: A Study of Family Size in a Group of University of Chicago Faculty Wives Born 1900–1934" (Weiner 1983). Each of these descriptive articles showed whether the women in question conformed to or differed from general economic or demographic trends.

Finally, *French Historical Studies* and the *Journal of Social History* reflected the domestic interests of many scholars researching women's past. The former included a study of "Protecting Infants: The French Campaign for Maternity Leaves, 1890's–1913" (McDougall 1983), which traced how arguments stressed the child's needing its mother at birth and ignored women's rights in the political debate. The latter journal published an article on "Domestic Servants and Households in Victorian England" (Higgs 1983), which focused more on servants' work than on their significance for the lives of middle-class women, a focus the author contends has too heavily dominated the research on servants.

Works in women's history continue to make the field a patchwork quilt of topics, times, and places. Theoretical controversies within the field are numerous, but not sufficiently focused so that an overview of all materials published in women's history during a single year could pinpoint a single, significant area of debate. As noted in *Feminist Studies*, questions are developing about the focus on maternity, domestic life, and sexuality that could lead women's history into differing directions. Historical journals, more than women's studies journals, continue to place women's experience into a context outside of their lives, seldom from the perspective of women's own interests. Whether the women's studies journals and the historical ones will move closer together in the next decade to integrate women's history into understandings of general historical phenomena in positive ways is uncertain.

Philosophy

Two important collections, *Discovering Reality: Feminist Perspectives on Epistemology, Metaphysics, Methodology, and the Philosophy of Science*, edited by Sandra Harding and Merrill B. Hintikka, and *Beyond Domination: New Per-*

spectives on Women and Philosophy, edited by Carol C. Gould, appeared during 1983. Carol Gould's work is a collection of papers presented at a conference on the philosophy of women held in 1980. Available in paperback, this collection includes essays on a proposed value framework for feminism; sex, gender, and women's identity; women and spirituality; domination; work; personal relations; political life; law; ethics; and public policy. Its breadth of coverage makes it an ideal reader for classes in the philosophy of women or in feminist theory generally. Individual essays are well-written by authors obviously familiar with women's studies across a range of disciplines. Sometimes abstract and difficult for the nonphilosopher, it is nonetheless a collection that deals thoughtfully with current and historical problems related to women, and it provides probing analysis sometimes lacking in general women's studies readers.

The Harding and Hintikka collection is a work less accessible to students of women's studies generally. It is a difficult and sophisticated work of greatest use to graduate students and faculty in philosophy and political theory. Including a variety of topics ranging from Aristotle's treatment of women to discussions of Charlotte Perkins Gilman and a psychoanalytic perspective on epistemology, the work deals with issues of fundamental importance to the intellectual constructs of "male," "female," and "human." The last two essays by Nancy Hartsock and Sandra Harding are especially valuable feminist analyses of historical materialism and the evolving definition of the sex/gender system. The general interest of Harding's argument lies in its breadth: "The sex/gender system appears to be a fundamental variable organizing social life throughout most recorded history and in every culture today. Like racism and classism, it is an *organic* social variable—it is not merely an 'effect' of other, more primary, causes."

In addition, a number of works deal with philosophical, theological, and moral aspects of women's lives. These include Rosemary Radford Ruether's *Sexism and God-Talk: Toward a Feminist Theology*, which analyzes religion's conception of woman as body, nature, and exploited labor. She pinpoints three levels of women's subjugation including control over the womb which leads to control over the person which ultimately results in exploited female labor, similar to the exploitation of peasants and workers generally. This work is as much a personal as a scholarly view of women's inferior treatment in varying cultures. Carol Ochs's *Women and Spirituality* possesses a similar breadth and deals with varieties of religious experience including ecstasy, guilt, and solitude. It discusses the basic issues of human life: love, birth, death, unity, and so on. A somewhat predictable collection, Ochs has produced social and moral commentaries as much as a work of scholarly research.

Linda A. Bell's edition of *Visions of Women* includes philosophical treatments of women by authors from Plato to C.S. Lewis and Simone de Beauvoir. It raises contemporary issues, such as the ethics involved in biomedical research, and suggests additional readings related to the printed texts. Mary Briody Mahowald's *Philosophy of Woman: An Anthology of Classic and*

Current Concepts suffers from an unorthodox organization. Beginning with current feminist works, it next moves to nineteenth-century thinkers, and then backward to Plato and Aristotle, with a final section on Freud. The reason for this structure is not clear, which makes it the least useful of the philosophical works discussed here.

Art and Music

There was little written on women in these fields during 1983, especially in the scholarly areas of art history and musicology. Serious questions about the basis of aesthetics and art criticism, similar to those raised in *Old Mistresses: Women, Art, and Ideology* (Parker and Pollock 1981) have generated short essays such as "Cognitive Function and Women's Art" (Kraft 1983). The *Woman's Art Journal* included the articles, "Lady Elizabeth Thompson Butler in the 1870s" (Lalumia 1983); "O'Keeffe's Art: Sacred Symbols and Spiritual Quest" (Weisman 1983); and "Painter and Patron: Collaboration of Mary Cassatt and Louisine Havemeyer" (Faxon 1983). Although interesting, each of these articles is brief and without the detailed explorations raised in women's literature or history. *Women Artists News*, as could be expected, focuses more on issues of importance to contemporary artists, but does include some discussion of historical topics.

Two books, valuable primarily as reference works and informational guides, appeared on women in music. They are Mildred D. Green's *Black Women Composers* and Judith Tick's *American Women Composers before 1870*. Other works on women in music covered particular musicians, such as Heidi Von Gunden's book on Pauline Oliveros and D. Antoinette Handy's history of the International Sweethearts of Rhythm, a mostly black jazz band of the 1940s. Unsurprisingly, the depth of material and the types of analyses were less advanced than in the more investigated areas of women's studies.

References

Art

FAXON, A. 1983. Painter and patron: Collaboration of Mary Cassatt and Louisine Havemeyer. *Woman's Art Journal* 3, no. 2:15–20.

KRAFT, S. 1983. Cognitive function and women's art. *Woman's Art Journal* 4, no. 2:5–9.

LALUMIA, M. 1983. Lady Elizabeth Thompson Butler in the 1870's. *Woman's Art Journal* 4, no. 1:9–14.

PARKER, R., and G. POLLOCK. 1981. *Old mistresses: Women, art, and ideology*. New York: Pantheon Books.

WEISMAN, C. 1983. O'Keeffe's art: Sacred symbols and spiritual quest. *Woman's Art Journal* 3, no. 2:10–14.

History

BAILEY, S.F., ed. 1983. *Women and the British empire: An annotated guide to sources.* New York: Garland.

BEDDOE, D. 1983. *Discovering women's history.* London: Routledge and Kegan Paul.

BELL, S.G., and K.M. OFFEN. 1983. *Women, the family, and freedom: The debate in documents.* Vol. 1: 1750–1880; Vol. 2: 1880–1950. Stanford, Calif.: Stanford University Press.

BOYD, L.H., and R.D. BRACKENRIDGE. 1983. *Presbyterian women in America: Two centuries of a quest for status.* Westport, Conn.: Greenwood Press.

BRENZEL, B.M. 1983. *Daughters of the state: A social portrait of the first reform school for girls in North America, 1856–1905.* Cambridge, Mass.: MIT Press.

BUHLE, M.J. 1983. *Women and the American left: A guide to sources.* Boston: G.K. Hall.

CAZDEN, E. 1983. *Antoinette Brown Blackwell: A biography.* Old Westbury, N.Y.: Feminist Press.

CHAMBERLAIN, M. 1983. *Fenwomen: A portrait of women in an English village.* Boston: Routledge and Kegan Paul.

COWAN, R.S. 1983. *More work for mother: The ironies of household technology from the open hearth to the microwave.* New York: Basic Books.

DUDDEN, F.E. 1983. *Serving women: Household service in 19th century America.* Middletown, Conn.: Wesleyan University Press.

EISENSTEIN, S. 1983. *Give us bread but give us roses: Working women's consciousness in the United States, 1890 to the First World War.* Boston: Routledge and Kegan Paul.

FALK, J.D. 1983. The new technology for research in European women's history: "Online" bibliographies. *Signs* 9, no. 1:120–33.

FOLBRE, N. 1983. Of patriarchy born: The political economy of fertility decisions. *Feminist Studies* 9, no. 2:261–84.

FOX-GENOVESE, E., and S.M. STUARD, eds. 1983. *Restoring women to history: Materials for Western civilization I.* Bloomington, Ind.: Organization of American Historians.

GLUBKA, S. 1983. Out of the stream: An essay on unconventional motherhood. *Feminist Studies* 9, no. 2:223–34.

GREEN, H. 1983. *The light of the home: An intimate view of the lives of women in Victorian America.* New York: Pantheon Books.

GROSSBERG, M. 1983. Who gets the child? Custody, guardianship, and the rise of a judicial patriarchy in nineteenth-century America. *Feminist Studies* 9, no. 2:235–60.

HELSINGER, E.K., R.L. SHEETS, and W. VEEDER, eds. 1983. *The woman question: Society and literature in Britain and America, 1837–1883.* 3 vols. New York: Garland.

HIGGS, E. 1983. Domestic servants and households in Victorian England. *Social History*, May, pp. 201–10.

HOLMS, K.L., ed. 1983. *Covered wagon women: Diaries and letters from the western trails, 1840–1850*. Glendale, Calif.: Arthur H. Clark Co.

HOUSTON, R.A. 1983. Marriage formation and domestic industry: Occupational endogamy in Kilmarnock, Ayrshire, 1697–1764. *Journal of Family History* 8, no. 3:215–29.

JONES, K.W. 1983. Sentiment and science: The late 19th century as mother's advisor. *Journal of Social History* 17, no. 1:79–96.

KING, M.C., and A. RABIL, eds. 1983. *Her immaculate hand: Selected works by and about the women humanists of quattrocento Italy*. Binghampton, N.Y.: Medieval and Renaissance Texts and Studies, no. 20.

KLEINBAUM, A.W. 1983. *The war against the Amazons*. New York: New Press.

LEAVITT, J.W. 1983. "Science" enters the birthing room: Obstetrics in America since the eighteenth century. *Journal of American History* 70, no. 2:281–304.

LELOUDIS, J.L. 1983. School reform in the new south: The Woman's Association for the Betterment of Public School Houses in North Carolina, 1902–1919. *Journal of American History* 69, no. 4:886–909.

LEVENSTEIN, H. 1983. "Best for babies" or "preventable infanticide"? The controversy over artificial feeding of infants in America, 1880–1920. *Journal of American History* 70, no. 1:75–94.

LEVINE, S. 1983. Labor's true woman: Domesticity and equal rights in the Knights of Labor. *Journal of American History* 70, no. 2:323–39.

LEWIS, J.S. 1983. Maternal health in the English aristocracy: Myths and realities, 1790–1840. *Journal of Social History* 17, no. 1:97–114.

McDOUGALL, M.L. 1983. Protecting infants: The French campaign for maternity leaves, 1890's to 1913. *French Historical Studies*, Spring, pp. 79–105.

MARSHALL, R.K. 1983. *Virgins and viragos: A history of women in Scotland from 1080 to 1980*. Chicago: Academy Press.

MOYNIHAN, R.B. 1983. *Rebel for rights: Abigail Scott Duniway*. New Haven, Conn.: Yale University Press.

PAYNE, K., ed. 1983. *Between ourselves: Letters between mothers and daughters, 1750–1982*. Boston: Houghton Mifflin.

ROTH, D.R. 1983. Growing like topsy: Research guides to women's history. *Journal of American History* 70, no. 1:95–100.

SCHARF, L., and J.M. JENSEN, eds. 1983. *Decades of discontent: The women's movement, 1920–1940*. Westport, Conn.: Greenwood Press.

SIEVERS, S.L. 1983. *Flowers in salt: The beginnings of feminist consciousness in modern Japan*. Stanford, Calif.: Stanford University Press.

SMITH, R.J. 1983. Making village women into "good wives and wise mothers" in prewar Japan. *Journal of Family History* 8, no. 1:70–84.

SPENDER, D. 1983. *There's always been a women's movement this century*. Boston: Pandora Press.

STAFFORD, P. 1983. *Queens, concubines, and dowagers: The king's wife in the early Middle Ages*. Athens, Ga.: University of Georgia Press.

WARNICKE, R.M. 1983. *Women of the English Renaissance and Reformation*. Westport, Conn.: Greenwood Press.

WEINER, N.F. 1983. Baby bust and baby boom: A study of family size in a group of University of Chicago faculty wives born 1900–1934. *Journal of Family History* 8, no. 3:279–91.

WINTER, J. 1983. Widowed mothers and mutual aid in early Victorian Britain. *Journal of Social History* 17, no. 1:115–25.

Literature

ABEL, E., M. HIRSCH, and E. LANGLAND, eds. 1983. *The voyage in: Fictions of female development*. Hanover, N.H.: University Press of New England.

BARR, M., and N.D. SMITH, eds. 1983. *Women and utopia: Critical interpretations*. Lanham, Md.: University Press of America.

BORNSTEIN, D. 1983. *The lady in the tower: Medieval courtesy literature for women*. Hamden, Conn.: Archon Books.

DONOVAN, J. 1983. *New England local color literature: A women's tradition*. New York: F. Ungar Publishing Co.

DUKE, M., J.R. BRYER, and M.T. INGE, eds. 1983. *American women writers: Bibliographical essays*. Westport, Conn.: Greenwood Press.

GELFAND, E.D. 1983. *Imagination in confinement: Women's writings from French prisons*. Ithaca, N.Y.: Cornell University Press.

HERZOG, K. 1983. *Women, ethnics, and exotics: Images of power in mid-19th century American fiction*. Knoxville: University of Tennessee Press.

HUDSPETH, R., ed. 1983. *The letters of Margaret Fuller: Vol. 1, 1817–1838*. Ithaca, N.Y.: Cornell University Press.

HUF, L. 1983. *A portrait of the artist as a young woman*. New York: Frederick Ungar Publishing Co.

JARDINE, L. 1983. *Still harping on daughters: Women and drama in the age of Shakespeare*. Totowa, N.J.: Barnes and Noble.

JUHASZ, S., ed. 1983. *Feminist critics read Emily Dickinson*. Bloomington: Indiana University Press.

KENNEDY, P.S., and G.H. O'SHIELDS, eds. 1983. *We shall be heard: Women speakers in America*. Dubuque, Iowa: Kendall Hunt Publishing Co.

LITTLE, J. 1983. *Comedy and the woman writer: Woolf, Spark, and feminism*. Lincoln: University of Nebraska Press.

MARCUS, J., ed. 1983. *Virginia Woolf: A feminist slant*. Lincoln: University of Nebraska Press.

OSTRIKER, A. 1983. *Writing like a woman*. Ann Arbor: University of Michigan Press.

RUSS, J. 1983. *How to suppress women's writing*. Austin: University of Texas Press.

Music

GREEN, M. 1983. *Black women composers*. Boston: Twayne.

HANDY, D.A. 1983. *The International Sweethearts of Rhythm*. Metuchen, N.J.: Scarecrow Press.

TICK, J. 1983. *American women composers before 1870*. Ann Arbor, Mich.: University Microfilms.

VON GUNDEN, H. 1983. *The music of Pauline Oliveros*. Metuchen, N.J.: Scarecrow Press.

Philosophy

BELL, L.A. 1983. *Visions of women*. Clifton, N.J.: Humana Press.

GOULD, C.C. 1983. *Beyond domination: New perspectives on women and philosophy*. Totowa, N.J.: Rowman and Allanheld.

HARDING, S., and M. HINTIKKA, eds. 1983. *Discovering reality: Feminist perspectives on epistemology, metaphysics, methodology, and the philosophy of science*. Boston: D. Reidel.

MAHOWALD, M.B. 1983. *Philosophy of woman: An anthology of classic and current concepts*. Indianapolis: Hackett Publishing Co.

OCHS, C. 1983. *Women and spirituality*. Totowa, N.J.: Rowman and Allanheld.

RUETHER, R.R. 1983. *Sexism and God-talk: Toward a feminist theology*. Boston: Beacon Press.

Bibliography

ANDORS, PHYLLIS. *The Unfinished Liberation of Chinese Women, 1949–1980*. Bloomington: Indiana University Press, 1983. Examines the impact of the stages of modern Chinese policy development on women; looks at rural and urban women, changes in family structures, employment.

ATKINSON, CLARISSA. " 'Precious Balsam in a Fragile Glass': The Ideology of Virginity in the Latter Middle Ages." *Journal of Family History* 8, no. 2 (1983):131–43.

BITTON-JACKSON, LIVIA. *Madonna or Courtesan? The Jewish Woman in Christian Literature*. New York: Seabury Press, 1983.

BORENSTEIN, AUDREY. *Chimes of Change and Hours: Views of Older Women in Twentieth-Century America*. Rutherford, N.J.: Fairleigh Dickinson University Press, 1983. Basically a sociological study, but with extensive analysis of the image of older women in literature, and the artist/writer as an older woman.

BRAND, PAUL A., and PAUL R. HYAMS. "Seigneurial Control of Women's Marriages." *Past & Present*, May 1983, pp. 123–32.

De CARO, FRANCIS A. *Women and Folklore: A Bibliographic Survey*. Westport, Conn.: Greenwood Press, 1983.

DEMETRAKOPOULOUS, STEPHANIE. *Listening to Our Bodies: The Rebirth of*

Feminine Wisdom. Boston: Beacon Press, 1983. A mixture of philosophy, theology, and psychology; women's experience of life cycles, spirituality.

DINER, HASIA R. *Erin's Daughters in America: Irish Immigrant Women in the Nineteenth Century*. Baltimore: Johns Hopkins University Press, 1983. Using primary sources and published materials mostly for the Boston area, Diner skillfully recreates the lives of Irish immigrant women who, in numbers much greater than other ethnic groups, came to this country alone and unmarried.

FAIRBANKS, CAROL, and SARA BROOKS SUNDBERG. *Farm Women on the Prairie Frontier: A Sourcebook for Canada and the United States*. Metuchen, N.J.: Scarecrow Press, 1983. Useful collection of essays and annotated bibliographies, covering fiction and nonfiction.

FOSTER, SHIRLEY. "Female Januses: Ambiguity and Ambivalence towards Marriage in Mid-Victorian Women's Fiction." *International Journal of Women's Studies* 6, no. 3 (1983):216–29.

GOLDIN, CLAUDIA. "The Changing Economic Role of Women: A Quantitative Approach." *Journal of Interdisciplinary History*, Spring 1983, pp. 707–35.

HANSSON, CAROLA, and KARIN LIDÉN. *Moscow Women: Thirteen Interviews*. New York: Pantheon Books, 1983. Translation, in question-answer format, of interviews with ordinary women (not arranged via official channels). Grouped by themes such as work, sexuality, divorce, and so on.

HOLDEN, PAT, ed. *Women's Religious Experience*. Totowa, N.J.: Barnes and Noble, 1983. Essays on a wide variety of world traditions, for example, Islam in Turkey and Indian and African religions; critique of male dominance; and insight into women's use of religion to explore their social roles.

HOLLAND, CAROLINE, and G.R. GARETT. "The 'Skirt' of Nessus: Women and the German opposition to Hitler." *International Journal of Women's Studies* 6, no. 4 (1983):363–81.

HUTCHESON, JOHN. "Subdued Feminism: Jane Austen, Charlotte Bronte and George Eliot." *International Journal of Women's Studies* 6, no. 3 (1983):230–57.

JAMESON, ELIZABETH, ed. *Western Womantalk*. Denver, Colo.: Loretto Heights College, Research Center on Women, 1983. Proceedings of a conference on oral history in the Rocky Mountains/Southwest.

JOHNSON, JULIE GREER. *Women in Colonial Spanish American literature: Literary Images*. Westport, Conn.: Greenwood Press, 1983. Survey of images of women in prose, poetry, drama, essays, between 1492 and 1800, within the context of general Spanish literature and mythologies of the New World.

JOHNSON, KAY ANN. *Women, the Family and Peasant Revolution in China*. Chicago: University of Chicago Press, 1983. Similar to Andors's book; analysis of women's roles under both traditional and revolutionary regimes.

LAUTER, PAUL. "Race and Gender in the Shaping of the American Literary Canon: A Case study from the Twenties." *Feminist Studies* 9, no. 3 (1983): 435–463. Analyzes forces that shaped the current academic literary canon beginning in the 1920s, showing the progressive exclusion of women authors.

LUCAS, ANGELA M. *Women in the Middle Ages: Religion, Marriage, and Letters*. New York: St. Martin's Press, 1983. Broad historical study, mostly about upper-class women; good source for Anglo-Saxon women.

MULLANEY, MARIE MARMO. *Revolutionary Women: Gender and the Socialist Revolutionary Role*. New York: Praeger, 1983. How Alexandra Kollontai, Rosa Luxembourg, and others were affected by their female roles, despite their rejections of feminism per se.

O'BRIEN, PATRICIA. "The Kleptomania Diagnosis: Bourgeois Women and Theft in Late 19th Century France." *Journal of Social History* 17, no. 1 (1983):65–78.

PATAI, DAPHNE. "Beyond Defensiveness: Feminist Research Strategies." *Women's Studies International Forum* 6, no. 2 (1983):148–69.

PERADOTTO, JOHN, and J.P. SULLIVAN, eds. *Women in the Ancient World: The Arethusa Papers*. Albany: State University of New York Press, 1984. Includes a sixty-page bibliography on women in classical antiquity, by Sarah B. Pomeroy.

RAYNER, WILLIAM P. *Wise Women: Singular Lives That Helped Shape Our Century*. New York: St. Martin's Press, 1983. Twenty-one journalistic profiles of "successful" women in a variety of endeavors.

ROSE, PHYLLIS. *Parallel Lives: Five Victorian Marriages*. New York: Knopf, 1983. Sex roles, balance of power, nature of relationships in five upper-class intellectual couples: Jane Walsh and Thomas Carlyle, Effie Gray and John Ruskin, Catherine Hogarth and Charles Dickens, George Eliot and George Henry Lewes, Harriet Taylor and John Stuart Mill.

SPENCER, MARY L., MONIKA KEHOE, and KAREN SPEECE. *Handbook for Women Scholars: Strategies for Success*. San Francisco: Center for Women Scholars, American Behavioral Research Corporation, 1982. Current information and source book with addresses of advocacy groups, professional caucuses, research centers. Short papers on topics such as minority women, getting funding.

TAYLOR, BARBARA. *Eve and the New Jerusalem: Socialism and Feminism in the Nineteenth Century*. New York: Pantheon, 1983. Attempts to understand why women's rights were dropped from socialist-leftist agendas late in the nineteenth century, when there had been such a strong conjunction of the two in the Owenite movement.

WALKER, BARBARA G. *The woman's Encyclopedia of Myths and Secrets*. New York: Harper & Row, 1983. Massive (1,115 pages) compilation of short articles and entries on saints, goddesses, religious traditions, folk remedies, customs and symbols, with brief documentation and bibliography. Useful reference tool for verifying names, movements, terminology.

WANDOR, MICHELENE, ed. *On Gender and Writing*. Boston: Pandora Press, 1983. Collection of essays on modern British writers.

WOODBRIDGE, LINDA. *Women and the English Renaissance: Literature and the Nature of Womankind, 1540–1620*. Urbana: University of Illinois Press, 1983. Using prose, poetry, sermons, treatises, the author seeks to distinguish between literary creation and women's actual lived experience.

YALOM, MARILYN, ed. *Women Writers of the West Coast: Speaking of Their Lives and Careers*. With photographs by Margo Davis. Santa Barbara, Calif.: Capra Press, 1983. Combines interviews, photos, and text selections to give portraits of such women as Tillie Olsen, Maxine Hong Kingston, Ursula LeGuin, Judy Grahn, Susan Griffin, and others.

International Issues

Mary O'Callaghan

Women internationally become increasingly interdependent. Is our consumer life-style a cause of malnutrition and starvation of women and children in other parts of the world? Are government budget shifts to defense and nuclear weapons weighing more heavily on American women and children or on our sisters in the Third World areas where UN and regional or unilateral aid programs have been cut? Are multinationals in which we hold stock related to human rights violations? More and more interlocking women's issues blur distinctions of local, national, or international. What are the priority issues on which women agree?

Women across nations want peace, human rights, and a clear recognition and respect of women's rights. They want health care, education, job opportunities, equal pay, appropriate technology, and a fair division of work between the sexes; without these, they cannot benefit from any improvement in economic conditions. As economic crises rock both the industrialized and developing worlds, loans made by governments and by international financial institutions cause runaway inflation. The interdependence of rich and poor nations becomes clearer and has a severe impact on women, who traditionally are placed at the lowest levels of society.

Women are becoming more conscious both of their oppression and of their ability to educate and organize others. One of the achievements of the women's movement is the bonding of diverse women, transcending in many ways racial, ethnic, religious, and economic differences. Women workers without formal Western education, or with very little, are able to verbalize their situations and rally others to their side.

This essay will discuss efforts to improve the conditions of Third World women in agricultural and industrial development, to expose the exploitation of women by multinational corporations, to secure support from the United Nations (UN) and its agencies, and to promote international dialogue among women. It will review and evaluate the meetings of the UN Decade for Women and will describe women's work for peace and human rights.

Women in Development

In 1961, President John F. Kennedy, in his first address to a plenary session of the UN, called for a "decade of development." The UN agreed and subsequently extended the time into a second development decade during the 1970s and a third in the 1980s. Women were overlooked in the first decade, when increased international trade was to lift the GNP of developing countries. This became clear when in 1970, agriculture and population expert Ester Boserup published *Women's Role in Economic Development*. This was a seminal work for American women, showing how development up to that point had adversely affected the lives of most women in developing countries. The study was based on global statistics that were admittedly incomplete, both because developing countries did not have the resources to gather and compile complex census information and because women did not figure in the labor categories of the time, which looked only to productivity outside the home or village community. Boserup brought out parallels in the development process in Africa, Asia, and Latin America (Boserup 1970; Boulding 1983). In the same year, Barbara Ward called attention to the discrimination against women in an article called "Women and Technology in Developing Countries," while Carmen Deere's "Rural Women's Subsistence Production on the Capitalist Periphery" appeared in 1976 (Ward 1970; Deere 1976).

Boserup's continued usefulness is indicated by its being listed first among three texts in a 1982 *Syllabus on Women in Development* (Henderson 1982). However, later studies, cited throughout this essay, are based on newer, more complete statistics and in some cases on life among the people discussed. The statistical difficulties encountered by Boserup and others are addressed by Elise Boulding, who would add to current census categories certain classifications reflecting women's work: "home production worker: home agriculture; home services; home craft producing; home-based barter" (Boulding 1983).

In the third development decade, Arvonne Fraser with the Agency for International Development's Office for Women in Development won the right to monitor every program proposal to ensure the inclusion of practical programs for women. Proposal writers immediately began to integrate women into AID planning; otherwise the proposal was returned to the agency or the would-be contractors. To name but two of the results: Paula Roark's *Successful Rural Water Supply Projects and the Concerns of Women* and Irene Tinker's *Women and Energy: Program Implications* both appeared in

1980. With the advent of the Reagan administration and funding reductions in the office, Fraser returned to Minneapolis where she is directing the preparation of a book, *Women Affecting Public Policy Worldwide*, to be completed in time for the Nairobi conference evaluating the UN Decade for Women.

At the same time as Fraser was integrating Third World women into the AID, Barbara Good, a career foreign service officer, reaped the fruit of her efforts to improve the possibilities for women in diplomatic careers (Good 1983).

The third development decade's concern with basic needs, the quality of life, and the New International Economic Order (NIEO) reflected the need to move from abstraction to reality. Elise Boulding argued that life expectancy and literacy are meaningless if "a human being's value is measured primarily in terms of availability to participate in the labor force. To ensure that women are not only integrated into the development process, but also benefit from such integration, the focus as well as the measures of development must change" (Boulding 1983). For example, time budget studies and time use surveys, made by field workers who listened to the stories of women and translated them into terms understood by Western economists, have both strengths and weaknesses. They need to be supplemented by analysis of the needs and contributions of each member of the family.

Work

The work that women and children do in and around the home is not included in the definition of employment by the International Labor Organization (ILO), yet fetching water for drinking, cooking, and washing may take as much as a third of a woman's day (Roark 1980). Gathering, bundling, and transporting firewood is another necessity, and in denuded areas it may take 20 percent of a family's income to buy fuel to cook food. Because they are the poorest in all societies, Boulding has dubbed women and children "the fifth world" (Boulding 1980; Beneria 1982).

Considered as an unused labor resource, they were drafted for work outside the home in fields or factories, with little if any lessening of their former work. Food production on family holdings suffered, as cash crops for export zoomed among official priorities. Peasants' and agricultural workers' cooperatives were commandeered by government; loss of control and corruption often followed.

After these initial errors, "appropriate technology" to suit the locale and to meet the needs of women came later in the second decade of development (Carr 1978). In first sending machines or tools more suited to men than women, traditional roles were threatened and women's place in society endangered. Technology benefits an area only when it encourages the productive use of all human resources. *Women and Technological Change in De-*

veloping Countries looks at technology for improving health, the production and preparation of food, housing, and fertility, and examines the needs of women as members of families, heads of households, and agents of change (Dauber and Cain 1981).

Borreman distinguishes two kinds of research being conducted on appropriate tools for women. The first is done by women themselves and is eminently creative and practical, such as using an engine gear box as an oven. The second kind is the work of men who often produce "intermediate" technology which, after brief experiments, women refuse to use. Grain mills that are too heavy for them to hold will not replace the time-consuming, rugged work of pounding grain by hand. Instead of leaving it to men to do the difficult work of climbing trees to gather honey from wild bees, women have become expert in, and have earned income from, keeping bees in simply constructed hives three feet above the ground (Borreman 1982–83). Women have become more literate, reading material on how to construct filters in an experimental UNESCO project in Upper Volta, for example (UNESCO 1975). The ILO is now conducting studies of women's work and of appropriate technology to help them.

It is generally agreed that women do between 60 and 80 percent of the agricultural subsistence work in Africa; an estimate for Latin America is 40 percent. Gayatri Spivak stated that 84 percent of women's labor in India is done by illiterate peasants (Disch 1983). Even when food production changes because of the introduction of new technology, the percentage of agricultural work done by women may remain the same. Steel-plated plows require the strength of men, and Western donors often consider tractors proper only for men. Women's work may actually increase as men consider tasks like weeding to be women's responsibility. Colombo-Sacco found in one African region that women performed 55 percent of the agricultural work in a traditional village and 68 percent in a "modernized" one (Colombo-Sacco and Lopez-Morales 1975).

A booklet from the Food and Agricultural Organization (FAO), *The Missing Half: Woman 1975* (Colombo-Sacco and Lopez-Morales 1975), states that "most projects have been planned, formulated or implemented with scant regard for the employment of women or their production or income." Dr. A. Boerma, a former director-general of the FAO, is quoted in a 1978 publication as saying, "It is important to remember that most of the problems we have been facing for years would not have become as serious as they have if, in tackling them, we had concerned ourselves more with the women of the developing world" (Carr 1978).

Health

Women in developing countries are often unable to make any kind of progress because of poor health. Contaminated water, poor food supplies, and the dangers of constant childbearing are some of the problems (Blair 1981;

Harrington 1983). The UN Water Decade, if it succeeds, can do much for the improved health of women. Its objective—clean drinking water and adequate sanitation for all by 1990—may result from global conservation and improvement of water supplies. Women and children, because of their greater malnutrition, are more susceptible to the diarrhea and cholera with attendant dehydration and skin diseases caused by polluted water. Malaria, eye infections, gastroenteritis, and long-term enervating fevers are endemic.

The deepening drought and famine throughout the "shank" of Africa and its eastern areas is expected by most meteorologists to continue for two more years, four in all. Thirty-one countries are involved; the most severely stricken are Mozambique, Ghana, Mauritania, and northern Ethiopia. Besides the immense amount of human suffering this will entail, some new governments may be unable to survive (Southern Africa . . . 1984; Dash, Frankel, and Fitzgerald 1984; Chevre 1984). Since men traditionally receive the first choice of food, women and children are nearer starvation and are the first victims of famine brought on by drought. Whole villages of the dead and dying have been left by fleeing men.

An increase in the number of live births and children who live beyond the age of five would lighten the burden of providing children to the clan, a woman's first duty in traditional societies. The Worldwatch Institute finds that one in ten babies worldwide dies before its first birthday (Infant Mortality 1981). Fran Hosken also charges that female children are neglected and left to starve, and that female infanticide continues in many societies (Symposium . . . 1981).

Family planning or birth control programs in Third World countries have met with different receptions in different places. It has been found that if local women are used as paramedics or work with expatriate teams, the programs gain more acceptance. The experts now realize that traditional contraceptives and abortives may be used at the same time as modern pills and other contraceptive devices, and that the validity of family planning statistics must be checked by someone living among the people. National population objectives vary widely, however. China now restricts couples to one child and uses traditional communal observation and reporting to authorities to monitor births (Corry 1984). Other nations, whose populations have suffered through war or natural disasters, want more children and offer incentives for large families.

Daily living presents many health problems for women in Third World countries. Often breast feeding continues for 1½ or 2 years, which drains the mother's body and leads to constant fatigue, frequent exhaustion, stillborn babies, and infant deaths, especially in times of famine. In areas where clitoridectomy or infibulation is practiced, women may suffer lifelong pain; infections that often prove fatal and births that endanger children are common (Hosken 1982). Contrary to the stereotype, though these crude operations occur chiefly in Muslim areas of Africa and Indonesia, they are not part of Islam; rather, they antedate it. African and Asian women with wider educations are now trying to halt these attacks on women. Some progress is being made—Kenya outlawed clitoridectomy in 1982. Another health problem occurs in areas where purdah prevails; there are taboos against women being treated by male doctors who are not members of the family.

Education

Next to health care, improved education is most important for changing women's status and enriching their lives. Roughly two-thirds of all illiterate people in the world are women. Literacy and education, however, are not synonymous, as the academic Woodrow Wilson pointed out. Training in values, customs, and skills fits women for life in traditional societies. But today, literacy is increasingly necessary for human dignity in interacting with literate husbands and children, and for reading government forms and regulations, health indications and contracts. In some Third World countries, young, educated women both help and defer to older women without Western educations.

Education in these countries tends like most other goods to go first to men. Boys will be sent to school first, if the family, because of its labor needs or the costs of travel and clothing, must make a choice. Less developed countries are not able to provide free public education for all children (Smock 1981; Kelly and Elliott 1982; Women and Education . . . 1980).

Women and Multinationals

Transnational corporations, or multinationals (Richard Barnet's term), looking for profit maximization realized early that labor in Third World countries is far cheaper than in industrialized countries (Barnet and Muller 1974). Multinationals from American, European, or Japanese bases now proliferate in Mexico and the rest of Latin America, Southeast Asia (especially the Philippines), and Taiwan. Among the most docile workers, and the most proficient where manual dexterity is required, are young women who move into big cities as family holdings are taken over by large landowners and fewer workers are needed at home. Companies first deny health hazards and then try to cover them up, sometimes employing violence and armed forces to stop activist-organizers. Multinationals also are able to move their operations when women suffering from low wages or threatening health conditions organize or seek government help. Several writers, such as Annette Fuentes and Barbara Ehrenreich (1983) and Helen Safa (1981), have studied the particular impact on women of these employment practices. The Institute for Policy Studies in Washington, D.C., also sponsored a series of seminars on women in the international economy (Sorrel 1983).

Now that the production of electronics equipment has been separated into different components, the most demanding visual and wiring work is often done by young women in South Korea, the Philippines, Taiwan, and islands over which Japan exercises economic control. The microchips and software of the burgeoning computer indutry are produced by these women. Often their eyesight is ruined, and their general health suffers. For some five or six years, women withstand the hazardous conditions: noxious fumes, crowding, lack of ventilation, unsafe and outdated equipment, eye-strain from microscopic work, inadequate medical care, and little or no union representation. This plentiful and easily replaceable work force of young women has increased the numbers of unemployed men (AFSC-NWP 1981c).

Moreover, Japanese and American advertising companies bombard these young women with images of white women as sex objects to awaken desires for soft drinks, cosmetics, and a consumer life-style far beyond their means (Gay 1983). If the ads succeed, their wages are spent as a gamble on attracting a husband rather than as a contribution to family income. If they lose at this ploy, prostitution may often be the only alternative for survival.

The United Nations

When the United Nations charter was first written in 1945, human rights and fundamental freedoms were assured without distinction as to race, sex, language, or religion. At the beginning Bertha Lutz noticed that the use of the generic term *men* had precluded women from taking part in public af-fairs. Only 1 percent of the delegates were women and none was in the UN policymaking body. Thirty-five years later, the increase in the number of women in professional UN positions was only 0.7 percent a year. At that rate, it would take forty-one years for women to reach 50 percent (Nicol and Croke 1978; Sohm 1980).

The UN Commission on the Status of Women, founded in 1946, was set up under the auspices of the Economic and Social Council, but it was to meet less frequently than other commissions. It is still not as powerful within UN politics as are other bodies, but it has actively worked on the conferences of the the Decade for Women and may yet see future growth in affecting policy (Galey 1979; UN Commission 1983; *U.N. Chronicle* 1984).

The UN Voluntary Fund for the Decade for Women makes modest grants for women's projects—small, feasible projects that can be carried out and evaluated without the bureaucratic delays that too often provide help only after the need has changed (*U.N. Chronicle* 1984). The fund counts among its accomplishments the support of village women's income-raising activities. For example, in the Philippines, shrimp-drying, shingle-making, and garment-sewing projects were implemented, as was fish cultivation in

India's Orissa State. In Korea, 120 piglets were distributed among forty women in four pilot areas; study tours gave Thai women the opportunity to visit other areas of their country and to learn other work processes; Sri Lankan women learned how to grow flowers for export. Other regional groups are developing similar projects suited to their women's needs.

UNESCO (United Nations Educational, Scientific, and Cultural Organization) has carried out long-term programs to create equal educational opportunities for women, sponsoring projects in Africa, Asia, and Latin America (UNESCO 1975). Since the advent of the UN Decade for Women, the organization has integrated Decade activities into its overall planning (UNESCO 1980, 1983).

In 1983, years of preparation culminated in the opening of the UN International Research and Training Institute for the Advancement of Women (INSTRAW), with headquarters in Santo Domingo in the Dominican Republic. The Institute will collect, classify, and analyze information on research programs related to women, and will further the development of additional research on the economic and educational status of women, through a network of cooperating agencies and commissions (*U.N. Chronicle* 1984).

International Women's Year

International Women's Year, an event long in the making, worked its way through UN channels from the Status of Women Commission to the General Assembly, where 1975 was proclaimed as the International Women's Year (IWY). Its purpose was to intensify action:

- to promote equality between men and women
- to ensure the full integration of women in the total development effort
- to recognize the importance of women's increasing contribution to the development of friendly relations and cooperation among states and to the strengthening of world peace

An international conference was held in Mexico City, 19 June-2 July 1975, with over a thousand delegates in attendance from 125 nations (about 30 percent were men). Another five thousand women and men, among them members of 113 nongovernmental organizations (NGOs), also attended.

Among the central issues at the conference were the North-South conflict, the struggle of developing countries for the adoption of the NIEO (New International Economic Order) which would provide aid and favorable terms of trade to offset the rape of nonrenewable raw materials and the exploitation of their labor forces. The all-inclusive programs of a proposed World Plan of Action would require large government expenditures for the elimination of racism, apartheid, colonialism, alien domination, and the acquisition of territory by force, as well as the removal of obstacles to equal rights, opportunities, and responsibilities. The World Plan of Action mirrored the tensions in the understanding of objectives, with industrialized countries loath to admit guilt or pay damages. Israeli and other Jewish women and organizations were resentful of the extension and interpretation of "racism." Delegates balked if their cultures were unready to face the equality of women, protesting in some instances that their religious liberty was threatened (World Conference . . . 1976). Simone de Beauvoir denounced IWY as a disaster, a plan by men to confuse women (Russell and Van de Ven 1976). If only official delegates bound by the instructions of their governments had attended, her pessimism would have been more meaningful. The U.S. meeting to implement the World Plan of Action was held in Houston, Texas, in 1976. All states and outlying islands were represented. The Equal Rights Amendment, equal pay and equal opportunity, health care for and by women, aid for welfare mothers and for the handicapped and elderly were among the long list of objectives that ranged from the controversial to the generally accepted. Abortion rights advocates and lesbians were well organized and vocal (Bird 1979; U.S. National Commission . . . 1976).

IWY lengthened into a decade, with a mid-term meeting held in Copenhagen in 1980. The UN Decade for Women: Equality, Development, Peace developed the subthemes of education, health, and employment, on which studies were conducted in preparation for the Copenhagen meeting. President Carter's personal liaison for women's issues, Sarah Weddington, headed the American delegation. Much preparation went into the selection of delegates and the framing of issues as part of the strategy to avoid "politicization" (as any condemnation of Israel was called). The Tribune, a convocation of nongovernmental organizations, met in an alternative gathering place that made it possible to discuss at length issues not allowed on the official conference floor. Some observers estimated that American hopes were routed and that Arab women came away with more than they had dreamed. There was agreement that while progress had been made in the first half of the decade, it was not sufficient. Even the UN itself had not moved far in increasing the number of women representatives in policy-making places. A 218-paragraph Program of Action for the second half of the decade was approved (Lynn 1984; *World Conference* 1980).

The Commission on the Status of Women has decided to continue the subthemes of the Copenhagen meeting during an evaluation conference to be held in Nairobi in July of 1985 (*U.N. Chronicle* 1984). Areas of special concern are the gap between women's legal rights and their actual condition, problems faced by rural women, education and training for girls, and misuse of world resources to fuel the arms race. The degree of optimism present at the beginning of the Decade may not be present now, but like the ERA in this country, the struggle will continue (*U.N. Chronicle* 1984). Although IWY and its decade prove that all women are not in the same place (had anyone still doubted it), the series of national and international meetings have brought together so many women that the experience of being a woman has taken on new depth and meaning.

Human Rights

A growing body of international human rights laws and an increasing readiness of nations to boycott national offenders or ostracize them from international society have been aided by the Charter of the United Nations, 1945, its Declaration of Human Rights, 1948, and successive covenants. The International Covenant on Economic, Social, and Cultural Rights, 1966, was ratified by thirty-five countries in 1975. The International Covenant on Civil and Political Rights brought the Human Rights Committee of the UN into being 23 March 1976, with an all-male membership elected in September 1976 (Whittick 1979). The 1952 Convention on the Political Rights of Women won 46 votes in the General Assembly, with no votes opposed and 11 abstentions, 6 of whom later signed.

The Declaration of Human Rights did not have the force of law, but states with radically opposed ideologies were able to sign it for different reasons. Enforcement is weak partly because of the nature of the UN, where there is a reluctance to accuse a member state of violations that are often denied.

International bodies of lawyers and jurists and groups like Amnesty International and Human Rights Internet make transgressions known. Countries like South Africa spend large sums to improve their image, while Communist countries accuse capitalist governments of gross crimes to divert attention from their own. Mass arrests, torture, forced movements of peoples, and imprisonment without trial continue.

A UN Convention on the Elimination of All Forms of Discrimination against Women was adopted by the General Assembly on 18 December 1979 (U.N. Working Group . . . 1979; *U.N. Chronicle* 1984). The Carter administration and many organizations of American women and others tried to win its ratification by the United States in 1980 (Lawyers . . . 1983). The present climate is not favorable here, though enough other nations have assented for it to have gone into effect.

An unofficial International Tribunal on Crimes against Women met in Brussels, 4–8 March 1976 (Russell and Van de Ven 1976). Almost three hundred pages of edited testimony has detailed the experiences of witnesses. Scholars and activists in this country continue to examine the international infringements of women's human rights and the prospects for addressing those infringements either through law or through nongovernmental actions (Hevener 1982; Symposium . . . 1981).

Boycotts internationally can be effective. For example, though the malnutrition and deaths of babies on diluted infant food formulas may be due to complex reasons, the campaign against Nestlé and other producers grew in force, until the advertisements suggesting to Third World women that breast feeding is traditional and bottle feeding is "modern" gave way to other devices. The World Health Organization drew up a code of conduct for marketing infant formula, but it was opposed in the United States by three formula producers. The Reagan administration supported them, voting against the code and calling it unenforceable and a violation of anti-trust laws. The United States was the only country to vote against it, and the Nestlé Company agreed to follow the WHO guidelines in early 1984 (AFSC-NWP 1981a; Thorkelson 1984). This was an issue that appealed directly to many American women across political lines and helped to raise the awareness of links between multinationals in Western countries and the lives of Third World women.

Early UN studies and, more recently, documentary films have shown the particular impact of apartheid on women (U.N. Secretary-General 1978). Apartheid oppresses women in ways that need not be spelled out for Americans familiar with the injustices black women have suffered in this country. In South Africa, the demand for miners and other laborers in areas where they are not allowed to bring their wives or children reduces women to heads of miserably poor households. Men are allowed to return only once a year or every two years if they are working at a considerable distance, sometimes abroad. Frequently, the women are forced to live in bantustands, areas with poor soil and extremes of harsh weather. Women often go to the cities, trying to find their men. If they refuse to carry the hated "pass," identification required by the government, they may be imprisoned for several months for a first offense. Women prisoners may be kept in solitary confinement, denied adequate food, and allowed only one half-hour of exercise during which they are also supposed to wash their clothes (AFSC-NWP 1982).

Members of the U.S. Congress are trying to offer honorary U.S. citizenship to Winnie and Nelson Mandela, leaders of women's resistance and of the African National Congress, respectively (Crocker 1983). Independently, boycotts of South Africa by entertainers and athletes are being led in the United States by Harry Belafonte and Arthur Ashe. Artists and Athletes Against Apartheid, inspired by TransAfrica, is making known the UN-sanctioned ban on South African tours. In the case of performers who persist in going, the amount of money they receive, as much as $2 million, is publicized. When they promise in writing not to return to South Africa, the boycott-breakers' names are removed from the list (Verdon 1983; *Washington Notes* 1983).

An ambitious case involving international police brutality was brought by Dr. Myrna Cunningham (a Nicaraguan citizen who is half Miskito Indian) and Sanchez Espinosa against President Reagan, Secretary of State Shultz, CIA Director Casey, and Nicaraguan exile organizations; it was entered in the Washington, D.C., District Court in 1982. The plaintiffs were joined by six other Nicaraguans and Congressman Ronald Dellums. They alleged torture, kidnapping, and murder by counterrevolutionaries operating from Honduras, and charged the actions of the contras to the U.S. National Security Council. The case was dismissed by the court because of the "delicate foreign relations" matters involved. It is on appeal by the Center for Constitutional Rights, the New York law firm acting for Dr. Cunningham and her associates (Dellums 1982; Center for Constitutional Rights 1983).

International law is woefully underdeveloped in regard to refugees, who are overwhelmingly women. Pregnant women and women with small children, often trying to care for other family members, are among the poorest, and they are apt to have fewer language and labor skills than men. In most countries, girl refugees are less welcome than boys. What are the rights of "boat people"? Some nations, reluctant to have their GNP dissipated, have refused asylum. Others, even the United States, sometimes treat refugees as though they were criminals, interning them in camps long after screening for health hazards is past, and making it difficult for them to communicate with lawyers and to receive information about members of their families or friends. An internationally accepted definition of *refugee* is needed to prevent governments from making invidious distinctions between "political refugees" and "economic illegal workers" who are deported.

The UN High Commission for Refugees (UNHCR) attempts to secure the physical safety of refugees. The high commissioner's funds are placed at the service of refugees in areas where a receiving government may be overwhelmed by the numbers of aliens suddenly flooding across its borders. This is especially true in Africa, which has two-thirds of the world's refugees, as UNHCR counts them.

Women's rights also are violated by the tourist industry in East and Southeast Asia which generates millions of dollars yearly. Many of these trips, especially those organized in Japan, are designed to exploit women as sex objects. Women tour guides and flight attendants are part of the publicity; prostitutes are provided at stopovers. The costs are high and the profits go to the travel agencies and middlemen. In tours to the Philippines and Thailand, Japanese men form 80 percent of the groups. In Bangkok, there are 1,157 places of entertainment offering sex services, and employing a reported 30,000 women. The Third World Movement against the Exploitation of Women, based at Quezon City in the Philippines, has won international support. This group persuaded the Filipino National Union of Workers in Hotel Restaurant and Allied Industries to pass a resolution opposing sex tourism and to actively campaign against it (AFSC-NWP 1981b, 1983; Neumann 1984). Women from twenty-four countries met in Rotterdam at the Erasmus University, 6–15 April 1983, to form the International Feminist Network against forced prostitution and all forms of female sexual slavery. Regional centers were organized throughout the world, furthering the possibility of global strategies. If these women succeed, women who escape from sexual slavery will be given the status of refugees (Fighting sexual . . . 1983).

Among other gross violations of women's rights are female infanticide, the barter of women, the international slave trade, imprisonment without arrest or charge, and other violations of the international penal code such as rape and torture. Word of the suffering of women is moving through both open and secret channels. Solidarity groups, statements that emerge from countries continents away, actions before corporate meetings and embassies of oppressive governments, and gatherings before UN meetings attest to the growing force.

The International Conference on Human Rights in 1968 asked the Secretary General of the UN to study respect for the privacy of individuals, the sovereignty of nations, protection of human personality and physical integrity in the light of advances in biology, medicine, and biochemistry, auditory and visual surveillance, psychological invasion, and misuse of computer data files (*U.N. Chronicle* 1983a). The last report makes clear why prisoners prefer death to torture.

Peace Movements

Work for peace became an important objective of women's organizations founded in the nineteenth and early twentieth centuries. The International Women's Council, the International Alliance of Women, and the Women's International League for Peace and Freedom (WILPF) formed to improve conditions for women, to win the vote, and to work singly and together to achieve peace negotiations. Their histories inspire contemporary efforts and offer documentary sources for women's and peace researchers. They participated in the League of Nations and now with the United Nations. Three of their officers received Nobel Peace prizes. The first female member of Congress and the only one to vote against U.S. entry into World Wars I and II, Jeanette Rankin, served only in those critical sessions.

Between the world wars, women's organizations for regional good will supported the victims of fascism and Nazism and tried to bring together leaders and peoples with polarized ideologies. In 1971, WILPF's mission to North and South Vietnam in the midst of the war brought women to sign a separate treaty of peace. Church women of all faiths are exercising leadership in peace prayer, research, writing, and activism, fostering the growing demand among peoples that nuclear weapons be abandoned.

More recently, Helen Caldicott has lectured fearlessly about the effects of a nuclear blast and its medical consequences. At first, she met opposition, but then she was joined by Physicians for Social Responsibility, an international organization. She became its president emeritus in 1983 to give full time to Women's Action for Nuclear Disarmament which she also founded.

Women have taken an active stance in the 1980's protests against nuclear weapons. Although many protests have occurred at the cruise missile site in England, Greenham Common is the only camp maintained solely by women (Cook and Kirk 1983). "I was tired of governments, tired even of peace movements, when I went to Greenham Common for direct action," one of their number told Americans celebrating the 400th anniversary of the coming of Mennonites and Friends to Pennsylvania after refusing, because of religious conviction, to bear arms in Germany. Peace camps have been placed in northern Germany, Norway, Sicily, Sweden, and the United States (D'Adesky 1983.) The Greenham Common camp was disbanded by force in April 1984 (Hoyle 1984).

Admiration for the Greenham Common women brought them an invitation to speak and participate in the Seneca Falls Women's Camp in New York in the summer of 1983. This town, an army depot housing Pershing II missiles for deployment in England and other European countries, in 1848 hosted the first American meeting for women's civil and political rights. Peace was the priority of the 1983 campers, but many other women's issues were addressed (Hutchins 1983).

It is not easy to assess these efforts. The persistent public prayer of no-nuke peace activists, their leafletting at the Pentagon and picketing of the White House and State Department draw indifference, scorn, abuse, and arrests. Subconsciously, however, it may all have an effect. Feminist groups nevertheless have pushed forward and expanded their analysis of the fundamental issues involved. British women especially have been active in writing about women, peace, and antimilitarist organizing (Cambridge . . . 1983; Jones 1983). In the United States, Women's Pentagon Action and many other groups have formed new coalitions to fight nuclear weapons (Bullard 1983).

Working more quietly for peace and development are women in the Peace Corps, founded by President Kennedy in 1961 and one of the best opportunities middle-class American women, minority women, college graduates, and professionals of all ages have had to live and work with Third World women. About a third of the Peace Corps are and have been women. Young women who teach mathematics and science are an amazement as possible role models to the Third World girls they serve. Highly qualified women medical personnel, teachers, administrators, agronomists, and forestry specialists win admiration and illustrate how women can be educated and work in other societies. Throughout its existence the Peace Corps has been modified according to the requests of receiving governments. After the Percy amendment to the U.S. Foreign Aid Act of 1973, there has been more emphasis on basic needs and the training of poor women and their daughters (Cohn, Wood, and Haag 1981; Rice 1981). Though women's groups lobbied earnestly for the Percy amendment, women-specific projects are now under attack by a few who argue that they simply continue the separation and now virtual isolation of women; it is more important, they say, to integrate them as equals into a society of women and men (Borreman 1982–83).

International Dialogue

A number of international conferences have brought First and Third World women together. These conferences reflect the ongoing creative clash of ideas; scholars and activists in both First and Third World countries have modified their ideas and strategies over the years, but they still present many conflicting theories.

EPOC, the Equity Policy Center, chose health for its concentration before the UN Mid-Decade meeting in 1980. It sponsored an international symposium on health issues of women as workers and as mothers, on health systems' responses to women's needs, and on women as members of health care teams. Irene Tinker, director of EPOC, feels that the two sets of ideas that inspired the conference were (1) the statement that all are entitled by the year 2000 to a "level of health that will permit them to lead a socially and economically productive life" (International Conference on Primary Health Care, Alma Ata, U.S.S.R. 1978) and (2) the concepts of the women's health movement of the last decade. In the resolutions, they reached out to women refugees, recognizing both their mental stress and their need for primary health care (Blair 1981).

An international conference on Women and Food: Feminist Perspectives, claiming to be the first of its kind, was held at the University of New South Wales, 25–27 February 1982. Dr. Lenore Manderson of the school of sociology at the university and three other Australian women organized the meeting which drew 250 delegates from around the world. Women as producers, preparers, providers, and consumers of food were discussed.

Participants in another conference, Common Differences, Third World Women, and Feminist Perspectives at the University of Illinois, Urbana-Champaign, 9–13 April 1983, tried to find common ground. Isabel Letelier, Chilean exile and director of the Third World Women's Project at the Institute of Policy Studies, Washington, said in a keynote address that many women in Latin America are doing important things for women, but they do not call themselves feminists. The word *feminist*, she reportedly said, implies alignment with a bourgeois movement in an imperialist country. Other speakers felt that First World women's inability to deal with racism and class struggle needs to be changed. Bell Hooks called for a political ideology that unites all women rather than union based on common oppression (Disch 1983). *off our backs*, on the same page as this story, noted ten articles it had published from April 1979 to June 1983 that dealt with different areas and issues of Third World women.

The Women's Center of the University of California–Berkeley sponsored a conference on Women and Work in the Third World, 11–15 April 1983. Scholars and representatives of business, labor, activist organizations, and funding agencies came from around the world. More regionally specific explanations of women's situations were demanded, and Third World women challenged established theories. Linda Lim of Singapore and Neuma Aguiar of Brazil rejected the idea that women's participation in agriculture has declined; marginality and a "reserve army of labor" are nonspecific concepts. Lim feels that the multinationals' influence in creating negative conditions for women has been greatly exaggerated; international theories of superexploitation might better look to internal sociopolitical forces in Singapore and Malaysia. Aguiar wants to break through Marxist analysis to see the dynamics of what is happening in noncapitalist sectors. Women workers in Islamic countries are easily coopted into the traditionally conservative system, reported Mervet Hatem, an Egyptian political scientist. Hanna Papanek, an outstanding scholar, called for facing facts— there are no conveniently available theoretical frameworks for research on women who are not all in the same place (*Feminist Forum* 1983).

The first International Conference on Research and Teaching Related to Women in Montreal (Concordia University, Simone de Beauvoir Institute) heard Third World delegates criticize their Western hosts' failure to understand the cultures they were investigating and their ignorance of the problems of working-class women.

The 1983 conference of the National Women's Studies Association sparked similar protests during the plenary session on the "international feminization of poverty." Although speakers addressed substantive issues of women's economic oppression, the audience soon became enmeshed in accusations of racism and condescension within the association. The numbers of minority women who attend NWSA conferences have dropped significantly, for both financial reasons and differences in outlook and agenda (Lootens 1983).

How can we sum up "women and international affairs"? Clearly we know more about one another than we did before; pioneering works are now outdated, corrected in part by more specialized studies. Interviews and case studies with Third World women refract rich perspectives. Some of these women live in both the near Stone Age and the Space Age and interact comfortably with both. Can we, conditioned by our cultural baggage, travel backward *and* forward with them?

References

American Friends Service Committee. 1982. *South Africa: Challenge and hope*. Philadelphia and Bloomington: AFSC and African Studies Program, Indiana University.

AFSC-NWP. 1981a. World health assembly condemns infant formula abuse. Spring-Summer.

———. 1981b. Mobilization against sex tourism in Asia. Spring-Summer.

———. 1981c. Asian electronics workers expose conditions and management control methods. Spring-Summer.

———. 1983. International feminist network fights traffic in women. Vol. 4, no. 1.

BARNET, RICHARD J., and RONALD E. MULLER. 1974. *Global reach: The power of multinational corporations.* New York: Simon and Schuster.

BARRY, K. 1981. Female sexual slavery—understanding the international dimensions of women's oppression. *Human Rights Quarterly* 3, no. 1 (Spring): 44–52.

BENERIA, L. 1982. *Women and development: The sexual division of labor in rural societies.* New York: Praeger.

BIRD, C. 1979. *What women want: From the official report to the president, the Congress, and the people of the United States.* New York: Simon and Schuster.

BLAIR, P. 1981. *Health needs of the world's poor women.* Based on proceedings of the International Symposium on Women and Their Health, 8–11 June 1980. Washington, D.C.: Equity Policy Center.

BORREMAN, V., 1982–83. Technique and women's toil. *Cross-currents* 32, no. 4 (Winter): 420–29.

BOSERUP, E. 1970. *Women's role in economic development.* New York: St. Martin's Press.

BOULDING, E. 1980. *Women; the fifth world.* Foreign policy association headline series, no. 248, February New York: Foreign Policy Association.

———. 1983. Measures of women's work in the Third World: Problems and suggestions. In *Women and poverty in the Third World,* edited by Mayra Buvinic, Margaret Lycette, and William McGreevy. Baltimore: Johns Hopkins University Press.

BULLARD, L. 1983. Who's mobilizing? *Ms.,* August, p. 86.

BUVINIC, M. 1983. Women's issues in Third World poverty: A policy analysis. In *Women and poverty in the Third World,* edited by Mayra Buvinic, Margaret Lycette, and William McGreevy. Baltimore: Johns Hopkins University Press.

Cambridge Women's Peace Collective. 1983. *My country is the whole world: An anthology of women's work on peace and war.* Boston: Pandora Press.

CARR, M. 1978. *Appropriate technology for African women.* Addis Ababa: United Nations, Economic Commission for Africa, African Training and Research Centre for Women.

Center for Constitutional Rights. 1983. *The illegal U.S. war against Nicaragua.* New York: Center for Constitutional Rights.

CHEVRE, G. 1984. Drought: A new challenge . . . . *Africa News* 22, no. 7–8:11–12.

COHN, S., R. WOOD, and R. HAAG. 1981. U.S. aid and Third World women: The impact of Peace Corps programs. *Economic Development and Cultural Change* 29 (July): 795–811.

COLOMBO-SACCO, D., and G. LOPEZ-MORALES. 1975. *the missing half: woman, 1975.* Rome: Food and Agriculture Organization.

COOK, A., and G. KIRK. 1983. *Greenham women everywhere*. Boston: South End Press.

CORRY, J. 1984. Birth curb in China. *New York Times*, 14 February.

CROCKER, G. 1983. House Joint Resolution 240 and 241. Release from the congressman's office.

D'ADESKY, A-C. 1983. Peace camps: A worldwide phenomenon. *Ms.*, December, p. 108.

DASH, L., G. FRANKEL, and M.A. FITZGERALD. 1984. Drought maims, kills in growing swath of Africa. *Washington Post*, February 27.

DAUBER, R., and M.L. CAIN, eds. 1981. *Women and technological change in developing countries*. Boulder, Colo.: Westview Press.

DEERE, C. 1976. Rural women's subsistence production in the capitalist periphery. *Review of Radical Political Economics* 8, no. 1:9–17.

DELLUMS, R. 1982. Press release and statement on joining suit to challenge Reagan administration's illegal acts to destabilize Nicaragua. Washington, D.C.: Office of Congressman Dellums, 10 Nov.

DISCH, E. 1983. Common differences: Third World women and feminist perspectives. *off our backs*, July, pp. 4–6.

Feminist forum. 1983. Supplement to the *Women's Studies International Forum* 6, no. 3:iv–v.

Fighting sexual slavery globally. 1983. *off our backs*, July, p. 18.

FUENTES, A., and B. EHRENREICH. 1983. *Women in the global factory*. Boston: South End Press.

GALEY, M.E. 1979. Promoting nondiscrimination against women: The U.N. Commission on the Status of Women. *International Studies Quarterly* 23 (June): 273–302.

GAY, J. 1983. Sweet darlings in the media. *Multi-national Monitor*, August, pp. 19–21.

GOOD, B. 1983. Women in the U.S. Foreign Service: A quiet revolution. In *Face to face*, edited by Meg McGavran Murray. Westport, Conn.: Greenwood Press.

HARRINGTON, J. 1983. Nutritional stress and economic responsibility: A study of Nigerian women. In *Women and poverty in the Third World*, edited by Mayra Buvinic, Margaret Lycette, and William McGreevy. Baltimore: Johns Hopkins University Press.

HENDERSON, H. 1982. Syllabus on women in development. *Women's Studies Quarterly*, January, pp. 28–30.

HEVENER, N.K. 1982. *International law and the status of women*. Boulder, Colo.: Westview Press.

HOSKEN, F.P. 1982. *The Hosken report: Genital and sexual mutilation of females*. 3d ed. Lexington, Mass.: Women's International Network News.

HOYLE, R. 1984. Breaking camp at Greenham: Britain ends a protest as the Netherlands hesitates over missiles. *Time*, 16 April.

HUTCHINS, L. 1983. Seneca: Summer of action and learning. *off our backs*, October, pp. 3–6.

Infant mortality. 1981. *Washington Post*, 13 December.

JONES, L., ed. 1983. *Keeping the peace: Women's peace handbook I*. London: Women's Press.

KELLY, G.P., and C.M. ELLIOTT, eds. 1982. *Women's education in the Third World: Comparative perspectives*. Albany: State University of New York Press.

Lawyers' Committee for International Human Rights. 1983. Letter asking lobbying support for ratification of Covenant on the Elimination of Discrimination against Women. New York: Lawyers' Committee for International Human Rights.

LOOTENS, T. 1983. The international feminization of poverty. *off our backs*, August-September, pp. 5–6.

LYNN, N., ed. 1984. The United Nations Decade for Women World Conference: Copenhagen, Denmark. *Women & Politics* 4, no. 1:whole issue.

NEUMANN, A.L. 1984. Scandal in Manila, the X-rated business trip. *MS.*, February, pp. 99–102.

NICOL, D., and M. CROKE, eds. 1978. *The United Nations and decision-making: The role of women*. New York: U.N. Institute for Training and Research.

REANDA, L. 1981. The United Nations approach: Commission on the Status of Women. *Human Rights Quarterly* 3, no. 1:11–31.

RICE, G. 1981. *Twenty years of the Peace Corps*. Washington, D.C.: Government Printing Office.

ROARK, P. 1980. *Successful rural water supply projects and the concerns of women*. Washington, D.C.: U.S. Agency for International Development, Office of Women in Development.

RUSSELL, D.E.H., and N. VAN de VEN. 1976. *Crimes against women: Proceedings of the International Tribunal*. Millbrae, Calif.: Les Femmes-Publications.

SAFA, H.I. 1981. Runaway shops and female employment: The search for cheap labor. *SIGNS* 7, no. 2:418–33.

SMOCK, A.C. 1981. *Women's education in developing countries: Opportunities and outcomes*. New York: Praeger.

SOHM, E.D. 1980. *Status of women in the professional category and above: A progress report*. Doc. A/35/182. New York: United Nations.

SORREL, L. 1983. Women subsidize global economy. *off our backs*, June, pp. 1, 17.

Southern Africa food needs acute. 1984. *Africa News*, 27 February.

Symposium: Women and international human rights. 1981. *Human Rights Quarterly* 3 (Spring):whole issue.

THORKELSON, W. 1984. A boycott that worked: Nestlé bites the bullet. *National Catholic Reporter*, 24 February.

TINKER, I. 1980. *Women and energy: Program implications*. Washington, D.C.: Office of Women in Development, Agency for International Development.

U.N. Chronicle. 1983a. Science, technology, human rights: The web of modernity. April, pp. 25–40.

———. 1983b. Exploitation and traffic in women. July.

————. 1984. Issues relating to women. January, pp. 46–47.

U.N. Commission on the Status of Women. 1983. *Report of the Commission on the Status of Women acting as the preparatory body for the World Conference to Review and Appraise the Achievements of the United Nations Decade for Women on its first session.* Doc. A/CONF.116/PC/9. New York: United Nations.

U.N. Secretary-General. 1978. *The effects of apartheid on the status of women in South Africa, Namibia, and Rhodesia.* Doc. E/CN.6/619. New York: United Nations.

U.N. Working Group of the Whole on the Drafting of the Convention on the Elimination of Discrimination against Women. 1979. *Draft convention . . . report.* Doc. A/34/60. New York: United Nations.

UNESCO. 1975. *Women, education, equality: A decade of experiment.* Paris: UNESCO.

————. 1980. *Half of the world: UNESCO activities for the advancement of women.* Paris: UNESCO.

UNESCO: A course for the future. 1983. *UNESCO Courier*, January:whole issue.

U.S. National Commission on the Observance of International Women's Year. 1976. *". . . to form a more perfect union . . .": Justice for American women.* Washington, D.C.: Government Printing Office.

VERDON, L. 1983. Boycotting South Africa. *Washington Post*, 13 September.

VON HAHMANN, G. 1981. *Women and world issues: An action handbook for your community.* Washington, D.C.: Overseas Education Fund.

WARD, B. 1970. Women and technology in developing countries. *Impact of Science on Society* 20, no. 1:93–101.

Washington notes on Africa. 1983. Washington Office on Africa.

WHITTICK, A. 1979. *Woman into citizen.* London: Atheneum Publishing Co.

Women and education in the third world. 1980. *Comparative Education Review* June:whole issue.

Women and food: Feminist perspectives. 1982. Conference papers. Available from Dr. Lenore Manderson, School of Sociology, University of New South Wales, P.O. Box 1, Kensington, N.S.W., 2033, Australia.

World Conference of the International Women's Year, Mexico City. 1976. *Report.* Doc. E/CONF.66/34. New York: United Nations.

World Conference of the United Nations Decade for Women: Equality, Development, and Peace, Copenhagen. 1980. *Report.* New York: United Nations.

Bibliography

ANAND, ANITA. "The International Economy and Models of Development: Help or Hindrance to women?" Paper presented at the Conference on Women and International Development in the 80's, November 1983. Washington, D.C.: Association for the Advancement of Policy, Research, and Development in the Third World.

BARRIOS DE CHUNGARA, DOMITILA. *Let Me Speak: Testimony of Domitila, a Woman of the Bolivian Mines.* New York: Monthly Review Press, 1978.

BLACK, NAOMI, and ANN BAKER COTTRELL, eds. *Women and World Change: Equity Issues in Development*. Beverly Hills, Calif.: Sage, 1981. Individual articles and case studies based on work in many world regions.

BOULDING, ELISE, et al., eds. *Handbook of International Data on Women.* Beverly Hills, Calif.: Sage, 1976. Although out of date, still helpful for locating types of sources.

BUVINIC, MAYRA. *Women and World Development: An Annotated Bibliography*. Washington, D.C.: Overseas Development Council, 1976.

CASSIDY, SHEILA. *Audacity to Believe: An Autobiography*. Cleveland: Collins World, 1978. British M.D. working in Chile, 1971–75; she was arrested and tortured for treating a wounded revolutionary.

Catholic Institute for International Relations. *South Africa in the 1980's*. London: The Institute, [n.d.]. Documents transgressions of human rights.

CHAPMAN, WILLIAM. "Women's March into Workforce Changes Social Structure." *Washington Post*, 29 February 1984. In Japan, "computer ladies."

Columbia Human Rights Law Review. *Law and the Status of Women: An International Symposium*. New York: United Nations Centre for Social Development and Humanitarian Affairs, 1977.

CURTIN, LESLIE B. *Status of Women: A Comparative Analysis of Twenty Developing Countries*. Washington, D.C.: Population Reference Bureau, 1982. Uses data from the world fertility survey over the past twenty-five years to analyze women's education and employment patterns.

DANFORTH, SANDRA C. *Woman and National Development*. Monticello, Ill.: Vance Bibliographies, 1982. Thirty-five-page bibliography.

HOSKEN, FRANZISKA P. *International Directory of Women's Development Organizations*. PB-292 854. Washington, D.C.: National Technical Information Service, 1977. Compiled under contract from the Agency for International Development, this directory lists over 300 organizations from 133 countries.

Hunter College and the National Council for Research on Women. *Women in Development: Theory and Practice*. New York: National Council for Research on Women, 1983. Proceedings of a conference, with keynote addresses by Florence Howe, Hanna Papanek, and Nadia Youssef.

HUSTON, PERDITA. *Third World Women Speak Out: Interviews in Six Countries on Change, Development, and Basic Needs*. New York: Praeger, in cooperation with the Overseas Development Council, 1979. A classic work.

IGLITZIN, LYNNE B., and RUTH ROSS. *Women in the World: A Comparative Study*. Santa Barbara: ABC-Clio, 1976. Heavily documented essays on the social and political role of women in different countries.

Independent Commission on International Development Issues. *North-South, a Program for Survival*. Cambridge, Mass.: MIT Press, 1980. Also called the "Brandt Report" after chair Willy Brandt.

International Council of Women. *Women in a Changing World: The Dynamic Story of the International Council of Women since 1888*. London: Routledge and Kegan Paul, 1966. Documents early organizing among women internationally.

ISIS Women's International Information and Communication Service. *Women in Development: A Resource Guide for Organization and Action*. Geneva and Rome:

ISIS, 1983. Excellent, thorough guide with essays, bibliographies, directories. State of the art.

KENWORTH, ELDON. "Our Colleague [Jeane] Kirkpatrick." *Latin American Studies Association (LASA) Forum* 14, no. 4 (Winter 1984): 23–24. Scholarly note on Ambassador Kirkpatrick as a political scientist, not a Latin American specialist.

KOHN, WALTER S. *Women in National Legislatures: A Comparative Study of Six Countries.* New York: Praeger, 1980.

LERNOUX, PENNY. *Cry of the People: The Struggle for Human Rights in Latin America—the Catholic Church in Conflict with U.S. Policy.* New York: Penguin, 1982. Important for understanding current directions.

LILLICH, RICHARD B., and FRANK C. NEWMAN. *International Human Rights: Problems of Law and Policy.* Boston: Little, Brown & Co., 1979. Text with case studies.

LINDSAY, BEVERLY, ed. *Comparative Perspectives on Third World Women: The Impact of Race, Sex, and Class.* New York: Praeger, 1980. Cross-cultural reviews of women in Africa, Asia, and the Americas, focusing on racism and colonialism; draws on statistics, film and literature, national ideologies.

"The New Arms Technology and What It Means." *Nation,* 9 April 1983. Special issue.

NEWLAND, KATHLEEN. *The Sisterhood of Man.* New York: Norton, 1979. From the Worldwatch Institute. Comparative analysis of health, political status, work, media, law, education, and family roles; a readable, well-documented study.

off our backs, 1841 Columbia Road N.W., #212, Washington, DC 20009. Major feminist newspaper with extensive international coverage.

PEREZ ESQUIVEL, ADOLFO. *Christ in a Poncho, Witnesses to the Nonviolent Struggles in Latin America.* Maryknoll, N.Y.: Orbis Books, 1982. Nobel Prize–winning poet; see especially pp. 43–57, "The Mothers' Courage of Buenos Aires."

PEZULLO, CAROLINE. *Women and Development: Guidelines for Programme and Project Planning.* Santiago, Chile: United Nations, 1982. A tool to help design and implement women's programs at the community, national, regional, and international levels.

RIHANI, MAY, with JODY JOY. *Development as If Women Mattered: An Annotated Bibliography with a Third World Focus.* Washington, D.C.: Overseas Development Council, 1978. Good supplement to Buvinic.

SIGNS: Journal of Women in Culture and Society. 7, no. 2 (Winter 1981). A special issue on development and the sexual division of labor.

STAUDT, KATHLEEN A., and JANE S. JAQUETTE, eds. "Women in Developing Countries: A Policy Focus." *Women & Politics* 2, no. 4 (Winter 1982): whole issue. Articles and book reviews; feature on databases for WID research.

STOCKLAND, TORIL, MALLICA VAJRATHON, and DAVIDSON NICOL, eds. *Creative Women in Changing Societies: A Quest for Alternatives.* Dobbs Ferry, N.Y.: Transnational Publishers, 1982. 1980 seminar proceedings of the UN Institute for Training and Research (UNITAR).

TARANGO, S. YOLANDA. "The Undocumented: An Interview with Bishop Flores." *probe* 9, no. 8 (June 1979): 3–5. National Assembly of Women Religious.

TINKER, IRENE, MICHELE BO BRAMSEN, and MAYRA BUVINIC, eds. *Women and World Development.* New York: Praeger, 1976. Proceedings of a seminar cosponsored by the American Association for the Advancement of Science and various branches of the UN. Includes papers by leading authorities, proposed UN activities, annotated bibliography.

United Nations Centre against Apartheid. *Register of Entertainers, Actors, and Others Who Have Performed in Apartheid South Africa.* New York: United Nations. Recurring report, first issued October 1983.

U.S. Agency for International Development. *Women in Development 1980.* Report to the Committee on Foreign Relations, U.S. Senate, and the House Committee on Foreign Affairs. Washington, D.C.: Government Printing Office, 1980.

U.S. Agency for International Development. *Women in Development, a Pocket Guide to Women in Development Resources in the United States.* Washington, D.C.: AID, [1983]. Small but very handy list of organizations.

Women Affecting Public Policy Worldwide. Study in progress by Arvonne Fraser at the Humphrey Institute of Public Affairs at the University of Minnesota. Results to be available for the 1985 UN Decade for Women conference in Nairobi, Kenya.

"Women and Mission." *International Bulletin of Missionary Research* 8, no. 1 (January 1984): whole issue. Articles by women of different faiths.

"Women and National Development." *SIGNS: Journal of Women in Culture and Society* 3, no. 1: whole issue.

Women in Dialogue. Inter-American meeting, Puebla, Mexico, 27 Jan.-13 Feb. 1979. Notre Dame, Ind.: Catholic Committee on Urban Ministry, 1979. Translation of seminars held "outside the walls" during CELAM III, Third Conference of Latin American Bishops.

Resources

American Friends Service Committee, *National Women's Project Newsletter.* Third World Women Newsletter included. 1501 Cherry St., Philadelphia, PA 19102.

Association for Women in Development, founded 1982, by women scholars, practitioners, and policymakers. Its goals are to increase interaction among women in both the public and private sectors to strengthen research and action in WID; to improve the integration of women as agents and beneficiaries of development by multilateral, unilateral, and private institutions; to provide improved communication to a widening audience on problems and solutions relating to WID. Their 13–15 October 1983 first annual conference was devoted to food and energy. Suite 300, 1900 Pennsylvania Ave., N.W., Washington, DC 20006.

Center of Concern, Women's Project, 3700 13th St., N.E., Washington, DC 20017. Staff members travel to TWC or bring TWC women here to know conditions as they are experienced by the chief actors, work with them toward solutions. N.G.O. status with U.N. Newsletter, memoranda, conferences here and abroad.

Connexions. Journal published by feminists of diverse nationalities and political perspectives committed to the international women's movement, with translations of women's writing not easily available in the United States. Each issue of *Connexions* focuses on a different theme: older and younger women, migrant/refugee, for example. 4228 Telegraph Ave., Oakland, CA 94609.

Coalition of Women in Development (CWID). 3700 13th St., N.E., Washington, DC 20003. Monthly meetings include presentation by an expert, questions, comments, exchange of information, new developments, future meetings and conferences, publications of members, research opportunities.

Equity Policy Center (EPOC). Publications, conferences, clearinghouse. Directed by Irene Tinker, an early women-in-development specialist, with an outstanding staff. Reprints of journal articles available. 1525 Eighteenth St., N.W., Washington, DC 20036.

Human Rights Internet Directory. Separate volumes on Latin America, Africa, Asia; North America; Eastern Europe. *Reporter*, published five times a year, c. 225 pp. an issue. Over 2,000 individuals and organizations contribute to the network. Founded 1976. 1338 G St., S.E., Washington, DC 20003.

Human Rights of Women, Packet Service Center, Board of Global Ministries, 7820 Reading Rd., Cincinnati, OH 45237 ($3.95 plus $1 postage.) Ten specific areas, twelve articles: UN Declarations, Sterilization Abuse, Effects of Apartheid on Women, Housing, Torture, Job Stress, Prisons, Physical Abuses, Brown Lung, Alternative Futures.

Institute for Policy Studies (IPS). Third World Women's Project. Isabel Letellier, assisted by Jill Gay. Booklet. 1901 Q St., N.W., Washington, DC Research, lectures from political leaders, scholars, women members of national legislatures, labor leaders, films, traveling exhibits.

International Labor Office, Washington Branch. Numerous reports include *Women, Work and Development*, a new serial; separate books on issues and regions; studies of women's economic contributions and the change in women's roles as the result of their own efforts; policy changes in government and private sector, new technologies, demographic change, degree of equality in the domestic sphere and labor markets. *Women at Work*, a new bulletin begun in 1983, 2 issues a year. It is devoted to questions concerning the economic and social contribution of women to society. 1750 New York Avenue, N.W., Washington, DC 20006.

International Women's Tribune Center. *Tribune: A Women and Development Quarterly.* Continues work of the autonomous meetings of the Tribune which met in Mexico City, Copenhagen. Networks with national women's centers. International Women's Tribune Center, Inc., 305 E. 46th St., New York, NY 10017.

ISIS, Women's International Information and Communications Service, Resource and Documentation Service. *Women's International Bulletin.* English, Spanish, and Portuguese. Offices in Geneva (P.O. Box 50, Cornavin, 1211 Geneva 2, Switzerland) and Rome (Via S. Maria dell'Anima 30, 00186 Roma, Italy).

Secretariat for Women in Development, New Transcentury Foundation, 1789 Columbia Road N.W., Washington, DC 20009. Works with private and voluntary agencies to integrate women into overseas programming; publications include bibliographies, lists of funding sources, directories of projects.

Washington Office on Africa (WOA) and Washington Office on Latin America (WOLA). 110 Maryland Avenue N.E., Washington, DC 20002. These two separate offices offer briefings, publications, and country expertise.

Women Strike for Peace. 145 South 13th St., Philadelphia, PA 19107. Founded 1961, active in demonstrations.

Women's International League for Peace and Freedom, U.S. Section. 1213 Race St., Philadelphia, PA 19107. Founded in 1916, still going strong. Supports protest actions, worldwide network, wide variety of programs and publications. Newsletter *Peace and Freedom.* WILPF presidents have included Nobel Prize winners Jane Addams and Emily Balch; the organizational archives are now available on microfilm.

Women's International Network. 187 Grant St., Lexington, MA 02173. Publishes *WIN News,* quarterly report on all aspects of women and development, peace and militarism, health, labor, the UN, etc.

Women's International Resource Exchange, Inc. (WIRE). Issues translations of articles concerning women: oppression by governments, transnational corporations, struggles for liberation, health. Special packets and catalog. 2700 Broadway, #7, New York, NY 10025.

Film and Video

American Friends Service Committee. *In Their Own Words: Salvadoran Refugees in Honduras.* Based on children's drawings, with narration by refugee teachers.

Are You Listening? Series of half-hour videotapes, includes many international topics: women in Java, Egypt, Colombia, China, Jamaica; IWY interviews, etc. Martha Stuart Communications, P.O. Box 127, Hillsdale, NY 12529.

BARRIOS, JAIME, et al. *Missing Persons.* 1979. 26 min., B/W, in Spanish and English. Three women tell about repression in Chile. From Women Make Movies, P.O. Box 315, Franklin Lakes, NJ 07417.

BRIGGS, RAYMOND. *When the Wind Blows.* About an elderly British couple who symbolize gently but powerfully the incomprehensibility of nuclear war. American premiere, March 1984.

British Broadcasting Company. *China's Only Child.* Documentary on China's new population policy, aired on PBS in the United States in February 1984.

FRIEDKIN, WILLIAM. *The Deal of the Century.* Hollywood, Warner Brothers, 1983. Satire on the international arms industry.

The Global Assembly Line. 1983. 60 min., color. Part of the "Hidden from History" series, with accompanying study packets, this film looks at women in the international work force. From New Day Films, P.O. Box 315, Franklin Lakes, NJ 07417.

MACLAINE, SHIRLEY, and CLAUDIA WEILL. *The Other Half of the Sky: A China Memoir.* Color, 75 min. Women's film crew went to China in 1973. New Day Films, P.O. Box 315, Franklin Lakes, NJ 07417.

MARTIN, PAT H. *Bases of Our Fears.* Filmstrip, 25 min. How presence of U.S. Navy bases in the Philippines changes the regional economy, exploits women. Mennonite Central Committee Audiovisuals, 21 S. 12th St., Akron, PA 17501.

Refugee Women. Sixty-slide set from the UN High Commission on Refugees, N.Y.

Selected Films on Women in the World. Resource Packet #2. Secretariat for Women in Development, New Transcentury Foundation, 1789 Columbia Road, N.W., Washington, DC 20009.

We Have Struck a Rock. Struggles of South African women. Distributed by California Newsreel, 630 Natoma St., San Francisco, CA 94103.

Women Today. Series of six films about women in Afghanistan, Bolivia, Kenya, China; women in development. Wheelock Educational Resources, P.O. Box 451a, Hanover, NH 03755.

The World's Uprooted Refugees. Filmstrip, 15 min. Lutheran World Relief, 475 L'Enfant Plaza, S.W., Washington, DC 20024.

YOUNG, DICK. *Journey for Survival.* Fifteen min. 1981 UN Water Decade film. Also *Water* and *Water More Precious Than Oil*, videocassettes. All from Global Water, 2033 M St., N.W., Washington, DC 20036.

Lesbians

Judith Schwarz

This is the fourth edition of *The Women's Annual*, yet the first to devote a chapter to lesbian issues. While works about lesbianism were discussed in previous editions within chapters on such matters as health or psychology, little attention was given to the complexities or major issues of our lives as lesbians in Western society. As in most reference and scholarly works, we have been merely an afterthought, a footnote to the major body of work on heterosexual existence. I am pleased to begin the challenging work of recognizing lesbian concerns in an entire chapter devoted to 1983's events, writings, and issues. Readers will find information related to lesbians in other sections as well.

The greatest difficulty in attempting an overview of lesbian life in any given year is not in synthesizing the rich mother lode of material published by and about lesbians. It is, rather, that for all the great strides we have made since the convergence in 1969 of the women's and gay liberation movements, most lesbians are still invisible. Many of us live under the public assumption of heterosexual disguise rather than face the extreme prejudices of the sexual majority in power. This often forces us to live our emotional, affectional, political, and sexual lives behind a surface blandness within our work places, our schools, and our biological families. Yet behind this surface blandness, lesbians have created a diverse network of alternative methods and publications to communicate our concerns to one another, essentially bypassing most of the heterosexual world while still reaching many, though certainly not all, lesbians. This is especially remarkable in view of the fact that when we speak of "the lesbian community," we are speaking really on two levels: referring in a universal, national way to all lesbians, as well as to small clusters of lesbians acquainted with one another through social, political, or cultural groupings with only one or two members linking the clusters within geographic or interest boundaries. Recognizing this, it is amazing how well communication of vital information related to our lives as lesbians travels its circuitous but well-organized route from one small cluster to local, national, and international lesbian communities.

News about child custody cases; grand jury investigations; violence against lesbians; military witchhunts; traumatic illnesses; job discrimination or firings based on sexual preference; political battles over lesbian and gay rights; work involving lesbian affiliation groups on such issues as racism, nuclear disarmament, peace, environment, incest, and sexual harassment; success stories; new creative work by lesbian artists, musicians, and writers; disability issues; and social and cultural events journeys beyond lesbian friendship circles via the grapevine (a traditionally rich source of communication among women often disparagingly referred to as "gossip"). Discussion groups, informal support networks, letters, and the telephone wires carry our individual or local concerns to an ever-larger audience.

Within a month or two of any localized news, a multitude of lesbian and feminist newsletters pick up the theme. They range from small vibrant publications like Roanoke, Virginia's *Skip Two Periods* to the national newsletter *Lesbian Connections* with a readership in the tens of thousands. *Common Lives/Lesbian Lives*, *Sinister Wisdom*, and other periodicals continue the process, along with workshops at annual lesbian and so-called women's music festivals and conferences. It may take two to three years between the time issues of importance first receive local attention and the day they appear in book form. The excellent but financially pressed lesbian publishers, distributors, and mail order catalogs then carry the information back into the women's, lesbian and alternative bookstores that are the final link providing a general forum for discussion and debate.

Only rarely will lesbian issues or news circumvent the information flow described above. More rarely still can we count on gathering pertinent news from the mass media. Rarest of all are books from mainstream non-lesbian or feminist publishers that recognize a potentially strong market for sales and introduce new ideas, research, or issues back into lesbian communities.

References cited in this chapter are very difficult to find outside of women's or alternative bookstores. Small press publications go out of print quickly because of the economic realities of underfinanced publishers, few copies initially run, and homophobic or distribution problems with regular bookstores which refuse to carry small-press or self-published books about lesbians. Moreover, despite the encouraging work of the American Library Association's Gay Task Force, you may well have some difficulty finding references in your local or academic library. This is another reason lesbian and gay archives and libraries devoted to collecting this material are so essential. Lesbians have done so much, written about it so well, but little is readily available. Yet, a thought-provoking and challenging world awaits you if you go to the trouble of seeking it out.

Definition, Differentness, and Diversity

Who is a lesbian? A standard historical definition states that she is "a woman whose primary erotic, psychological, emotional and social interest is in a member of her own sex, even though that interest may not be overtly expressed" (Martin and Lyon 1972). But as pioneer lesbian researcher Jeannette Foster noted, "In popular usage [lesbian] implies overt sexual expression" (Foster 1956). Throughout the 1970s, published material both within and without the lesbian community presented a stereotypical lesbian who was college educated, unmarried, childless, movement oriented, downwardly mobile, denim wearing, physically strong, of middle-class background, white, and fairly young. Her main goal in life was to radically change women's status and living conditions in our society. If she slept with women, so much the better, but she seldom wrote about it, and it was never a requirement. Women who fit the rest of the categories could and did choose the political label of "lesbian" without regard to whether they had ever tasted the pleasures of another woman sexually. References to lust, sexual styles, or the desire for power in relationships; or more than a token recognition of lesbians who were working class, disabled, Republicans, married, practicing sado-masochism, were religious or ambitious, or in prison, had children, preferred make-up and dresses over jeans, were downplayed or eliminated in discussions and written material by and about lesbians for nearly a decade. Lesbians of color were tentatively welcomed and acknowledged, but only so long as they acted "white."

Coming from a historical position of total isolation into the relative sunlight of lesbian feminism, it is no wonder that lesbians felt such a need to present a monolithic front to our powerful political foes. However, as long as we stayed so preoccupied with a unified "sisterhood," we were not willing to devote much attention to the growing rage of lesbians who did not fit the stereotype. Rather than face the great uneasiness and pain so evident among women from different class, educational, geographic, racial, and cultural backgrounds, the lesbian community tended to focus energy on struggling against racism and economic inequalities in the larger society.

In the 1980s, we have begun to face hard internal questions within our communities and ourselves. Racism and fear of "the other" can no longer be chalked up to ignorance, since a distinguishing feature of recent lesbian writing has been the desire to recognize and gain new strength from our very diversity. The enormous pain, anger, and rejection felt by so many for so long has erupted into the most exciting, creatively challenging writing seen in lesbian publications for a long time. There is a sense of cautious celebration—perhaps overly optimistic—in the air. Lesbians everywhere have seen that acting, speaking, thinking, and dressing as if we all came from the same cookie cutter hasn't got us anywhere in either the straight world or the one we've been working so hard to create. The demand for "politically correct" sameness has denied us the rich complexities of lesbian existence.

Asian-American, black, Latina, and Native American lesbians as well as Jewish lesbians have consistently been in the forefront of this new dialogue, doing prolific and creative hard work. A few have reminded us of lessons learned in our recent past that we have already forgotten. Audre Lorde tells us that in the 1950s, "There was a loose group of young lesbians, white except for Flee and I, who hung out together, apart from whatever piece of the straight world we each had a separate place in. . . . However imperfectly, we tried to build a community of sorts where we could, at the very least, survive within a world we correctly perceived to be hostile to us; we talked endlessly about how best to create that mutual support which twenty years later was being discussed in the women's movement as a brand-new concept. Lesbians were probably the only Black and white women in New York City in the fifties who were making any real attempt to communicate with each other; we learned lessons from each other, the values of which were not lessened by what we did not learn" (Lorde 1983, 179). In 1983, works by black poets Cheryl Clarke, Pat Parker, and Michelle Parkerson, novelists Ann Shockley, Audre Lorde, Becky Birtha, and black lesbian writers Anita Cornwall, Barbara Smith, and Gloria Hull have taught us lessons on black lesbian experience, relationships, humor, and oppression. Alice Walker's Pulitzer Prize novel *The Color Purple* continued to make new audiences aware of women-loving-women.

Kitchen Table Press was founded to publish works by and about women of color. During the past year, lesbians contributed many powerful, sensuous tales to their anthologies *Home Girls* (Smith 1983) and *Cuentos: Stories by Latinas* (Gomez, Moraga, and Romo-Carmona, 1983) as well as the reprint edition of *This Bridge Called My Back: Writings by Radical Women of Color* (Moraga and Anzaldua 1983). Latina, Chicana, and Puerto Rican women have consistently emphasized the wealth of language resources available to them through their bilingual heritage. They sweet-talk their way into women's hearts first in Spanish, then in English, and then back again to Spanish—all in the course of a couple of sentences. Cherríe Moraga, who coedited *This Bridge* and *Cuentos*, has added an exceptionally provocative and thoughtful voice to lesbian literature in her collection *Lo Que Nunca Paso Por Sus Labios—Loving in the War Years*.

Also in 1983, New York Asian lesbians began the first known search for forgotten lesbian foresisters throughout the many cultures and countries of Asia. Sifting through the collections at the Third World Women's Archives and the Lesbian Herstory Archives, the Asian Women's Herstory Project has already uncovered fascinating evidence of lesbian communities in Japan and China, though sometimes stymied by language barriers and the extreme homophobia they face within their own Chinese-American and Japanese-American cultures. Kitty Tsui's *The Words of a Woman Who Breathes Fire* (1983) and the writings of Barbara Noda, Merle Woo, and Michiyo Cornell (Fukaya) inspired the organization, Asian Lesbians on the East Coast, to produce its first newsletter this year.

Native American lesbians Joy Harjo and Paula Gunn Allen added *She Had Some Horses* (Harjo 1983) and *The Woman Who Owned the Shadows* (Allen 1983) to the very small body of literature on lesbians in Native American cultures. *Sinister Wisdom* contributed "A Gathering of Spirit—North American Indian Women's Issue" to our limited knowledge in 1983 as well.

Throughout the 1970s, Jewish lesbians have been visible, valuable, and politically aware shapers of lesbian communities and culture. Women like songwriter/performer Maxine Feldman, photographer JEB (Joan E. Biren), writers Elana Dykewomon, Melanie Kaye, Martha Shelley, Adrienne Rich, Lesbian Herstory Archives cofounders Joan Nestle and Deborah Edel, and so many, many more have made enormous contributions. In 1982, Jewish lesbians began to speak, meet, and write much more frequently about their unique, complex lives, their humor, their pain at sometimes being "the only lesbian among Jews, the only Jew among lesbians, the only Jewish lesbian of color among white Jewish lesbians, the only Sephardic Jew among Ashkenazi" (Beck 1982). *Nice Jewish Girls: A Lesbian Anthology* proved to be the first book to examine the place of lesbians in Jewish culture along with the many ways in which Jewish lesbians have experienced anti-Semitism in the women's and lesbian movement. Many of the lesbians included in the anthology continue to inform non-Jewish lesbians, particularly Irena Klepfisz in *Keeper of Accounts* and Alice Bloch and Batya Bauman in *On Being a Jewish Feminist: A Reader* (Heschel 1983).

Issues around class status—the class we were raised in as well as that in which we may have moved up or down as adults—have been addressed passionately by lesbians since the beginnings of the women's movement. The eloquent voices of Sharon Isabell, Judy Grahn, Ann Shockley, Linda Marie, and of course, Rita Mae Brown's earliest writings were all sharp reminders that many of us did not grow up within the middle-class nuclear family so treasured by the mass media. Many who did may have lost what little privilege girl children enjoyed in that class, particularly if we spent much time working for low wages for women's movement causes, refused to marry men even though it may have been the economically healthy thing to do, did marry and have children whom we are now raising as divorced mothers without child support, or chose to live as "out," visible lesbians with fewer job options available to us. The oft-heard "joke" that "I'm a bag lady in waiting" only slightly masks the unease that many of us feel as we realize how precarious our economic existence really is.

The periodical *13th Moon* published an excellent special issue in late fall 1983 on the "Working-Class Experience" (Hacker 1983–84). Lesbians and other women wrote of their lives as single parents, prisoners, unemployed, and/or women of color in working-class America. This will surely continue to be an issue that draws ever more attention as lesbians who came out in the early women's movement and the many who came out in the bars before them grow older in a society that is increasingly hostile to helping the less advantaged or enacting a national health care system.

Sexuality

Since lesbians are largely defined by what we do in bed together and are still considered sexual outlaws by much of heterosexual society, the unknowing reader might think that publications written, illustrated, and published by lesbians would be rife with sexual references. This is, unfortunately, not so. In fact, references to explicit sexual behavior before 1979 were few, particularly when you consider the large number of references available in the same time period on lesbians in organizations, for example. Among the most notable contributions were the delightfully humorous *What Lesbians Do* (Gayle 1975), Tee Corinne's erotic drawings of labias in the *Cunt Coloring Book* (Corinne 1975), and the warm, sensuous *Loving Women* (Nomadic Sisters 1975). Tee Corinne's traveling slide show of lesbian erotic images in art have had a cultural impact all their own, sparking discussion groups in city after city as well as influencing contemporary lesbian artists to portray their own sexual fantasies. Her *Sinister Wisdom* cover photograph-turned-poster of a woman entering another woman can be found in countless lesbian homes and private spaces throughout the country.

In 1979, an anthology of lesbian erotica called *A Woman's Touch* (Ceder and Nelly 1979) was published by a lesbian press. That same year, the seldom discussed topic of lesbian sadomasochism burst into view with the publication of a small pamphlet by Samois, a northern California s/m group, called *What Color Is Your Handkerchief? A Lesbian S/M Sexuality Reader*. One of Samois's most outspoken and articulate members, Pat Califia, then compiled *Sapphistry* in 1980, which is still the most comprehensive and challenging handbook on lesbian sexuality. She writes of s/m practices as well as erotic images, masturbation, sex for disabled lesbians, and myriad other aspects of sexuality. The year 1981 saw the publication of *Heresies* magazine's sex issue, which pulled together a number of important and controversial articles on lesbian butch-fem relationships, lesbian sex in black herstory, and the silence around sex among the feminist community. Samois published their second book, an anthology titled *Coming to Power: Writings and Graphics on Lesbian S/M*.

These publications, plus the increasingly hostile stance by Women Against Pornography members and other feminists in New York City particularly, set the stage for open confrontation at the April 1982 Barnard

College Scholar and the Feminist Conference, "Towards a Politics of Sexuality" (Towards . . . 1982). The Barnard conference continues to have an enormous impact on lesbian and feminist discussions of sex roles, power within sexual relationships, public sex, what pornography is and who uses it, sadomasochist sex, and all other aspects of the debate over women as powerful sexual beings with control over how, when, and where they wish to act out their desires versus a concept of feminism or "politically correct" sex which places limits on sexual freedom. Women who presented papers or led workshops at the conference on some of these issues were picketed and harassed by other feminists (including some lesbians) from Women Against Pornography.

Since then, *The Diary of a Conference on Sexuality* (Alderfer, Jaker, and Nelson 1982), once banned as too controversial by Barnard officials, has sparked the flame that produced *Powers of Desire* (Snitow, Stansell, and Thompson 1983), a provocative anthology on issues of sexuality, power, and gender. "Confessions of a Butch Dyke" (Mushroom 1983) and the writings of Joan Nestle, which combine so well her work on lesbian history with her "memory of being a queer, my inheritance from the fifties" (Nestle 1983, 35), complement the work of butch and fem support groups and such groups as the Lesbian Sex Mafia in furthering the debate. Women who consider much of this emphasis on "deviant" sex unfeminist have produced *Against Sadomasochism* (Linden et al. 1982), along with lengthy opinion pieces in *off our backs* and other feminist periodicals. This debate is obviously only in the beginning stages and certainly promises to intensify in 1984.

Living Our Lives

Once lesbians come out, many of us find our lives completely altered by the simple fact that we are a hidden minority in a predominantly heterosexual, homophobic society. *One Teenager in Ten* (Heron 1983) tells the stories of lesbian and gay youth as they find themselves forced to either tell their parents and friends or live a lie. The founders of Parents of Gays give clear advice in *Now That You Know* (Fairchild and Hayward 1979) to parents who have problems understanding what makes their child "that way." A lesbian who is herself a mother more often than not finds herself the object of society's harshest strictures. *Rocking the Cradle: Lesbian Mothers—a Challenge in Family Living* (Hanscombe and Forster 1982) is a ground-breaking study of the problems lesbian mothers and children of lesbians face through the courts and institutional structures of a culture that cannot bear to think of a lesbian and a mother as one and the same person. Based on interviews on England and Wales, this is a fascinating book. It also gives one of the clearest explanations of artificial insemination techniques yet published anywhere. Lesbian mothers, their lawyers, parents, and friends will find the bibliography *Lesbian Mothers and Their Children* (Hitchens and Thomas 1983) extremely helpful.

Another good legal resource for lesbians is the recently revised *The Rights of Gay People* (Boggan 1983), which continues the very useful American Civil Liberties Union series of handbooks aimed at various subcultures in America. Even the growing number of lesbian lawyers agree that lesbians have had little reason to trust that the law will be used for us rather than against us. Witness the court-martial sentence of six years at hard labor given Air Force Lieutenant Joann Newark on charges of sodomy (sex with a woman lover) and drugs (smoking marijuana in her own home). The harsh sentence drew strong public reaction from both the straight and the gay publics, which eventually convinced military officials to release Lieutenant Newark on parole by the end of 1983 (Gervasoni and McKnight 1983).

That the sentence was reconsidered would give some of us hope that things are indeed changing slowly, if not for the frightening experience that recently affected the lives of hundreds of Northampton, Massachusetts, lesbians. It began with a long series of threatening phone calls received by area lesbians and the New Alexandria Lesbian Library, a well-known, greatly respected institution in the community. The callers stated that they were members of a group calling themselves SHUN—Stop Homosexual Unity Now. Women in the community demanded an investigation by local police and politicians, but little attention was paid to the protest until two local lesbians were raped and a third severely beaten. Furthermore, when the police and state troopers did begin to look into the violent threats and actions, an FBI agent used the situation to question area lesbians about unrelated radical and political cases (Goldsmith 1983). A lone male suspect was finally arrested, but only after unrelenting pressure was applied through organized marches, demonstrations, and other tactics by local lesbians to keep the issue in the public eye.

Neither the women directly involved in these incidents nor their supporters have accepted the role of passive victims. Activist fighters for lesbian and women's rights have found the anthology *Fight Back: Feminist Resistance to Male Violence* (Delacoste 1981) to be an excellent primer on strategies for rape crisis centers, battered women's shelters, self-defense instruction, help for incest victims, and other issues related to violence against women. *Voices in the Night* (McNaron and Morgan 1983) adds much needed information to the long-silenced subject of incest victims and the torment they continue to suffer long after sex with male relations has stopped.

In the political arena, 1983 was another year of battle against President Reagan's politics, particularly his defense policies. Seneca Falls, New York, Greenham Common, England, and missile sites in Germany were scenes of women's peace encampments protesting the deployment and stockpiling of American nuclear weapons. Lesbian baiting was a common tactic used by pro-Reagan supporters against the protesters, yet for once the tactic seemed to draw lesbians and straight women together more than it caused a split (Hutchins 1983). Many encampment participants may have read Pam McAllister's fine anthology *Reweaving the Web of Life: Feminism and Nonviolence* (McAllister 1982), which contains several essays by lesbians on applying nonviolent principles to antiwar and pacifist actions. Finally, lesbian feminists Charlotte Bunch and Marilyn Frye published long-awaited works on *Going Public with Our Vision* (Bunch 1983) and *The Politics of Reality: Essays in Feminist Theory* (Frye 1983).

Struggling year after year against the same political issues and enemies, many lesbians have become aware of a more personal struggle to stay well, stay optimistic, and keep up their energy. As the more visible lesbian leaders who came out in the late 1960s and early 1970s feel the first inkling of middle-age mortality, the earlier "preliberation" group now in their fifties and sixties are a more visible presence in our communities than ever before. Fortunately, we are also seeing a greater emphasis on and consciousness of the fact that health is not a given. Some of us were never able to be the athletic, ideal dyke because of health "defects" or later illnesses and injuries. Most important, instead of wondering where all the old lesbians have disappeared to, we are learning directly from women who know best that aging has its rewards as well as its problems. In June 1983, the National Association for Lesbian and Gay Gerontology (NALGG) met in San Francisco to discuss the work of Senior Action in a Gay Environment (SAGE) and other groups formed within the homophile community to support and respond to the needs of older gays and lesbians (Cook 1983). Publications such as *SAGE Writings* (Baracks and Jarratt 1980), *Aging Lesbians and Gay Men* (Wolf 1983), and the wonderfully personal *Look Me in the Eye: Old Women, Aging and Ageism* (Macdonald and Rich 1983) have allowed women to face their fears of what it means to be an old woman and an old lesbian with much more information than before.

Our community's continuing problem with an ideal of beauty embodied in the stereotype of a slender young able-bodied woman is expressed well in several other new books. *Shadow on a Tightrope: Writings by Women on Fat Oppression* (Schoenfielder and Wieser 1983) is a collection by fat women about living in a society obsessed with thinness. *Lesbian Health Matters!* (O'Donnell et al. 1983), *Out from Under: Sober Dykes and Our Friends* (Swallow 1983), and *Woman/Doctor: The Education of Jane Patterson, M.D.* (Patterson and Madaras 1983) are excellent new works on lesbians and the health care system.

These books and others such as *Images of Ourselves: Women with Disabilities Talking* (Campling 1981) build on the ground-breaking work of the *off our backs* special issue on illness and disability (1979). Cancer, in particular, has taken its toll among our friends, a sad fact reflected in Audre Lorde's *The Cancer Journals* (1980), Alice Bloch's *Lifetime Gurantee* (1981), and many articles on lesbians dying of cancer in *Common Lives/Lesbian Lives* (see especially "The Connie Journals" [Newomon 1983] for a moving description of lesbian extended families and burial rituals). Not least of the many books in 1983 that were the first to deal with certain subjects is *I Thought People Like That Killed Themselves: Lesbians, Gay Men and Suicide* (Rofes 1983). Rofes discusses gay suicide both historically and politically in this important, helpful book.

Imagination: Present and Past

Anyone interested in studying the rich detail and diversity of lesbian literature is almost forced to do their reading in a lesbian or gay archives or one of the few major research libraries that purchase lesbian writing on a regular basis. Still, each year, new works appear to replace the rapidly out-of-print works from the year before. In studying this topic, Jeannette Foster's *Sex Variant Women in Literature* (1975), *The Lesbian in Literature* (Grier 1981), and *Black Lesbians: An Annotated Bibliography* (Roberts 1981) are absolutely vital references. One of the best cross-cultural bibliographies appeared in Canada in the lesbian issue of *Resources for Feminist Research/Documentation Sur la Recherche Féministe*. Naiad Press has reprinted several of the most beloved pre-1970s lesbian paperback classics in 1983, particularly Valerie Taylor's *Journey to Fulfillment* series and the Ann Bannon Beebo Brinker series. These are lusty reminders of 1950's lesbian bars in the Village, butch/fem sex with and without relationships, as well as of a time when self-hatred was rampant along with alcoholism and violence in the lesbian world. No longer do we need to search these books out in dusty shops selling used books. For all the difficulties they present to contemporary lesbian feminists, they are true to their time. Best of all, writers like Ann Bannon knew how to write a good sex scene, full of passion and longing—something many postfeminist lesbian novels have not had.

Other important new novels published in 1983 were *Toothpick House* (Lynch 1983) about a butch cab driver and her academic lover; *The City of Hermits* (Covina 1983), based in California after the next earthquake; *Saturday Night in the Prime of Life* (Azpadu 1983), from the rare viewpoint of an older Sicilian-American lesbian; *Relatively Norma* (Livia 1983) about an English lesbian in Australia; and a new Sarah Aldridge suffrage romance, *Madame Aurora* (1983). Even Rita Mae Brown published a new novel, this one on the tennis circuit, titled *Sudden Death* (1983). Two literature anthologies were published: *Mae West Is Dead: Recent Lesbian and Gay Fiction* (Mars-Jones 1983) and *New Lesbian Writing* (1983) by Margaret Cruickshank, whose previous anthology, *Lesbian Studies: Present and Future* (1982), was concerned both with lesbian academics and how lesbians are studied in the college curriculum. Last but not least, Renée Vivien's short stories were collected and published for the first time in English in *Woman of the Wolf and Other Stories* (1983).

Lesbian poetry has been a mainstay of our writings since Sappho wrote her first ode. But it took *Lesbian Poetry: An Anthology* (Bulkin and Larkin 1981) to make many of us see the power and beauty of the images produced by lesbian poets.

In 1983, new volumes of poetry were rare but wonderful, particularly Judith McDaniel's *November Woman*, black filmmaker poet Michelle Parkerson's *Waiting Rooms*, and Pat Parker's reprinted *Movement in Black*. In local communities, lesbian poets and writers have had more difficulty in recent years finding places in which to read their work, but whenever a woman's bookstore or center could offer space, large audiences turned up to show their appreciation of new creative work.

Biographies of past lesbians—the more massive the better—have always fascinated us, particularly since lesbian history has been so hidden and inaccessible. Jill Johnston's *Motherbound: Autobiography in Search of a Father* (1983) was the first volume of her autobiography, covering her childhood and teenage years. Biographies were published in 1983 on the lives of writers Djuna Barnes (Field 1983), Willa Cather (Robinson 1983), and Vita Sackville-West (Glendinning 1983), as well as bisexual artist Frida Kahlo (Herrera 1983) and Paris bookstore owner Sylvia Beach (Fitch 1983). But these works examine only the more privileged and better-known women in lesbian history. Only recently have researchers begun the process of searching out lesser known, less accessible women whose letters weren't usually saved.

The growth of regional and national lesbian and gay archives over the last fifteen years has facilitated extensive research on our collective history. Among work by gay and lesbian historians, Jonathan Katz's *Gay American History: Lesbians and Gay Men in the USA* (1976) is still the definitive collection of original historical documents from 1566 to the present, including a section on "Passing Women," women who lived their lives passing as men. His new *Gay/Lesbian Almanac* (1983) continues where the other left off, while developing a new theme of homosexual and lesbian lives as socially constructed experiences largely affected more by society's strictures, morals, and political climate than by the expression of our sexuality. Lillian Faderman's new work *Scotch Verdict* (1983) researches the actual trial in Scotland on which Lillian Hellman's popular play "The Children's Hour" was based. Faderman's *Surpassing the Love of Men: Romantic Friendship and Love between Women from the Renaissance to the Present* (1981) documents female friendship and cases of romantic love.

Two other historical studies of homosexuals and lesbians in the twentieth century are John D'Emilio's *Sexual Politics, Sexual Communities: The Making of a Homosexual Minority in the United States, 1940–1970* (1983), and Allen Berube's article in *Mother Jones* on lesbians in the Women's Army Corps and homosexuals in the military during World War II (1983). This last work is based on Berube's research and slide show, "Marching to a Different Drummer," which has inspired and affected thousands of us in cities across the country over the last two years. In fact, the absence of positive or even truthful lesbian and gay images in the more accessible public media such as television and movies has led to the great popularity of several other historical slide shows, including Canadian Frances Rooney's "Finding Lesbian History," Tee Corinne's and JEB's shows on lesbian photography, photographers, and artists, as well as others on the wealthy American lesbians in Paris, gays and lesbians in Harlem, and lesbians in Greenwich Village. The contact information for these is listed in the March 1983 lesbian issue of *Resources for Feminist Research/Documentation Sur la Recherche Féministe*.

We study the collective past of individual lesbians and lesbian institutions and communities in order to gain new insight into our own era and possible futures. By learning our history, we become more aware of the ever-changing attitudes of society at large toward sexuality in general, as well as toward those who deviate from the particular standards of behavior in any society at any given time. It is important and directly relevant that lesbians learn more about laws and attitudes affecting all women who have openly enjoyed their sexuality in any form, whether as lesbians, bisexuals, homosexuals, passing women, spinsters, or other independent women who refused to accept limitations placed on their sexual and affectional lives.

This chapter has touched upon the many works and topics it is possible to cite in a lesbian overview of 1983. By consulting the works listed as references, you will be able to find leads to new directions in research, as well as more information on the subjects covered. You will find lesbian and gay archives and bookstores helpful resources in future searches for information on this often inaccessible topic.

Acknowledgments

Without the help of Deborah Edel and Joan Nestle and the collection available to me at the Lesbian Herstory Archives, this chapter could not have been completed. I also appreciate the warm support of Karyn London of Womanbooks in New York City, as well as the vital feedback and verbal hugs given by Linda Levine, Sarah Watstein, and Kathleen C. during the long process.

References

ALDERFER, HANNAH, BETH JAKER, and MARYBETH NELSON. 1982. *Diary of a conference on sexuality*. New York: Faculty Press.

ALDRIDGE, SARAH. 1983. *Madame Aurora*. Tallahassee, Fla.: Naiad Press.

ALLEN, PAULA GUNN. 1983. *The woman who owned the shadows*. San Francisco: Spinsters Ink.

Asian lesbians of the east coast newsletter. 1983. New York: ALOEC. Available from ALOEC, C/O K. Hall, 320 Eastern Parkway, Brooklyn, NY 11225.

AZPADU, DODICI. 1983. *Saturday night in the prime of life.* Iowa City, Iowa: Aunt Lute Books.

BANNON, ANN. 1982. Beebo Brinker series. Tallahassee, Fla.: Naiad Press.

BARACKS, BARBARA, and KENT JARRATT, eds. 1980. *Sage Writings.* New York: Teachers and Writers Press.

BECK, EVELYN TORTON, ed. 1982. *Nice Jewish girls: A lesbian anthology.* Watertown, Mass.: Persephone Press.

BERUBE, ALLAN. 1983. Coming out under fire: The untold story of the World War II soldiers who fought on the front lines of gay and lesbian liberation. *Mother Jones,* February-March, pp. 23–29.

BIRTHA, BECKY. 1983. *For nights like this one: Stories of loving women.* East Palo Alto, Calif.: Frog in the Well Press.

BLOCH, ALICE. 1981. *Lifetime guarantee.* Watertown, Mass.: Persephone Press.

BOGGAN, E. CARRINGTON. 1983. *The rights of gay people.* Rev. ed. New York: Bantam.

BRANT, BETH, ed. 1983. *Sinister wisdom: A gathering of spirit—North American Indian women's issue,* No. 22–23.

BROWN, RITA MAE. 1983. *Sudden death.* New York: Bantam.

BULKIN, ELLY, and JOAN LARKIN, eds. 1981. *Lesbian poetry: An anthology.* Watertown, Mass.: Persephone Press.

BUNCH, CHARLOTTE. 1983. *Going public with our vision: Feminism in the 1980's.* Denver, Colo.: Antelope Press.

CALIFIA, PAT. 1980. *Sapphistry.* Tallahassee, Fla.: Naiad.

CAMPLING, JO, ed. 1981. *Images of ourselves: Women with disabilities talking.* Boston: Routledge and Kegan Paul.

CEDER and NELLY, eds. 1979. *A woman's touch.* Grants Pass, Oreg.: Womanshare Books.

CLARKE, CHERYL. 1982. *Narratives: Poems in the tradition of black women.* New Brunswick, N.J.: Sister Books.

Common lives/lesbian lives. P.O. Box 1553, Iowa City, IA 52244.

COOK, LOREE. 1983. Lesbians and gays discuss aging. *off our backs,* October, pp. 20–21.

CORINNE, TEE. 1975. *Cunt coloring book.* San Francisco: Pearlschild Productions. Reprinted.

———. 1981. *Labiaflowers: A coloring book.* Tallahassee, Fla.: Naiad.

COVINA, GINA. 1983. *The city of hermits.* Berkeley, Calif.: Barn Owl Books.

CRUIKSHANK, MARGARET, ed. 1982. *Lesbian studies: Present and future.* Old Westbury, N.Y.: Feminist Press.

———. 1983. *New lesbian writing.* San Francisco, Calif.: Grey Fox.

DELACOSTE, FREDERIQUE, and FELICE NEWMAN, eds. 1981. *Fight back! Feminist resistance to male violence.* Minneapolis, Minn.: Cleis Press.

D'EMILIO, JOHN. 1983. *Sexual politics, sexual communities: The making of a homosexual minority in the United States, 1940–1970.* Chicago: University of Chicago Press.

FADERMAN, LILLIAN. 1983. *Scotch verdict.* New York: William Morrow.

————. 1981. *Surpassing the love of men: Romantic friendship and love between women from the Renaissance to the present.* New York: William Morrow.

FAIRCHILD, BETTY, and NANCY HAYWARD. 1979. *Now that you know: What every parent should know about homosexuality.* New York: Harcourt Brace Jovanovich.

FIELD, ANDREW. 1983. *Djuna: The life and times of Djuna Barnes.* New York: Putnam.

FITCH, NOEL RILEY. 1983. *Sylvia Beach and the lost generation: A history of literary Paris in the 20's and 30's.* New York: Norton.

FOSTER, JEANNETTE. 1956. *Sex variant women in literature.* Washington, D.C.: Vantage Press. Reprinted. 1975. Baltimore: Diana Press.

FRYE, MARILYN. 1983. *The politics of reality: Essays in feminist theory.* Trumansburg, N.Y.: Crossing Press.

GAYLE, MARILYN. 1975. *What lesbians do.* Portland, Oreg.: Godiva Press.

GERVASONI, SHARON, and JEANNIE MCKNIGHT. 1983. Air Force upholds lesbian's sentence. *off our backs*, April, p. 5.

GITTINGS, BARBARA. 1982. *A gay bibliography.* Philadelphia, Penn.: American Library Association Gay Task Force. Available from ALA/GTF, P.O. Box 2383, Philadelphia, PA 19103, for $1.00.

GLENDINNING, VICTORIA. 1983. *Vita: A biography of Vita Sackville-West.* New York: Alfred A. Knopf.

GOMEZ, ALMA, CHERRÍE MORAGA, and MARIANA ROMO-CARMONA, eds. 1983. *Cuentos: Stories by Latinas.* Brooklyn, N.Y.: Kitchen Table Press.

GOLDSMITH, LARRY. 1983. FBI questions Northampton lesbians. *Gay Community News*, 24 September p. 1.

GRIER, BARBARA. 1981. *The lesbian in literature: A bibliography.* 3 ed. Tallahassee, Fla.: Naiad Press.

HACKER, MARILYN, ed. 1983–84. Working-class experience. *13th Moon* 7, no. 1–2.

HANSCOMBE, GILLIAN, and JACKIE FORSTER. 1982. *Rocking the cradle: Lesbian mothers, a challenge in family living.* Boston, Mass.: Alyson Publishers.

HARJO, JOY. 1983. *She had some horses.* New York and Chicago: Thunder's Mouth Press.

Heresies. 1981. Sex issue, no. 12.

HERON, ANN, ed. 1983. *One teenager in ten: Writings by gay and lesbian youth.* Boston, Mass.: Alyson Publishers.

HERRERA, HAYDEN. 1983. *Frida: A biography of Frida Kahlo.* New York: Harper.

HESCHEL, SUSANNAH, ed. 1983. *On being a Jewish feminist: A reader.* New York: Schocken Books.

HITCHENS, DONNA, and ANN THOMAS, eds. 1983. *Lesbian mothers and their children: An annotated bibliography of legal and psychological materials.* San Francisco: Lesbian Legal Rights Project.

HUTCHINS, LORAINE. 1983. Seneca—summer of action and learning. *off our backs*, October, pp. 3–6.

JOHNSTON, JILL. 1983. *Motherbound: Autobiography in search of a father.* New York: Alfred A. Knopf.

KATZ, JONATHAN. 1976. *Gay American history: Lesbians and gay men in the USA.* New York: Thomas Crowell Co.

————. 1983. *Gay/lesbian almanac: A new documentary.* New York: Harper & Row.

KLEPFISZ, IRENA. 1982. *Keeper of accounts.* Watertown, Mass.: Persephone Press.

Lesbian Connections Newsletter. Ambitious Amazons, P.O. Box 811, Lansing, MI 48823.

Lesbian Herstory Archives Newsletter. Lesbian Herstory Archives, P.O. Box 1258, New York, NY 10116.

LINDEN, ROBIN RUTH, et al., eds. 1982. *Against sadomasochism.* East Palo Alto, Calif.: Frog in the Well Press.

LIVIA, ANNA. 1983. *Relatively Norma.* London: Onlywomen.

LORDE, AUDRE. 1980. *The cancer journals.* Argyle, N.Y.: Spinsters Ink.

————. 1982. *Zami: A new spelling of my name.* Watertown, Mass.: Persephone Press. Reprinted. 1983. Trumansburg, N.Y.: Crossing Press.

LYNCH, LEE. 1983. *Toothpick house.* Tallahassee, Fla.: Naiad Press.

MARS-JONES, ADAM, ed. 1983. *Mae West is dead: Recent lesbian and gay fiction.* London and Boston: Faber & Faber.

MARTIN, DEL, and PHYLLIS LYON. 1972. *Lesbian/woman.* New York: Bantam.

McALLISTER, PAM, ed. 1982. *Reweaving the web of life: Feminism and nonviolence.* Philadelphia, Penn.: New Society Publishers.

McDANIEL, JUDITH. 1983. *November woman.* Glen Falls, N.Y.: Loft Press.

MACDONALD, BARBARA, with CYNTHIA RICH. 1983. *Look me in the eye: Old women, aging and ageism.* San Francisco: Spinsters Ink.

McNARON, TONI, and YARROW MORGAN, eds. 1983. *Voices in the night.* Minneapolis, Minn.: Cleis Press.

MORAGA, CHERRÍE. 1983. *Lo que nunca paso por sus labios—Loving in the war years.* Boston, Mass.: South End Press.

MORAGA, CHERRÍE, and GLORIA ANZALDUA, eds. 1981. *This bridge called my back: Writings by radical women of color.* Watertown, Mass.: Persephone Press. Reprinted. 1983. Brooklyn, N.Y.: Kitchen Table Press.

MUSHROOM, MERRIL. 1983. Confessions of a butch dyke. *Common Lives/Lesbian Lives*, no. 9 (Fall):39–45.

National Association for Lesbian and Gay Gerontology Conference, 24–25 June 1983. San Francisco.

National Gay Archives Newsletter. National Gay Archives, P.O. Box 38110, Los Angeles, CA 90038.

NESTLE, JOAN. 1983. Voices from lesbian herstory. *Body Politic*, September, pp. 35–37.

NEWOMON, STEELIE. 1983. The Connie journals. *Common Lives/Lesbian Lives* no. 7 (Spring).

Nomadic Sisters. 1975. *Loving women*. Sonoma, Calif.: Nomadic Sisters.

O'DONNELL, MARY, et al. 1979. *Lesbian health matters!* Santa Cruz, Calif.: Santa Cruz Women's Health Center.

PARKER, PAT. 1983. *Movement in black*. Trumansburg, N.Y.: Crossing Press.

PARKERSON, MICHELLE. 1983. *Waiting rooms*. Washington, D.C.: Common Ground Press.

PATTERSON, JANE, and LYNDA MADARAS. 1983. *Woman/doctor: The education of Jane Patterson, M.D.* New York: Avon.

Resources for Feminist Research/Documentation Sur la Recherche Féministe. (RFR/DRF). 1983. Lesbian issue, March.

ROBERTS, J.R., ed. 1981. *Black lesbians: An annotated bibliography*. Tallahassee, Fla.: Naiad Press.

ROBINSON, PHYLLIS. 1983. *Willa: The life of Willa Cather*. Garden City, N.Y.: Doubleday.

ROFES, ERIC E. 1983. *I thought people like that killed themselves: Lesbians, gay men and suicide*. San Francisco: Grey Fox Press.

SAMOIS. 1982. *Coming to power: Writings and graphics on lesbian s/m*. Rev. ed. San Francisco: Samois.

———. 1979. *What color is your handkerchief? A lesbian s/m sexuality reader*. Berkeley, Calif.: Samois.

SCHOENFIELDER, LISA, and BARB WIESER, eds. 1983. *Shadow on a tightrope: Writings by women on fat oppression*. Iowa City, Iowa: Aunt Lute Books.

Sinister Wisdom. P.O. Box 1023, Rockland, ME 04841.

Skip Two Periods. P.O. Box 3337, Roanoke, VA 24015.

SMITH, BARBARA, ed. 1983. *Home girls: A black feminist anthology*. Brooklyn, N.Y.: Kitchen Table Press.

SNITOW, ANN, CHRISTINE STANSELL, and SHARON THOMPSON, eds. 1983. *Powers of desire: The politics of sexuality*. New York: Monthly Review Press.

SWALLOW, JEAN, ed. 1983. *Out from under: Sober dykes and our friends*. San Francisco: Spinsters Ink.

TAYLOR, VALERIE. 1983. *Journey to fulfillment series*. Tallahassee, Fla.: Naiad Press.

Third World Women's Archives. P.O. Box 159, Bush Terminal Station, Brooklyn, NY 11232.

Towards a politics of sexuality: Conference report. 1982. *off our backs*, June, pp. 2–25.

TSUI, KITTY. 1983. *The words of a woman who breathes fire*. Argyle, N.Y.: Spinsters Ink.

VIVIEN, RENÉE. 1983. *Woman of the wolf and other stories*. Translated by Karla Jay and Yvonne M. Klein. New York: Gay Presses.

WALKER, ALICE. 1982. *The Color Purple*. New York: Washington Square Press.

West Coast Lesbian Collection. P.O. Box 23753, Oakland, CA 94623.

WOLF, DEBORAH. 1983. *Aging lesbians and gay men*. Berkeley: University of California Press.

Mass Media and Communications

Helen R. Wheeler

For the first time in the *Women's Annual* series, an analysis has been undertaken, from the feminist perspective, of work and influential developments in the field of mass media and communications. Advertising, books, films, periodicals, radio, and television, in delivering ideas to various groups of people, instruct not only with what they say, but how they say it. For the purposes of this chapter, mass media will be defined as "the various means used to convey information in a society, including magazines, newspapers, radio and television"; communication "involves making known, transmission, having an exchange, as of thoughts, ideas, or information, as by speech, signals or writing." These definitions are derived from the *American Heritage School Dictionary*, which has been well received by feminist parents, educators, and other communicators, and which, along with *Our Bodies, Ourselves*, has been banned from some schools and libraries! The omnibus scope makes comprehensive coverage impossible; "Popular Culture" chapters in previous annuals should also be consulted.

Newspapers

A newspaper research project sponsored by the Women Studies Program and Policy Center of George Washington University produced in 1983 a stunning report titled *New Directions for News* (East 1983). The project analyzed the coverage by ten major newspapers, including the *New York Times*, of six women's issues. Thousands of stories were analyzed and evaluated. It was determined that the legal impact of the ERA (one of the six issues), among the most fundamental, complex, and controversial legal issues of the 1970s, was not treated seriously by the newspapers in the study.

Other 1983 newspaper stories showed undercoverage and sensationalism in the nation's "coverage" of political activist and civil rights leader Ginny Foat, who was arrested in 1983 and accused by her ex-husband of participation in a 1965 murder. Similarly, most of what was heard about newswoman Christine Craft is either untrue, oversimplified, or out of context.

Women journalists continue their struggle for access to top jobs and stories. The professionalism of Helen Thomas (UPI) and Sarah McClendon (McClendon News Service) stands out among Washington reporters. In November 1983, a female-sex discrimination in employment class action initiated ten years before against the *Detroit News* was settled. In May 1982, the right-to-sue the *Cleveland Plain Dealer* was issued, based on findings that showed only 4 percent of top decision-making posts held by women over a seven-year period. The *New York Times*'s consent decree provided a four-year period to begin to rectify past discrimination, which is up; there has actually been a decline in the number of women in one job category (*Media report* . . . 1983, 1984).

Publishing

A "successful" woman, with two surnames and engaged in an enervating balancing act, reads books and periodicals that instruct in the maintenance of power, rather than its redistribution, and that emphasize the virtues of networking, role modeling, and mentors. When individual women realized that affirmative action and existing legislation would not take them far and concluded that they needed contact with the powerful, they began to replicate the "old-boy networks" through which powerful men have traditionally passed on their power to a select few. Women, by exercising their entrepreneurial skills, wielding power, and flexing their financial muscles, are joining the system, not changing it (Gordon 1983).

Since the nineteenth century, the periodical press has been producing quantities of magazines aimed at women, which serve as prescriptive models of whatever roles are currently desirable and as vehicles for promoting consumerism. The term *women's magazines* can now mean either traditional housekeeping and fashion magazines or newer feminist political and literary journals. The history of the impact of women's magazines is appearing in bits and pieces, with British publications the object of several book-length studies and a BBC program (Adburgham 1972; Dancyger 1978; Ferguson 1983; Recipes . . . 1983; White 1970). American publications, as a whole, have not received this kind of comprehensive treatment. However, research will be greatly aided by the appearance of a bibliography based on the extensive holdings of the University of Wisconsin and the State Historical Society of Wisconsin (Danky 1982).

Also from the University of Wisconsin is *Feminist Periodicals*, a quarterly that reprints the tables of contents of over fifty political and academic feminist periodicals with up-to-date addresses and ordering information. Complementing this is *The Annotated Guide to Women's Periodicals in the U.S.*, which appears twice a year and is particularly aimed at small-press and alternative magazines, explicitly excluding mainstream newsstand publications. Sources for the British women's movement today, as contrasted with the historical studies noted above, were reviewed this year in *off our backs* (Wallsgrove 1983), and some have been available for several years in microform in the Sexual Politics in Britain series from Harvester Press.

Several new feminist periodicals appeared in 1983 and late 1982. The *Women's Review of Books* is likely to become a mainstay. Its editorial policy is feminist but not restricted to any one conception of feminism, accepting all writing that is not sexist, racist, homophobic, or otherwise discriminatory. Each issue includes eight to ten lengthy reviews of feminist works across all disciplines. *Ikon*, first begun in 1967, has initiated a second series with poetry, prose, and graphics by noted feminist writers and artists, and in one issue is an interesting feature section on women and the computer. Visionary and multidimensional essays by Janice Raymond, Kathleen Barry, and others premiered *Trivia: A Journal of Ideas*, and Jane DuPree Begos launched *Women's Diaries*, a quarterly newsletter that grew out of her bibliography on the same topic. The editorial policies and styles of feminist literary journals were the focus of a survey reported by Mary Biggs (1983). Women academics, students, and feminist activists may find valuable information in *For Us Women Newsletter*, which started in 1983 and is billed as a guide to funding resources for women's self-development.

Harlequin Enterprises claims to sell millions of romances throughout the world annually. A dozen or so other paperback houses publish about six romance novels each month. That reading these novels functions to reinforce the status quo is recognized, but there have also been suggestions that they function for women readers (who generally purchase, rather than borrow them) in other ways as well. Escape or relaxation is their goal; their "ideal" romantic fantasy is tightly organized around the evolving relationship of a single couple composed of a beautiful, defiant, and sexually immature woman and a brooding, handsome man who is also curiously capable of gentle gestures (Radway 1983). It is also argued that Harlequin romances, gothic novels, and soap opera narratives are popular in part because they successfully speak to desires in today's women that our culture has found no other way of satisfying. Helen Hazen's *Endless Rapture* (1983) makes the questionable assertion that women are excited by violent romance and that the feminist movement has denied these needs. On the other hand, Tania Modleski's *Loving with a vengeance* (1982) sees Harlequins and gothic novels as a means of expressing fantasies of revenge against male dominance and as an outlet for women's fears and anger. The extent to which women's popular literature is a literature of subversion and protest was also examined at the 1983 Conference of the National Women's Studies Association.

Getting Published

The many women failing to gain serious consideration of their poetry, theses, monographs, novels, research, periodical literature, and so on, continue to bely the contention that women are underrepresented on publishers' lists and payrolls because they have not produced publishable (acceptable) manuscripts. Numerous women are employed in publishing, but as in academe, their roles are inferior to men's in policymaking and management, status and remuneration. Most publishers have their "women's books" and recognize the "women's reading" market. Publishers and bookstores have fostered creation of a euphemism known as the Women's Studies section. In the last decade, publishing houses and serials run by and for women came into existence, but in the present decade, many have disappeared (Persephone . . . 1983). Women's publishing is about feminist politics. Women in academe always have the problem of getting published in order to survive and advance; feminist academic women work within traditional disciplines and must adjust to the standard respectable concerns and methodologies while literally re-searching and reporting scholarship. Notably, although there are selective bibliographies of Women's Studies basics, feminist collections of titles in various fields, and library handbooks, there is no comprehensive publication for feminist researchers on a methodology that utilizes both standard resources and innovative ones. Works that seem at first to do this are either very theoretical (Stanley and Wise 1983) or more oriented to field and survey research in the social sciences (Roberts 1981). Female-sex discrimination does not make news, but the mere filing of a charge effectively blacklists a woman in academe (Wheeler 1983). Some tenured women have lost their professional lives. The current research of sociologist Athena Theodore for example, *Academic Women in Protest*, is unpublishable despite the commercial success of her earlier works, in particular *The Professional Woman* (1971).

It will be harder to deny the real problems of women writers in the face of a three works that appeared this year—Joanna Russ's *How to Suppress Women's Writing* (1983), Lynne Spender's *Intruders on the Rights of Men: Women's Unpublished Heritage* (1983), and a special issue of the *Women's Studies International Forum* on gatekeeping in publishing and academia (Spender and Spender 1983). All these authors make compelling analyses of the distortion, misattribution, trivialization, and dismissal that afflicts women's creative writing and research.

There are, however, positive developments. The first International Feminist Book Fair in June 1984 in London, England, was highly successful. Routledge & Kegan Paul have created the Pandora imprint to publish feminist books, and their selective distribution program for feminist bookstores includes discount and postage incentives and a catalog of their Women's Studies books listing bookstores carrying them. The International Women's Writing Guild has held twelve conferences, producing a videotape of the 1983 sessions in New York.

The Women's Institute for Freedom of the Press is a nonprofit organization founded in 1972 for research and educational purposes and for publishing works both theoretical and practical on the communication of information. WIFP employs three principles of feminist journalism: no attacks on people, more factual information, and people speaking for themselves. Their publication *Media Report to Women* and its annual index/directory are major sources for news and documentation on all aspects of women and media. This past year, WIFP sponsored its fifth annual conference on planning a national and international communications system for women.

Distribution

The WEEA Publishing Center, which has distributed nonprofit products of the Women's Educational Equity Act Program since 1977, has been funded at a lower level through September 1984. These products include print and nonprint resources for change developed under individual and group grants, the goal of which is educational equity for females in the United States. They represent an extraordinary value in these times of tight budgets: they are readily adapted to existing curricula, have a variety of uses in and out of the classroom, and involve parents and community members.

"Freedom of the press belongs to those who own the press!" has been the motto of KNOW, Inc., since its founding in 1969 by a group of Pittsburgh, Pennsylvania, NOW members. They bought an offset press to help spread the word about feminism, just as in another era, pamphleteers spread revolutionary unpublishable information. KNOW has kept in print numerous classics, including Pat Mainardi's *The Politics of Housework* and Judy Syfers's *Why I Want a Wife*.

A type of publication that has burgeoned at community levels is a Yellow-Pages format which lists mostly women-owned or -managed businesses, publications, services, and the like. They often do not purport to be feminist, although the advertiser may communicate feminism in her message. The 1984 Los Angeles–area *Women's Yellow Pages* is representative: it is a thick, useful compilation. Women knowing about, exchanging information with, and supporting other women's enterprises is important.

The New Technology

"Will Penelope and your new computer system get along?" asks a large ad in the *Chronicle of Higher Education* over a caricature of a maiden-lady type, brow furrowed and hands clenched, with ruffled neckline and a knitting needle thrust through the bun on her head, backing off so she can see. Although this stereotype has been very damaging to women, it is now being challenged as women's groups take technology into their own hands. The Women's Computer Literacy Project sponsors training courses for women to learn to use microcomputers, and the CompuServe computer information network has established a Women's Issues Special Interest Group. The National Woman's Party has been reaching the American public by cable television on the AM-Net circuit with a 7½-minute taped interview broadcast on several cable channels. Cable systems are being closely monitored by local women's groups to ensure fair access and responsive programming (Emmens 1983; Parkin 1983).

There is great need for a database accessing information about females and generating citations leading to publications conducive to change in the status of women, gender equity, enhanced coverage of events, and knowledge of and by females. The contents of many journals are retrievable by manual search of such indexes, abstracting services, and citation indexes like the *New York Times Index*, *Sociological Abstracts*, and *Social Sciences Citation Index*. Although online searching of the many indexes stored in computers is more efficient and productive, not all standard indexes are available for searching online, for example, *Alternative Press Index*, *Women Studies Abstracts*, and *Arts and Humanities Citation Index*. Published feminist scholarship is not adequately represented, and the alternative feminist press is almost invisible in existing printed indexes and online sources. Massive terminology and vocabulary problems exist when working with either women's media or feminist information sources, as women's reading, information about women, and feminist and Women's Studies information can vary greatly. Interdisciplinary approaches to all this information and to all these materials are required.

Joan K. Marshall's *On Equal Terms: A Thesaurus for Non-sexist Indexing and Cataloging* (1977) should be used by database producers as a guide for revision and construction of stereotype-free thesauri. In its attempt to remove sex bias from the influential *Library of Congress Subject Headings*, it automatically contributes to elimination of sexual and other social biases. A project to develop a stereotype-free thesaurus has been undertaken by a group sponsored by the National Council for Research on Women (NCROW), a consortium of women's research centers and programs largely but not totally affiliated with academic institutions and women's professional organizations. The Thesaurus Task Force is working toward publication in 1985 of a common set of index categories and descriptors for women's concerns and issues. NCROW has assigned a high priority to the establishment of a national cooperative information system in Women's Studies. It is to include research in progress and working papers issued by centers as well as directory-type data on individuals and organizations and citations to books and the contents of periodical literature.

The Catalyst Library and Audiovisual Center's collection of information on employment is recognized as one of the most current and comprehensive. Catalyst has entered the marketplace with production of the first specialized bibliographic database on women and employment, covering 1963 to the present. Called Catalyst Resources for Women, CRFW is accessed through the vendor Bibliographic Retrieval Services (BRS) and is searchable in most academic, special (corporate and institutional) and some public libraries, although anyone at a location with an online terminal and access to BRS databases can search it (Dadlez 1983). As an insight into the sexism possible in the library–information science press, an anonymous *Online Review* reporter's description of "New Sexist Database for Female Librarians" (June 1983, 200) elicited eighteen letters and numerous telephone calls to the international journal.

The Women's Educational Equity Communications Network (WEECN) served as a computer-based information acquisition and dissemination system for women's concerns in education from 1978 to 1980; it was operated by the Far West Laboratory for the U.S. Department of Education under the Women's Educational Equity Act. Some of its by-products can now be retrieved from the ERIC database. *Bibliofem*, a fiche product of the Fawcett Library and the British Equal Opportunity Centre's Information Centre is a current computerized bibliography of materials in their collections (Pritchard 1978). The National Women's Mailing List stores profiles of registrants and matches them against the information supplied to those who request a mailing list. The network is intended to match only those stated information needs with information supplied, and is seen as the beginning of a counter to right-wing mass mailings.

Librarians

Librarianship furthers the collection, organization, and dissemination of information, and is crucial to the growth of feminist scholarship. Ten years ago, feminist librarian and author Elizabeth Gould Davis declared, "Women need immediate help in the library profession before they go under irretrievably in the rising tide of masculinism" (Davis 1973). Librarianship and education for the profession constitute a setting comparable to most academic disciplines and to all the professions; the professional overlay can be generalized to all fields, whose associations, specialized accreditation agencies, editors, publishers, and executives are often active participants in the charade of gender equity.

Librarianship and feminism have not experienced the symbiotic relationship that might be possible were it not a so-called women's field. That is, for many years, most women librarians did not think they suffered from discrimination either as individuals or as a profession. Anita Schiller's careful research (1974) ended this myth in some areas, but annual reports in the American Library Association's *ALA Yearbook* show little progress. Although academic librarianship is more sexist than most types, college and university women librarians and library educators have rarely responded to personal discrimination based on their sex in employment. Last year, in a landmark *class action* first filed in 1974 on behalf of all women academicians employed or employable in the University of Minnesota system, the University of Minnesota at Minneapolis agreed to pay thirty-seven female librarians $900,000 in compensation for years of discriminatory salaries (University . . . 1983).

Early on, feminist librarians were aware of the pay equity issue (Galloway 1978). In 1981, workers in the city of San José, California, including significant numbers of library workers, won a strike for comparable-worth pay increases. The president of the ALA testified at the major congressional hearings on pay equity in September 1982, and in May 1983, fifty-one professional librarians (including two men) in Fairfax County, Virginia, filed a sex discrimination complaint with the Equal Employment Opportunity Commission, charging that the county underpays librarians in what it considers a "women's profession" (Zibart 1983). The U.S. Office of Personnel Management is seeking to redefine and lower the grade assigned to federal librarians, thus vitiating a form of existing comparable worth. Within librarianship, paraprofessional employees and volunteers are largely women; professional library periodicals tout volunteerism as an alleged economy. Volunteerism as an issue has received less feminist attention than some other issues; it is a highly respected aspect of the Reagan administration's place for women and social programs.

The women and men appointed to the ALA's Committee on the Status of Women in Librarianship (ALA-COSWL) monitor association policies and programs and produce research and resources for women in the profession (Fu 1983; Heim and Estabrook 1983; Williamson 1981). Two other groups, the Feminist Task Force of ALA and the independent Women Library Workers, publish *Women in Libraries* and the *WLW Journal*, which report not only on the status of women working in libraries but also on new and nontraditional materials to serve women library patrons, Women's Studies courses, and feminist activists.

As part of their commitment, feminist librarians are also aware of their responsibility to provide library services. These efforts include bibliographic control of Women's Studies materials, such as the current work on the women's database project; movement toward subject specialization in Women's Studies; cooperative work between teaching faculty and professional librarians to develop curricula in Women's Studies and to integrate research on women into already established courses; and outreach work in all types of libraries and across library boundaries to solve problems faced by women in acquiring knowledge and skills for whatever purpose (knowledge is power). The ALA-COSWL has produced a slide-tape package to point out these information needs and to suggest ways for librarians to address them, especially in public libraries (American Library Association 1983). There is little discussion of this in most programs of library education. The relatively low amount of online computerized-catalog use by female patrons (22.5 percent at UCLA and 33.1 percent in the entire University of California system (Broadus 1983)) implies that women students and faculty need some feminist impetus to encourage their knowledge and thus application of the new technology now common in libraries.

Film, Radio, and Television

Since Federal Communications Commission chairman Mark Fowler took office, he has pursued an "unregulatory philosophy": "I would abolish the equal time provision and the Fairness Doctrine, but these are issues the Congress must decide. . . . I am totally opposed to any and all content restrictions or mandatory programming requirements" (Pearce 1983). In the first major revision of its kind in thirty years, the FCC in 1983 proposed relaxing or eliminating restrictions forbidding ownership of more than seven television and radio stations by one entity.

The commission seems to be interested in encouraging women to enter the broadcasting business as owners and investors, judging from a 1982 study (ELRA Group 1982) and a September 1983 conference on Women in the Telecommunications Marketplace, cosponsored with the American Women in Radio and Television. However, these efforts represent an entrepreneurial, nonfeminist approach and obscure the fact that the lack of enforcement of many other regulations has already proven disastrous for women, especially in the area of programming. In the past, the networks were constrained by an FCC ruling that effectively barred them from airing presidential election debates unless sponsored by unaffiliated organizations. The League of Women Voters stuck to a format of panelists querying candidates within strict guidelines. The FCC has decided to allow the networks to run their own "debates" (show business). The poor coverage by television of news and policy issues of concern to and affecting women has not been the subject of the kind of analysis found in East and Jurney's newspaper study (1983). Most recent writing has focused on sexism in advertising, treated later in this chapter, or on the image of women in soap operas and prime-time dramas (Cantor and Pingree 1983; Cassata and Skill 1983; Meehan 1983).

Independent filmmakers legitimately hope public television will provide a way for their work to be seen by a larger audience. The connections among federal funding and the National Endowment for the Humanities, the National Endowment for the Arts, the Corporation for Public Broadcasting, the Public Broadcasting System (which actually buys and markets programs to the various stations), and the many individual public television stations foster general timidity and fear felt by these agencies and affect the television distribution of films and videotapes on radical topics. Data generated by the agencies may purport that "women's issues" are well represented, but these media convey the postfeminist or apolitical version of womanliness: humanitarian causes and concerns, arts and crafts, and non-threatening segments of the female population.

The year 1983 was difficult in the world of independent film for both filmmakers and distributors. A classic example, Serious Business Company, founded in 1972 to distribute the work of women filmmakers, closed its doors on 30 June. Remaining are four companies who distribute primarily "women's films": Second Decade Films, New Day Films, Iris Films, and Women Make Movies. Recognizable trends include more films made by minority women, for example, *Reassemblage; China: Land of My Father;* and the work of Christine Choy. In September 1983, Second Decade Films and the feminist journal *Heresies* cosponsored a four-day International Women's Film Festival in New York City. Filmmakers from the United States, China, Brazil, South Africa, Germany, and other countries presented and discussed documentaries, experimental films, features, and videotapes. Both the films and their producers/directors made strong political statements about the subject matter and about the difficulties in gaining access to commercial distribution channels (Rothaizer 1983).

Earlier films made by women reflected feminism's sense of expectation, potentiality, and clarity of purpose and displayed a kind of energy and grittiness missing in their current films; the marketplace has won, at least in terms of subject matter. Films that get distributed are slick productions on subjects for which there is a definite curricular or industrial use. Slowly but surely, they have become cosmetic, made to win social acceptance rather than to take a critical look at the existing order. It is always possible to accuse someone who makes this distinction of nitpicking; feminists acknowledge others' freedom to make such an accusation.

Some members of the Directors Guild of America are protesting a guild lawsuit against Warner Brothers. The suit charges that the studio unfairly discriminates against women and minorities in hiring, and it offers some damaging statistics to back up the claim. The group, which refuses to identify members, counters that guild members have been discriminated against so that women and minority members can be employed to "improve" the D.G.A.'s employment statistics.

Molly Haskell identifies in Hollywood commercial films the "open misogyny" in which the villain is a watered-down feminism (Haskell 1983). A new breed of Hollywood producers, directors, and screenwriters, most divorced at least once, are motivated by experiences that inevitably find their way into their movies. Simply by taking on the job of child rearing, as in the film *Kramer vs. Kramer*, men give it a dignity and status it never has when women do it.

Women in Film's Los Angeles chapter is the largest of a national, nonprofit organization for women in film and television whose purpose is to serve as a support group and act as a clearinghouse and resource of information on qualified professional women in the entertainment industry. The American Women in Radio and Television, Inc., does not consider itself "a strictly feminist organization and would not want it represented as such." The major project of the Women's Independent Film Exchange— *Pioneer American Women Filmmakers*—may yet come to pass; fund raising has been ongoing, and interviews are being taped, currently focusing on Frances Marion and other silent-era screenwriters who directed one or more Hollywood movies.

Sociolinguistics is an interdisciplinary area technically not encompassed by mass media and communications, but its significance concerns feminists working in these fields. Presumably one says what one means, and means what one says. The 35th annual Emmy Awards program in September 1983 on NBC declared that "the goal of TV has always been to make the common man into the uncommon man" (*View* 1983).

Music, Art, and Theater

The women's music business now has a real share of the independent record market in the United States (Kort 1983). Not to be confused with music made by women, "women's music" is an outgrowth of early 1970's feminism with a strong strain of lesbian consciousness. Because the media could organize and reach people, women's record companies were seen by their organizers as part of the movement rather than as a business. But a kind of professionalization has occurred, and distributors are now leaving the politics to the music itself. Well-known companies include Pleiades, Redwood, Women's Music Distribution Company, and Olivia Records, celebrating its tenth anniversary. Ladyslipper is a nonprofit organization involved in many aspects of women's music. Part of the Women's Independent Label Distributors (WILD) network, it promotes and distributes recordings by women especially through women's and alternative bookstores and, in 1982, brought out the first release on the Ladyslipper label. The *Ladyslipper Catalog* is an extensive guide to the women's music field.

The National Museum of Women in the Arts, thought to be the first of its kind, was established (on paper) in 1983. Devoted to art by women, it is scheduled to open in Washington, D.C., within three or four years. Founder Wilhelmina Holladay states the project is intended to fill a gap in the history of art, not to compare women's and men's work. In Los Angeles, the Women's Building, a public center for women's culture, has newly renovated its Gallery/Performance Space and seeks proposals for programming within it. The Women's Interart Center in New York has a year-round Media Artist-in-Residence. The Women's Caucus for Art is a feminist organization whose membership includes the Women Artists Documentation interest group.

A representative of the Women in the Arts Foundation testified in April before a U.S. House of Representatives subcommittee on the role of the National Endowment for the Arts in eliminating discrimination (Skiles 1983). Traditional patterns of operation and social networks by which public and private arts agencies and institutions do business normally preclude accomplished women artists from being proportionately represented both among the recipients of art fellowships, grants, and commissions to execute public art works and among artists represented by major galleries and shown in exhibitions and collections of institutions supported with public funds—often coming from the National Endowment for the Arts. The NEA-funded Corcoran Gallery included works by three women artists out of a total of thirty represented in its Biennial Exhibition despite the fact that women constitute 40 to 50 percent of all professional artists in the United States!

While radical feminist theater groups still struggle for existence, some women playwrights are finally breaking into the big time. Marsha Norman's receipt of the 1983 Pulitzer Prize for drama prompted an article in the *New York Times Magazine* (Gussow 1983), and British writers Caryl Churchill and Nell Dunn are making a mark on the New York theater scene with works that openly criticize women's images and roles (Goodman 1983). Karen Malpede's *Women in Theatre* (1983) presents a historical survey defining a feminist concept of theater under patriarchy, in which women are an alternative force promoting redefinition and change. Reflecting the interdisciplinary and multimedia connections that have enriched feminist analysis is a new journal, *Women & Performance*, which will address feminist issues in theater, dance, film, video, and ritual. This nexus has also evolved into "performance art," descended from the "happenings" of the 1960s and providing a creative framework for many women of whom Laurie Anderson is the most commercially successful. Moira Roth has edited an illustrated biographical-bibliographical review of women in this field (1983).

Image, Advertising, Pornography, and Violence

The most immediate impact of the mass media on women is through print and television advertising. There is a new emphasis on the full-bodied woman in advertising clothes; Macy's refers to "sensuous sweaters" for her. The authoritative, sometimes faceless male voice still narrates. Does less emphasis on thin-is-beautiful suggest recognition of the full-bodied woman or her purchase dollars? (Apparently airlines have not yet recognized females as a significant market, or else they consider their treatment of them already ideal.) The ad man is a powerful force in our society but he generally continues to fortify perceptions of traditional, limiting stereotypes of women and men; some feminists argue that advertising's effectiveness as a money-making tool is *also* limited by this. Activists, within and out the academy, have studied sexism in advertising, but there has been little positive change (Courtney and Whipple 1983; Women's Action Alliance 1980). Cigarette advertising is an excellent example of marketing products that damage the health of women and men, but it also demonstrates a particularly adverse impact on women. Surveys show that 50 percent of women do not know that smoking during pregnancy increases the risk of stillbirth and miscarriage. In 1980, when liberal-left magazine *Mother Jones*, edited by a feminist, ran a series of articles on the link between tobacco and cancer and heart disease, tobacco companies canceled their ads (Bagdikian 1983).

Feminists view pornography as violence against women perpetrated by the media. (See chapters on violence in previous issues of *The Women's Annual*.) *Chic, Gallery, High Society, Hustler, Oui, Penthouse, Playboy, Screw, Swank, Velvet*, and other magazines communicate that women deserve less respect than other people, and in so doing they are part of what keeps rape going. These, however, manage to keep above the level of other publications found in adult bookstores—*Big Brown Jugs, Bondage World, Bound to Please, Poppin Mammas, Teen Cream Puffs*—magazines so incredibly pornographic that smut, rather than the misleading term, *porn*, automatically comes to anyone's mind. *Playboy* and *Penthouse* have a combined readership of 29 million. Free-lance journalists are facing a crisis of survival currently; with magazines folding, they want assignments from a publication that will survive to print them. And skin magazines pay better (Miner 1981). Some magazines, *Mother Jones*, for example, receive crucial funding from the Playboy Foundation (Van Gelder 1983). Women Against Pornography opened an office in 1979 in the heart of Times Square, a few doors from the live peep shows, "adult" bookstores, and porn movie theaters that populate what is known as the pornography capital of the United States. Still going strong, it has become a national feminist voice against the pornography business. It has galvanized the feminist movement within New York City with its conferences, slide shows, demonstrations, and street tours, and it serves as a model for other communities. Demonstrations, such as that against *Deep Throat*, bring attention to the brutalization of women within the pornography industry, helping to explode the media myth that pornography is a harmless fantasy. The distinction between pornography and erotica wavers around the issues of mutuality, power, and coercion. There has been a notable increase of sex on television; the most explicit television porn comes in videotapes, and the hottest selling videocassettes are X-rated sex. Feminists and Native Americans spearheaded a successful protest against the pornographic video game "Custer's Revenge," which featured the rape of an Indian woman, but other such "games" remain on the market (jas 1983). The media's sexual exploitation of little girls, known as the Lolita syndrome, is also a dangerous trend. And it is a global issue: every large city in the non-Communist world has its district where theaters show pornographic films from the United States, Europe, and Japan. Women rarely have the opportunity or even impulse to see these, and the pornographic theater allows women as spectators only within the institution of the heterosexual couple.

By promoting the message that women are less than fully human, pornographic ads and media contribute to a cultural devaluation of women and legitimize sexual violence ranging from sexual harassment to rape. But the predominant image of women in advertising is that of the domestic drudge who finds fulfillment battling ring-around-the-collar. The old sexist stereotype has given way somewhat to a new, equally misogynistic one of women as exhibitionistic, vacuous sexual playthings. Hanes Corporation's double exploitation of women not surprisingly involves sexist advertising as well as working conditions affecting the health and safety of its female employees (Matusinka 1983).

Violence against women in and by means of popular music in the last twenty-five years has culminated in song lyrics, album covers, images in promotional videos, and the collaboration of media (radio, television) and corporate interests. Violent images abound in rock and roll. With the publication of a series of articles and bibliography entitled "Women and Pornography," *Jump Cut* magazine began an ongoing analysis of pornographic film from a radical and feminist perspective.

It has been possible to communicate the ideas that the ERA would do this or that, Ginny Foat was guilty until proven otherwise, nondiscriminatory affirmative action has improved the status of women significantly, and so on, via "coverage" provided by the mass media. At another level, the media have reinforced the status quo via denigration ("women's lib," for example), putdowns, and noncoverage, until dictionary words and terms communicate new, pejorative meanings. Consider the negative impact of *feminist* and *affirmative action*. That exceedingly threatening female, the single unmarried head of household, is virtually invisible other than the negatively stereotyped lesbian or unmarried mother; although she constitutes 38 percent of the population over eighteen years of age (as compared with 29 percent in 1965) (Statistical Abstract . . . 1982), she is an oddity. Still viewable only through a distorted lens is the never-married woman. Euphemisms have come into greater use by the mass media and by women—postfeminism, older woman, career woman, working woman—unfair and damaging, and representing only a very partial reality. Censorship in the media and in education, and restricted access to government information, are serious problems for women and other nonprivileged groups. The demise of many women-owned businesses and related publications, media, and organizations has come about. Some women have gone off into other, mainstream-liberal directions, church work, or volunteerism. Female feminists are burning themselves out, while the political scene that fosters this is able to coopt and exploit their issues. Too tired to fight anymore (and with a habit of not fighting), the women's community has not had a major impact on society with regard to the phenomena unique to feminism—issues of power and money and communication. The uncertain progress of women in relation to the mass media and communications makes it imperative for feminists to persist in their endeavors to change this field which is so central to the formation of our culture.

References

ADBURGHAM, A. 1972. *Women in print: Writing women and women's magazines from the Restoration to the accession of Victoria.* London: Allen & Unwin.

ALA Yearbook. 1976+. Chicago: American Library Association.

American heritage school dictionary. 1972. Boston: American Heritage Publishing Co.

American Library Association. Committee on the Status of Women in Librarianship. 1983. *Women as an underserved population.* Slide-tape program. Chicago: ALA.

Annotated guide to women's periodicals in the United States. Edited by Terry Mehlman, 5173 Turner Rd., Richmond, Ind. 47374.

BAGDIKIAN, B. 1983. *The media monopoly.* Boston: Beacon Press.

BIGGS, M. 1983. Women's literary journals. *Library Quarterly* 53, no. 1:1–25.

BROADUS, R. 1983. Online catalogs and their users. *College & Research Libraries* 44, no. 6:458–67.

CANTOR, M., and S. PINGREE. 1983. *The soap opera.* Beverly Hills, Calif.: Sage Publications.

CASSATA, M.B., and T. SKILL. 1983. *Life on daytime television: Tuning-in American serial drama.* Norwood, N.J.: Ablex.

COURTNEY, A.E., and T.W. WHIPPLE. 1983. *Sex stereotyping in advertising.* Lexington, Mass.: Lexington Books.

DADLEZ, E.M. 1983. Catalyst resources for women on BRS. *Database* 6, no. 4:32–43.

DANCYGER, I. 1978. *A world of women: An illustrated history of women's magazines.* Dublin: Gill & Macmillan.

DANKY, J.P., ed. 1982. *Women's periodicals and newspapers from the 18th century to 1981.* Boston: G.K. Hall.

DAVIS, E.G. 1973. Personal communication to the author, 14 March.

EAST, C., and D. JURNEY. 1983. *New directions for news.* Washington, D.C.: Women's Studies Program and Policy Center, George Washington University.

ELRA Group, Inc. 1982. *Female ownership of broadcast stations.* Washington, D.C.: Available from the Federal Communications Commission.

EMMENS, C.A. 1983. The cable underground. *Ms.*, April, p. 21.

FERGUSON, M. 1983. *Forever feminine: Women's magazines and the cult of femininity.* Exeter, N.H.: Heinemann.

FU, T.C., comp. 1983. *Directory of library and information profession women's groups.* 3d ed. Chicago: American Library Association.

GALLOWAY, S., and A. ARCHULETA. 1978. Sex and salary: Equal pay for comparable work. *American Libraries*, May, pp. 281–85.

GOODMAN, V. 1983. Britons generate excitement on NY stage. *New Directions for Women*, May-June, pp. 6, 17.

GORDON, S. 1983. The new corporate feminism. *Nation*, 5 February, pp. 1, 143, 146–47.

GUSSOW, M. 1983. Women playwrights: New voices in the theater. *New York Times Magazine*, 1 May.

HASKELL, M. 1983. Lights . . . camera . . . Daddy! *Nation*, 28 May, pp. 673–75.

HAZEN, H. 1983. *Endless rapture: Rape, romance, and the female imagination.* New York: Scribners.

HEIM, K.M., and L.S. ESTABROOK. 1983. *Career profiles and sex discrimination in the library profession.* Chicago: American Library Association.

jas. 1983. X-rated video games multiply. *off our backs* 13, no. 3:27.

KORT, M. 1983. Sisterhood is profitable. *Mother Jones*, July, pp. 39–44.

MALPEDE, K. 1983. *Women in theatre: Compassion and hope.* New York: Drama Book Publishers.

MARSHALL, J. 1977. *On equal terms; a thesaurus for non-sexist indexing and cataloging.* New York: Neal-Schuman.

MATUSINKA, A. 1983. Hanes' double exploitation of women. *Newsreport*, Spring-Summer, pp. 8–9. From Women Against Pornography, New York.

Media Report to Women. 1983. November-December, p. 4.

Media Report to Women. 1984. January-February, pp. 1, 15.

MEEHAN, D.M. 1983. *Ladies of the evening: Women characters of prime-time television.* Metuchen, N.J.: Scarecrow Press.

MINER, V. 1981. Fantasies and nightmares; the red-blooded media. *Jump Cut: A Review of Contemporary Cinema*, December, pp. 48–53.

MODLESKI, T. 1982. *Loving with a vengeance: Mass-produced fantasies for women.* Hamden, Conn.: Archon Books.

PARKIN, S. 1983. What *do* women want? NOW says less TV fluff. *Washington Post*, 26 January, p. Md10.

PEARCE, A. 1983. Mark Fowler. *View; the Magazine of Television Programming*, November, p. 47.

Persephone Press folds. 1983. *WLW Journal* 8, no. 4:26–27.

PRITCHARD, A. 1978. *Using BiblioFem: A joint library catalogue and continuing bibliography on women.* London: City of London Polytechnic.

RADWAY, J. 1983. Women read the romance: The interaction of text and context. *Feminist Studies*, Spring, pp. 53–78.

Recipes for being a woman. 1983. (London) *Times Educational Supplement*, 7 January.

ROBERTS, H., ed. 1981. *Doing feminist research*. Boston: Routledge and Kegan Paul.

ROTH, M. 1983. *The amazing decade: Women and performance art in America, 1970–1980*. Los Angeles: Astro Artz.

ROTHAIZER, S. 1983. 1983 International Women's Film Festival. *off our backs* 13, no. 10:21.

RUSS, J. 1983. *How to suppress women's writing*. Austin: University of Texas Press.

SCHILLER, A.R. 1974. Women in librarianship. In *Advances in Librarianship*, 4:103–47, ed. by Melvin J. Voigt. New York: Academic Press.

Sexual politics in Britain. 1972 + Sussex, England: Harvester Press.

SKILES, J. 1983. Testimony to the U.S. House of Representatives Committee on Appropriations' Subcommittee on the Interior and Related Agencies, 26 April. *Hue Points*, Spring-Summer, pp. 19–21.

SPENDER, D., and L. SPENDER, eds. 1983. Gatekeeping: The denial, dismissal, and distortion of women. *Women's Studies International Forum* 6, no. 5:whole issue.

SPENDER, L. 1983. *Intruders on the rights of men: Women's unpublished heritage*. Boston: Routledge and Kegan Paul.

STANLEY, L., and S. WISE. 1983. *Breaking out: Feminist consciousness and feminist research*. Boston: Routledge and Kegan Paul.

Statistical Abstract of the United States, 103 ed. 1982. Washington, D.C.: GPO.

THEODORE, A. 1971. *The professional woman*. Cambridge, Mass.: Schenkman.

University of Minnesota librarians win sex bias case. 1983. *Library Journal*, 1 June, pp. 1072–74.

VAN GELDER, L. 1983. Playboy's charity: Is it reparations or rip-off? *Ms*. 11 (June):78–81.

View; the Magazine of Television Programming. 1983. November, p. 27.

WALLSGROVE, R. 1983. British feminist publications. *off our backs* 13, no. 3:24–25.

WHEELER, H. 1983. Delay, divide, discredit: How uppity women are kept down, apart, and out of academe. *WLW Journal* 8, no. 3:1–5. Reprinted in *Alternative library literature: A biennial anthology*, edited by Sanford Berman and James Danky. Phoenix, Arizona: Oryx Press, 1984.

WHITE, C.L. 1970. *Women's magazines, 1693–1968*. London: Joseph.

WILLIAMSON, J. 1981. *Equality in librarianship: A guide to sex discrimination laws*. Chicago: American Library Association.

Women's Action Alliance. 1980. *The radio and television commercial monitoring project*. New York: Alliance.

ZIBART, E. 1983. Librarians in Fairfax seek to improve image—and their pay. *Washington Post*, 24 May.

Bibliography

Aegis; Magazine on Ending Violence against Women. Quarterly from the Feminist Alliance Against Rape, in cooperation with the National Coalition Against Domestic Violence and the Alliance Against Sexual Coercion, P.O. Box 21003, Washington, DC 20009.

BUTLER, MATILDA, and WILLIAM PAISLEY, eds. *Women and the Mass Media; Sourcebook for Research and Action*. New York: Human Sciences Press, 1979. First systematic study of the complex and changing roles of women in all phases of mass communication.

CLABES, JUDITH C., ed. *New Guardians of the Press: Selected Profiles of America's Women Newspaper Editors*. Indianapolis: R.J. Berg & Co., 1983.

Feminist Bookstore News. Bimonthly published and edited by Carol Seajay, P.O. Box 882554, San Francisco, CA 94188.

Feminist Collections; Women's Studies Library Resources in Wisconsin. Edited by Susan Searing, Women's Studies Librarian-at-Large for the University of Wisconsin System. 112A Memorial Library, 728 State St., Madison, WI 53706. Quarterly report of great value to *all* librarians in Women's Studies. Includes review essays, new periodicals, updates on publishers and bookdealers, much more.

Feminist Periodicals: A Current Listing of Contents. From the University of Wisconsin, same source as the above. The only way to keep up with both political and academic journals in Women's Studies and the feminist community.

FISHBURN, KATHERINE. *Women in Popular Culture: A Reference Guide*. Westport, Conn.: Greenwood Press, 1982. A series of chapter-essays with bibliographies, focusing on United States.

For Us Women Newsletter. P.O. Box 33147, Farragut Station, Washington, DC 20033. Guide to grants and other funding resources for women.

FRIEDMAN, LESLIE. *Sex Role Stereotyping in the Mass Media: An Annotated Bibliography*. New York: Garland, 1977.

HARTMAN, JOAN E., and ELLEN MESSER DAVIDOW. *Women in Print*. New York: Modern Language Association, 1982. Vol. I, *Opportunities for Women's Studies Research in Language and Literature;* Vol. II, *Opportunities for Women's Studies Publication in Language and Literature*.

HEIM, KATHLEEN M., ed. *The Status of Women in Librarianship: Historical, Sociological, and Economic Issues*. New York: Neal-Schuman, 1983. Essays on sex stereotyping, career patterns, problems of black and reentry women librarians, women administrators.

Heresies. Special issue, "Film Video Media." Fall 1983. Issue no. 16 (vol. 4, no. 4) of this feminist publication on art and politics. Heresies Collective, P.O. Box 766, Canal Street Station, New York, NY 10013.

Ikon: Creativity and Change. Edited by Susan Sherman, P.O. Box 1355, Stuyvesant Station, New York, NY 10009. New series of this feminist journal of literature and art.

KUHN, ANNETTE. *Women's Pictures: Feminism and Cinema.* Boston: Routledge and Kegan Paul, 1982. Examines the possibilities of feminist filmmaking.

Ladyslipper Catalog and Resources Guide of Records and Tapes by Women. P.O. Box 3124, Durham, NC 27705. Extensive listing produced by feminist music collective; a principal source for "women's music."

NAVARETTA, CYNTHIA. *Guide to Women's Art Organizations and Directory for the Arts.* New York: Midmarch Associates, 1982. Includes visual arts, mixed media, performing arts, film, writing; guide to organizations, funding, archives, local groups and publications.

New Directions for Women. National women's newspaper, bimonthly. 223 Old Hook Rd., Westwood, NJ 07675.

off our backs. 1841 Columbia Rd. NW, Rm. 212, Washington, DC 20009. Radical feminist newspaper; particularly strong for international news, conference reports, book and film reviews, women in prison, health issues.

PHENIX, KATHARINE. *Women in Librarianship: Bibliography 1983.* Chicago: American Library Association, Committee on the Status of Women in Librarianship, 1983. Update to previous books/bibliographies from COSWL.

Plexus. 545 Athol Ave., Oakland, CA 94606. West Coast women's press; see, for example, January 1984 issue: "High Technology in 1984: Will Women Control or Be Controlled?"

STRAINCHAMPS, ETHEL R., ed. *Rooms with No View: A Woman's Guide to the Man's World of the Media.* New York: Harper & Row, 1974. Anthology on discrimination in publishing and television. Appendix reprints landmark documents by groups of women at *Time, Newsweek,* CBS, AP. Compiled by the Women's Media Association.

Trivia: A Journal of Ideas. P.O. Box 606, Amherst, MA 01059. Began in 1982.

WHEELER, HELEN R. A Feminist Researcher's Guide to Periodical Indexes, Abstracting Services, Citation Indexes and Online Databases. *Collection Building* 5 (Winter 1983–84):3–24. Chapter from unpublished book, *Documentation for Human Equality: Doing Feminist Research—Strategy and Resources.*

WLW Journal: News-Views-Reviews for Women in Libraries. Women Library Workers, 2027 Parker, Berkeley, CA 94704.

Women & Performance: A Journal of Feminist Theory. Began in summer 1983. New York University, Tisch School of the Arts, Dept. of Performance Studies, 300 South Building, 51 W. 4th St., New York, NY 10012.

Women in Libraries. Edited by Leslie Kahn, 2 Manchester #2A, Newark, NJ 07104. Newsletter of the American Library Association's Feminist Task Force.

Women's Diaries: A Quarterly Newsletter. Began in spring 1983. Edited by Jane DuPree Begos, P.O. Box 18, Pound Ridge, NY 10576.

The Women's Review of Books: An Independent Journal. Began in summer of 1983. Edited by Linda Gardiner, 18 Norfolk Terrace, Wellesley, MA 02181.

Women's Studies in Communication. Journal of the Organization for Research on

Women and Communication of the Western Speech Communication Association. From the Department of Speech Communication, University of Denver, Denver, CO 80208.

Resources

American Library Association, 50 E. Huron St., Chicago, IL 60611. Includes the following groups related to the status of women, and Women's Studies: Committee on the Status of Women in Librarianship; Feminist Task Force (part of the Social Responsibilities Round Table); Women Administrators Discussion Group (Library Admin. and Mgmt. Assoc.); Women's Materials and Women Library Users Discussion Group (Reference and Adult Services Division); Women's Studies Discussion Group (Assoc. of College and Research Libraries).

Catalyst Library and Audiovisual Center, 14 E. 60th St., New York NY 10022. Focus on women's employment and career development; many publications.

HER SAY News Service, Women's News Institute, P.O. Box 11010, San Francisco, CA 94101. Weekly, twenty to thirty news stories.

International Feminist Bookfair, Room 306, 38 Mount Pleasant, London WC1, England.

International Women's Writing Guild, P.O. Box 810, Gracie Station, New York, NY 10028.

KNOW, Inc. P.O. Box 86031, Pittsburgh, PA 15221. Publishes pamphlets, resources.

National Center for Women in the Performing and Media Arts, Emerson College, 45 Beacon St., Boston, MA 02116.

National Council for Research on Women, Sara Delano Roosevelt Memorial House, 44-49 E. 65th St., New York, NY 10021. Umbrella group of research centers on women, both academically based and independent centers.

National Museum of Women in the Arts, 4590 MacArthur Blvd. NW, Washington, DC 20007.

National Women's Mailing List, 1195 Valencia St., San Francisco, CA 94110.

National Women's Studies Association, University of Maryland, College Park, MD 20742. Has national and regional conferences, newsletters; task forces include pre-K-12 teachers; librarians; lesbians; other interest groups.

Pacifica Tape Library, 5316 Venice Blvd., Los Angeles, CA 90119. Has archive of tapes and radio programs, many relating to women.

Serious Business Co., 1145 Mandana Blvd., Oakland, CA 94610. Freude Bartlett. Company papers now in the collection of the Bancroft Library at the University of California, Berkeley.

WEEA Publishing Center, 55 Chapel St., Newton, MA 02160. (800) 225-3088. Free catalog, "Resources for Educational Equity."

Women Against Pornography, 358 W. 47th St., New York, NY 10036. *Newsreport*.

Women Artists News Archives, GCT Box 3304, New York, NY 10163. Publishes *Women Artists News*, *Voices of Women*, and others.

Women in Cable, 2033 M Street NW, Suite 703, Washington, DC 20036.

Women in Communication, P.O. Box 9561, Austin, TX 78766. Monthly newsletter, *Pro/Comm*, covering trends in all areas of communications.

Women in Films, 8489 W. 3d St., Los Angeles, CA 90048. Publishes newsletter, sponsors internships, provides speakers' bureau.

WOMEN U.S.A. HOTLINE. (800) 221-4945. Ninety-second report on national women's issues.

Women's Caucus for Art, School of Art, Arizona State University, Tempe, AZ 85281.

Women's Computer Literacy Project, 1195 Valencia St., San Francisco, CA 94110.

Women's Institute for Freedom of the Press, 3306 Ross Pl. NW, Washington, DC 20008. Publishes *Index/Directory of Women's Media* (annual) and *Syllabus Sourcebook on Media and Women;* sponsors annual conference on planning an international communication system for women and media; collects syllabi and educational resources. Its *Media Report to Women* is a basic periodical; the 1983 issues included news reports under the following illustrative captions:
—90 percent of directing-editor jobs in nation's newsrooms are male
—censorship demands increase: monitor media, libraries, bookstores
—new media-video games used to teach men to hunt down women
—stations managed by women employ more women
—black women put in roles that bring in most revenue
—preteen romances, romance is big business
—mass media will continue their silence on actual words of the ERA
—pattern: men use their media to keep women down; New Zealand
—media not covering affirmative action now
—many women writers' best work is published by feminist small press
—Italy: feminist publishing market good, problem is distribution
—new periodicals mean outreach to more women
—translations: Beauvoir's *Second Sex*
—male editors, publishers, columnists, advertisers push acceptability of rape as joke
—nine women win "excellence in media" awards
—national festival of women's theater in Santa Cruz first in American history
—directing workshop for women
—radio-television jobs survey shows 85 percent nonclerical jobs in cable television go to men

Politics and Law

Cynthia E. Harrison

The political landscape in 1983 with respect to women confronts us with a paradox. For the first time, in November 1982, some elections turned on a distinctive women's vote. The gender gap in voting, which had emerged for the first time in 1980, had now been shown to have had a real impact on election outcomes. Yet—and here is the paradox—despite potential consequences for the election of 1984, Ronald Reagan and his Republican administration continued to decimate the federal effort on behalf of women's rights, and Congress defeated the Equal Rights Amendment. How could it come to pass that both the Congress and the administration in power could ignore not a small and isolated segment of voters, but a group that comprised more than half the electorate?

The Nature of the Gender Gap

Since its appearance in the election of 1980, analysts have debated the significance of the gender gap. Feminists argued that women, after more than a decade of activism and awareness devoted to women's issues, had decided to act in their own interests in the voting booth (Goldsmith 1983; Wilson 1983). In 1980, Republican presidential candidate Ronald Reagan and the Republican party had renounced support for the equal rights amendment, and Reagan had taken a vigorous stand against the right to terminate a pregnancy. In that election, 55 percent of the men but only 47 percent of the women voted for Reagan.

The disparity between the political views of men and women increased during Ronald Reagan's term in office. In January 1981, at the height of Republican party support in recent years, 42 percent of men had identified

145

themselves as Republicans as had 39 percent of the women. By September 1983, the percentage of men calling themselves Republicans had declined by 5 percentage points to 37, but only 30 percent of the women were now willing to adopt the Republican label, a decline of 9 points. Meanwhile, the proportion of women identifying themselves as Democrats grew from 50 percent in January 1981 to 59 percent in September 1983. The percentage for men had increased only 5 points, from 47 to 52 percent. In the 1982 election, in seventeen out of twenty-one races analyzed by the *New York Times*, women had voted Democratic in significantly higher numbers than did men and determined the outcome in at least two and as many as four governors' races.

But the polls disclosed some problematic data with respect to using women's issues to explain the gender gap. Men and women supported the equal rights amendment and the right to abortion in almost equal numbers. In fact, slightly more men than women favored both. In November of 1983, 54 percent of the men and 48 percent of the women said that another effort should be made to ratify the ERA. A poll conducted a few months earlier showed that only 3 percent more women than men were dissatisfied with Reagan's actions toward women. Reagan's overt antifeminism thus could not serve as a sufficient explanation for the gender gap.

Rather, the gap between men and women seemed to be based upon the traditional philosophical partisan positions that Reagan espoused and was implementing. Reagan enunciated a commitment to cutbacks in federal spending for domestic programs in order to reduce budget deficits, to restraint of government influence in private industry, to the market allocation of goods and services, and to an active anti-Communist position in the world arena. In a September 1983 poll reported in the *Washington Post* (8 October 1983), women strongly disapproved of Reagan's handling of the economy (54 percent to 40), whereas men just as vigorously approved (57 to 39). Both men and women objected to the way Reagan handled cuts in social programs, but women's dislike was stronger (66 percent of the women compared to 56 percent of the men). Women and men also divided sharply on defense issues: men supported the military budget, 52 to 43, whereas women opposed it, 47 to 38; men approved Reagan's nuclear policy 52 to 41, whereas women objected 50 to 39.

If a conscious commitment to women's issues could not account for the difference in the political perspective of men and women, other surveys revealed demographic factors that did seem suggestive. A poll conducted by the *New York Times* in November 1983 (in which 52 percent of the women and 38 percent of the men said that Ronald Reagan should not be reelected) indicated that marital status, employment, and income played a large role in voter opinion formation. Looking only at employment status, one sees that 60 percent of the men employed full time but only 37 percent of such women favored reelection for Reagan. Female heads of household showed greater dislike: only 17 percent of women who were unmarried, employed, and had children at home said that Ronald Reagan should be elected to a second term as president. Finally, income also proved a strong indicator: only 24 percent of women in families with incomes of less than $10,000 would reelect Reagan.

This data was consonant with the fact that Reagan's domestic program, revealed especially in his budget cuts, had disproportionately negative effects on women (Coalition . . . 1983; New budget . . . 1983). In 1982, women headed about 16 percent of all the nation's families, but 50 percent of the poor families in America. The Reagan budget requested cuts in most of the programs assisting poor families: WIC (Special Supplemental Food Program for Women, Infants and Children); aid to subsidized housing; and social services block grants, which include funds for child care services, meals for the elderly and infirm, and homemaker services. The Reagan budget would have completely eliminated the Women's Educational Equity Act program, legal services (over two-thirds of which went to women clients), and the Work Incentive Program. The voting behavior of low-income women accurately reflected the knowledge that their self-interest was not served by Republican policies. Analysts have attributed differences in support for Reagan's military policies to women's traditional pacifism, but the diversion of resources into military rather than domestic programs may also have played a role.

Although the voting pattern may not have sprung from a clear feminist commitment, it seems likely that women did view Ronald Reagan as hostile to women's interests overall. Women activists had access to the media and used it consistently to identify Reagan as insensitive to women's welfare. While the impact of such publicity is hard to gauge, it must, nevertheless, have had an impact on the consciousness of some women.

Reagan's own advisers took the view that the only part of the gender gap that mattered was comprised of women between the ages of twenty-five and forty who worked and who felt threatened by the president's economic policies, and of older women who feared Social Security cutbacks. This gap, which White House observers estimated at about 3 percentage points, could be closed by explaining the long-term beneficial effects of Reaganomics. Other anti-Reagan votes, they reasoned, came from feminists, liberals, and blacks who philosophically opposed Republican positions and who could not therefore be placated. Rather, they would be written off.

Viewed from this perspective, the gender gap did not constitute a problem for the Reagan administration, and his actions with respect to women's rights become comprehensible. His constituency supported his efforts to roll back federal activism concerning affirmative action and antidiscrimination efforts, and to undermine the Supreme Court decision granting women the right to choose abortion. Most of those who opposed him on economic issues did not seem especially concerned about women's equity issues, and Republican principles precluded expansion of the federal social welfare effort to win them over.

Democrats, on the other hand, found in the gender gap a valuable source of potential votes for the 1984 election. Democrats were committed both to an expanded role for the federal government in social assistance which would attract the disaffected women voters and to a full program of women's rights needed to win the support of activist women who often influenced the media. Among other things, 1983 was the prelude to an election year, and the political events with respect to women took place against the backdrop of the coming presidential campaign.

The Reagan Administration and Women

If Reagan was willing to write off the women voters who opposed him in the voting both, he could not so quickly dismiss the Republican women active in the party who demanded that he acknowledge them and who found women's lack of support for Republicans embarrassing. To meet these particular political needs, Ronald Reagan took refuge in a strategy of long standing. Accompanied by appropriate fanfare, he named women to some highly visible administration jobs.

When he took office in 1981, Reagan had neglected to appoint any woman to his cabinet, ignoring the precedent of the two presidents before him. In 1983, clearly in response to the need to show some concern for women in the face of the gender gap, he named two. The first appointment, of Elizabeth Dole, a White House adviser and former member of the Federal Trade Commission, to the position of secretary of transportation, was announced on 5 January. His nomination of Margaret Heckler—a former congresswoman from Massachusetts defeated at least in part because of her opposition to abortion rights—to the post of secretary of health and human services came only days later.

Neither appointment served the interests of women as defined by either economic or equity issues. As secretary of transportation, Dole had virtually no impact on any of the retrograde Reagan policies. Heckler, as secretary of health and human services, stayed true to her own philosophy and that of the president by affirming her opposition to abortion. She did divert some of the attention of her agency from the search for "waste, fraud and abuse" and did rescue a small program to enhance efforts to collect child support payments, a necessity for women only half of whom receive child support money due them from their former husbands. But her support of the Equal Rights Amendment or other women's equity issues brought no change in the White House. Another Reagan appointee, Faith Whittlesey, who replaced Elizabeth Dole in the White House, further angered women's groups by announcing that she had never been involved in women's issues. "Only when women get beyond women's issues and focus on the big questions will they be drawn into the general public debate" she asserted. (*NYT* editorial, 29 April 1983).

Whenever challenged on his record regarding women, Reagan fell back on his tally of appointments. In June, at the Republican Women's Leadership Forum, he asserted that he had appointed "more women to top policy positions in two years than did any previous administration" (*NYT*, 4 June 1983). Reagan referred not only to his two cabinet members (Dole and Heckler), to Jeane Kirkpatrick (U.S. ambassador to the United Nations, usually labeled "cabinet level"), and to Supreme Court Justice Sandra Day O'Connor—but to the one thousand other women he claimed to have named to policymaking positions.

Counting presidential appointments is a difficult business. All presidential appointments are not equal; some are to cabinet posts and some are to minor commissions that meet once a year for one day. Comparability is often determined by using only those appointments requiring Senate confirmation, but the Senate has to confirm not only Supreme Court justices, but also heads of local customs offices. Reagan's figure of 1,000 appeared to have included not only his appointments but the appointments made by his appointees. Using the standard of Senate confirmation, in fact, only 63 of 670 full-time appointments requiring Senate confirmation made during his first two years went to women, a total of 9 percent. In a comparable period, Jimmy Carter had appointed women to 15 percent of the positions. According to the *New York Times*, counting full- and part-time posts including those not requiring Senate confirmation, Reagan named 381 women in his first two years to Carter's 437. Reagan's record of judicial appointments, among the most significant appointments a president can make, was especially poor. Only 4.4 percent of Reagan's federal district court appointments went to women, compared to 12.5 percent for Carter. Overall, Reagan's judicial appointments went to women 6.9 percent of the time, compared to 15.8 percent for Jimmy Carter (U.S. Commission on Civil Rights 1983).

In any case, the number of appointments and their publicity did not seem to work as felicitously for Reagan as they had for former presidents. A more sophisticated public viewed the phenomenon with suspicion. An influential New York Republican woman, Muriel Siebert, commented to a group of her colleagues that the Republican women in Reagan's administration had "as much to do with leadership of the party as a mannequin has to do with the management of Bloomingdale's" (*NYT*, 5 April 1983). A poll released shortly after his two female cabinet appointments revealed that only 36 percent of the women surveyed approved of the way the president was performing his job.

Moreover, a serious attempt to sabotage the Commission on Civil Rights, an historically independent body set up by Congress to monitor progress on civil rights and to make policy recommendations, angered both

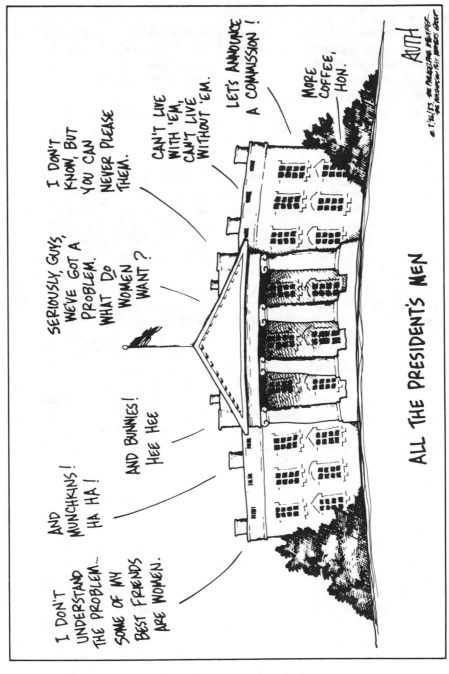

Courtesy Tony Auth

Republican and Democratic women, in addition to civil rights leaders and many members of Congress. The commission had six members evenly divided by party. In 1981, Reagan flouted the tradition that kept the commission outside of the usual political spoils operation and dismissed the moderate Republican chairman Arthur Flemming. He replaced him with a black Republican, Clarence Pendleton, who shared Reagan's antipathy for affirmative action and busing. In 1983, Reagan sought to pack the membership of the commission so that the majority would support the administration line. The effort, which began in May, went through several permutations before its conclusion in November, but the result was that two prominent Republican women members, feminist Jill Ruckelshaus and Mary Louise Smith, a former chair of the Republican National Committee and a strong advocate of women's rights, lost their positions on the commission, which now had a majority of members opposed to affirmative action. The new commission staff director, an Hispanic woman Democrat, Linda Chavez, shared this view.

The action suggested that the administration was willing to write off feminist Republicans as well as Democrats, liberals, and blacks. In August, the resignation of Barbara Honegger, a former Reagan campaign worker and then a Justice Department employee, placed the administration disregard for even Republican women center stage.

During the campaign, Reagan had asserted that he favored the "E" and the "R" but not the "A" in the Equal Rights Amendment, and as proof of that contention, he would institute a program to eliminate discrimination in the law on a statute-by-statute basis on both the federal and the state levels. The state program was called the Fifty States Project. Even before its inception, forty states had already instituted or completed efforts to remove discriminatory statutes; moreover, compliance was voluntary and the White House had no plan for implementation. The federal effort entailed a listing of discriminatory statutes compiled by the Justice Department for action by the Task Force on Legal Equity, which had twenty-one members, but no staff, no office, and no funds.

On 21 August, an article appeared in the *Washington Post*, written by Barbara Honegger, a special assistant in the Justice Department involved in the effort to identify sex discriminatory laws (Honegger 1983). Honegger claimed that in the year and a half since the project had been initiated, three quarterly reports had gone to the White House and not a single action had been taken. Her conclusion was that Reagan had reneged on his commitment to help women through an alternative to the ERA. The administration responded to Honegger's accusation with derision, claiming that she had no administrative responsibility, calling her names, and pointing to the long list of Reagan appointments of women. Women's organizations immediately rallied around Honegger, who resigned her administration post.

In a speech to Republican women shortly thereafter, Reagan promised to take action on the Justice Department reports. (President Reagan . . . 1983; U.S. Dept. of Justice 1983). His recommendations included altering a number of the laws, mostly to change gender-specific language to sex-neutral phraseology. Assistant Attorney General William Bradford Reynolds characterized the changes as "not substantial." The president declined to recommend revising statutes that favored women, or ones that stipulated differential treatment in the military, such as the law barring women from combat. NOW president Judy Goldsmith termed the president's response "so inadequate it is either arrogant or ignorant" (*NYT*, 8 September 1983). WEAL legislative director Pat Reuss observed: "The man is playing the tuba on the sundeck while the *Titanic* is sinking" (*Washington Post*, 9 September 1983).

Reagan's faith in his program prompted the administration to promise that the expected improvement in the economy, the decline in inflation, and tax reductions would all yield sufficient benefits for women so that special efforts to close the gender gap would be unnecessary. White House staff efforts to work with Republican women members of Congress lapsed because of administration reluctance to support the legislation they recommended. The executive departments followed the administration line, and agency after agency took stands directly counter to established federal policy with respect to women's rights.

Actions of Executive Departments

Department of Labor

In March 1983, the Office of Federal Contract Compliance published new and more lenient affirmative action rules for companies doing business with the federal government (St. George 1983). Under the new rules, 76 percent of these firms would be exempt from filing affirmative action plans and the government would no longer review affirmative action compliance before awarding contracts. Moreover, contractors would not be considered in violation of a contract solely because they had failed to meet affirmative action goals. In addition, only identified individuals who had suffered discrimination would be eligible for back pay awards, eliminating relief for classes of workers. Vigorous protest from women's organizations and civil rights groups prevented the implementation of the new regulations.

Department of Education

The Department of Education engaged in similar tactics. In his proposed budget, Ronald Reagan had eliminated funding for the Women's Educational Equity Act [WEEA] program, which supported programs designed to eliminate discrimination in educational institutions. Congress had declined to abolish this program and had maintained its funding. In August, the Department of Education fired five WEEA employees—all women—and left the program in the charge of the two remaining male employees, protected from dismissal by veteran's preference. This event is treated at greater length in the *Annual* chapter on education.

Department of Justice

The Department of Justice also followed Reagan's policy of aggressive reversal of equity policy. In August, the Justice Department filed a brief in a Supreme Court case involving compliance with Title IX of the Education Amendments of 1972, which reads: "No person in the United States shall, on the basis of sex, be excluded from participation in, be denied the benefits of, or be subjected to discrimination under any educational program or activity receiving Federal financial assistance." In 1978, Grove City College, in Pennsylvania, had refused to certify that it did not discriminate on the basis of sex on the grounds that it received no federal funds. The Department of Health, Education and Welfare, as it was then denominated, had threatened to cut off student aid to pupils enrolled at the college, and the case had gone to court. Lower court rulings had been inconclusive, and the case now awaited action by the Supreme Court. Counter to a decade-old department position and to the intention of Congress, the Justice Department brief argued that the college should be required to certify nondiscrimination only in the dispersion of financial aid, rather than throughout the institution.

Once again, the administration showed itself impervious to the requests of feminists of both political parties. A few days after the Justice Department brief was filed, fifty members of Congress led by Republican House member Claudine Schneider (R.I.) and including Republican senator Robert Dole (Kan.) filed a counter brief arguing that the intent of Congress had been to make the law apply to entire institutions. In November, the House passed a "sense of the House" resolution sponsored by Schneider that the federal courts should construe the legislation broadly. It was approved 414 to 8. Dozens of women's organizations and civil rights groups filed amicus briefs supporting that position. In February 1984, the Supreme Court ruled in favor of the Justice Department interpretation of the law. Sandra Day O'Connor was on the majority side of the 6 to 3 decision.

Department of Health and Human Services

The appointment of Margaret Heckler to replace Richard S. Schweiker led to minor changes in department policy. Acting in the wake of four unfavorable court decisions, the department rescinded a rule (the "squeal rule") that federally funded clinics dispensing birth control devices to teenage girls had to notify their parents. Secretary Heckler opposed the regulation, and the department therefore declined to appeal. In September, Heckler proposed legislation to strengthen federal action against fathers failing to meet child support payments. Although this measure would assist women responsible for raising children, it also appealed to conservatives who saw it as reducing demands on public assistance. The House passed the legislation unanimously in November and the Senate was expected to act favorably in 1984.

However, Heckler did little to stem the cuts for federal child care assistance. As a result of federal cutbacks totaling 21 percent over two years, three-quarters of church-run day care programs—the largest supplier of the service—had been eliminated. In New York State, for example, 42 percent of children outside New York City lost all or part of government-subsidized day care between 1981 and 1983.

Congressional Action

With the activity of the administration engendering widespread hostility on the part of women's rights organizations, Republicans in Congress sought to establish a record to protect themselves from allegations of insensitivity to women. Democrats likewise joined in efforts to distinguish themselves from the regressive Republican administration's actions toward women. However, Republican loyalty to the administration and desire on both sides of the aisle to cut deficits meant that the Congress as well as the administration had responsibility for the budget cuts that took a toll on women. Nevertheless, three specific legislative measures showed both the interest of congressional Republicans in doing something for women regardless of administration intentions, and the interest of Democrats in capitalizing on the Republican handicap with women voters.

Early in the session, Republican senator David Durenberger of Minnesota introduced a package of legislation identified as the Economic Equity Act. The package had several parts, including the revision of federal pension laws, tax breaks for displaced homemakers and single parents, the elimination of discrimination in insurance and pension plans, and the encouragement of day care center development (Paterson and Edmunds 1983; WEAL 1983). Durenberger explained his motivation: "I wouldn't want to be running in 1984, and have voters think that I was opposed to these issues or not interested in them" (NYT, 3 March 1983).

Congress addressed portions of the Economic Equity Act in separate bills. Both houses considered legislation to prohibit sex as a factor in determining insurance rates and benefits; Republican senator Robert Packwood (Ore.) served as chief sponsor in the Senate, and John D. Dingell, Democrat of Michigan, sponsored the measure in the House. The law would affect state and local governments offering plans to employees, and consumers purchasing automobile, life, health, disability, and annuity plans privately. Private employers were already required to offer sex-neutral insurance plans under Title VII of the Civil Rights Act of 1964. Although the insurance industry had initially seemed willing to negotiate an acceptable bill, in May the American Council of Life Insurance announced that it would oppose all such legislation, and it launched a million-dollar publicity campaign against it. No action had been taken by the end of the session.

If Republicans were willing to rally behind legislation prohibiting discrimination in insurance, a bill that would require little federal effort or cost to administer, the Democrats in the House seized on the issue of the Equal Rights Amendment to show women who their friends really were. On 3 January 1983, House speaker Tip O'Neill announced that the Equal Rights Amendment would be House Joint Resolution 1, the first piece of legislation in the new Congress. When introduced, the resolution had 221 cosponsors, of which a mere 31 were Republicans, representing only 18.5 percent of the 167 Republican House members. Democrats, on the other hand, had a showing of 71 percent of their ranks as cosponsors, a total of 190 of 267 members. The ERA was introduced in the Senate later that month with 55 cosponsors (among them only 20 of the Senate's 55 Republican members). Both bodies held hearings, with the speaker making an unusual appearance before the House Judiciary Subcommittee, while chief Senate sponsor Paul Tsongas (D., Mass.) faced hostile questioning from Senate Judiciary subcommittee chair and ERA opponent Orrin Hatch (R., Utah). The amendment passed through both the House Judiciary Subcommittee (6 to 2) and the full committee (21 to 10) with nine of the committee's 11 Republicans voting against, but the full committee vote took 5½ hours while the Democrats fought amendments on abortion, military service, insurance, veterans' benefits, and private single-sex schools. Fearful that amendments concerning abortion and the exclusion of women from combat would pass on the House floor, in November Speaker O'Neill brought the measure to a vote under a procedure called "suspension of the rules," which is usually reserved for noncontroversial matters; only twenty minutes of debate is permitted, and amendments are prohibited. The measure failed, 6 votes short of the two-thirds majority required by the Constitution. The 278 votes in favor included 225 Democrats and 53 Republicans. Thirty-eight Democrats and 109 Republicans opposed the amendment. Fourteen previous supporters voted against the measure, allegedly in protest against the unorthodox procedure utilized by the speaker.

The implications of this incident remain ambiguous. Republicans alleged that the speaker brought the measure to a vote, despite the certainty that it would fail under the suspension of the rules or be amended under normal voting procedures, because he wanted a clear partisan count in order to have a campaign issue for the following fall. The argument is a good one. Many women activists did not want the vote to take place, believing with some justification that yet another ERA defeat would do the women's cause no good. After the expiration of the ratification period, feminists had maintained that the next goal should be the replacement of anti-ERA legislators in the states, so that ratification could be achieved when state legislatures accurately reflected the sentiments of the voting public (Chisholm and Stewart 1983). Yet, NOW president Judy Goldsmith told NOW members in a special mailing after the vote that the count had been essential to determine who could be counted upon. In total, it seems more likely that the decision to bring the amendment to a vote came from the imperatives of Democratic decision makers, rather than women's rights activists. If Democrats were going to take up cudgels in support of women's issues, feminists would also have to serve Democratic party ends.

As 1983 drew to an end, it became clear that feminists were unwelcome in the Republican party whatever their other political views. In fact, at a December meeting of state legislators, an angry exchange erupted when White House spokespeople attempted to defend the Reagan program to the Republican women in the group. Despite the ire, and warnings from Republican politicos that the Republican party needed women as candidates and as party workers, the White House refused to make any concessions on women's issues.

Judicial Action

Though women gained ground neither in the executive branch nor in the Congress, ironically the one branch not susceptible to variations in voting by sex proved to be more sympathetic to women's rights (O'Connor and Epstein 1983a, 1983b). Key judicial decisions advanced women's job rights and protected their ten-year-old right to choose to terminate a pregnancy.

Employment

In June, the Supreme Court ruled in *Newport News Shipbuilding and Dry Dock Company* v. *EEOC* (Equal Employment Opportunity Commission) that, under the Pregnancy Discrimination Act of 1978, wives of male employees must be offered the same pregnancy-related insurance coverage as that offered to female employees. The decision affirmed that sex discrimination legislation offered benefits to men as well as to women, since the enhanced insurance coverage for dependents represented a benefit to male employees.

In July, the Supreme Court announced its verdict in *Norris* v. *Arizona*: that Title VII of the 1964 Civil Rights Act prohibits discrimination in premiums and benefits in pension plans. The Reagan administration argued in support of equal treatment in this case. However, the Court ruled that such discrimination could be banned only in the case of future contributions and benefits; relief would not be granted retroactively. The decision was expected to influence the outcome of the pending federal legislation to ban discrimination in pensions by public employers.

A case of particular significance not yet before the Supreme Court was decided in a federal court in Tacoma, Washington. In November, U.S. district court judge Jack Tanner ruled that the state of Washington had violated Title VII of the 1964 Civil Rights Act by undercompensating women employed in jobs that the state itself had deemed comparable to jobs held by men. In a related decision in December, he ordered the state to pay approximately $838 million in raises and back pay to more than fifteen thousand women state employees. The state planned to appeal, and the case is of special consequence in that it could establish an important precedent— that Title VII prohibits paying women less than men for jobs requiring comparable, rather than only identical, skills, training, and responsibility.

Meanwhile, the Republican administration settled another employment discrimination case out of court with less favorable results. The Equal Employment Opportunity Commission reached an out-of-court settlement with General Motors in October. The case had been pending against the nation's largest automobile manufacturer for ten years, alleging discrimination in hiring, training, and promotion of blacks, women, and Hispanics; in the agreement with the EEOC, GM admitted no wrongdoing, but agreed to lay out $42.5 million over five years, mostly for education and training. Only $4 million was set aside for back pay and individual relief, a small amount when compared, for example, with the 1973 settlement with A.T.&T. which resulted in $38 million to the company's workers.

An additional employment discrimination case was still pending on the Supreme Court docket at the end of 1983, one that would establish whether Title VII exempts partnerships, specifically law firms, from its provisions. Elizabeth Anderson Hishon sued the Atlanta law firm of King and Spaulding after they had declined to offer her a partnership (Horst 1983; Tybor 1983). The firm had never had a woman partner and had argued successfully before two lower courts that law firm partnerships were excluded from Title VII's purview. The attorney for the firm contended in oral arguments before the Supreme Court that law firms should be exempted because "they're essential to the enforcement of the Constitution." Newspaper accounts described the justices' response to this argument as "incredulous" (*NYT*, 1 November 1983). On May 22, 1984, the Court ruled unanimously against the law firm, stating that Hishon was entitled to sue under Title VII on the basis of sex discrimination.

Abortion

January 1983 was the tenth anniversary of *Roe* v. *Wade*, the major Supreme Court decision that prohibited federal and state governments from outlawing abortions. The decision did not stem the debate on the issue, which has continued to divide the public.

In the ten years since the decision, antiabortion activists have tried many strategies to negate the ruling, including constitutional amendments that would give states the right to legislate on abortion or that would define the meaning of *person* to include the conceptus. None has so far been successful. Legislation restricting federal and state funding for abortion services, on the other hand, has been enacted. In addition, abortion opponents have persuaded state legislatures to pass a number of statutes designed to limit access to abortion services.

On 15 June, the Supreme Court, in *Akron* v. *Akron Center for Reproductive Health*, vitiated this tactic and reaffirmed its decision in *Roe* v. *Wade*. Among the state regulations disallowed were those requiring a twenty-four-hour waiting period, those mandating that all abortions after the first trimester be performed in a hospital, and those compelling a physician to tell a woman that a fetus "is a human life from the moment of conception." Justice Sandra Day O'Connor dissented from the majority in this case; the state, she asserted, had an interest in protecting the life of the fetus "throughout the pregnancy," including its first weeks.

Ronald Reagan expressed "profound disappointment" at the Court's ruling and asked Congress to take action to overrule it. Among the anti-abortion amendments, one had been approved by the Senate Judiciary Committee; it read: "The right to abortion is not secured by this Constitution." A few days after the Supreme Court decision, the Senate considered the proposed amendment and voted it down, 50 against to 49 in support, 18 short of the two-thirds vote required for acceptance. Antiabortionist Republican Jesse Helms (N.C.) declined to vote in favor, on the grounds that the amendment would not end all abortions at once. The split in the antiabortion camp, preventing coalescence around one antiabortion strategy, thus worked in favor of prochoice advocates.

The administration continued to do what it could to limit access to abortion. The Office of Personnel Management barred Planned Parenthood from the Combined Federal Campaign, a joint charity appeal, but this action was overturned by a U.S. district court. In the fall, Congress passed legislation forbidding the use of health benefits for abortions by federal employees.

Consequences for the 1984 Presidential Campaign

The federal activity with respect to women provided much grist for the mill of women activists and Democratic presidential hopefuls gearing up for the 1984 campaign. Republican members of Congress, defensive and fearful about the gender gap on the local level, also looked ahead and sought ways to express concern about women in preparation for the coming election. By the end of 1983, it became clear that feminist organizations had defined

Ronald Reagan as the enemy, and Democrats had become newly vehement advocates of women's rights.

Republican efforts directed at 1984 were more circumscribed than Democratic ones, since the president had not yet announced his decision to seek reelection. However, Richard G. Lugar (Ind.), chairman of the National Republican Senatorial Committee, told the convention of the National Federation of Republican Women that female Republican candidates generally run 3 to 8 points better than males, and that the party had better seek such candidates. Linden Kettlewell, political director of the Republican National Committee, echoed his view; she opposed the Equal Rights Amendment and abortion, and claimed to have no position on the Economic Equity Act, but she supported the idea of Republican women running for office. The president himself asked Representative Claudine Schneider (R., R.I.) to run against Democratic senator Claiborne Pell, but Schneider declined, citing the difficulty in raising money for such a race.

Democrats, on the other hand, had no barriers to launching a presidential campaign and contenders filled the field, vying with each other for the support of feminist organizations who were committed to Ronald Reagan's defeat. In May, five Democratic candidates—Walter Mondale, Ernest Hollings, Gary Hart, John Glenn, and Alan Cranston—addressed the convention of the National Women's Political Caucus, each affirming support for the ERA, a nuclear arms freeze, pay equity, and a willingness to consider a woman as a running mate. Walter Mondale, widely regarded as the front runner, opened his speech by declaiming, "I am a feminist." In September, Gary Hart took the opportunity in a speech to the Americans for Democratic Action to assert that the Democratic party should make full equality for women its "principal interest."

In September, the National Organization for Women made headlines when it announced that, for the first time in its seventeen-year history, it would endorse a presidential candidate, part of its effort to oust Ronald Reagan, the group's priority for 1984. NOW president Judy Goldsmith emphasized "electability" as the group's major criterion for selecting a candidate to endorse. Six Democratic presidential candidates appeared at the NOW convention: Mondale, Hollings, Hart, Glenn, Cranston, and George McGovern. The major focus of NOW members' questions to them concerned the candidates' willingness to consider a woman as vice-president. All affirmed that they would. Hart stated that he would run with a woman on either end of the ticket, and Mondale promised that, male or female, he would choose only a feminist. Public opinion polls suggested that the presence of a woman on the ticket could help it, but in any case it seemed unlikely to do it harm. When black civil rights activist Jesse Jackson announced his candidacy in November, he promised to choose a woman as his running mate if selected to lead the ticket at the Democratic convention. All the candidates supported the full range of feminist planks, and all could point to women in key roles in their campaign organizations—more evidence of their interest in winning the women's vote.

In the end, NOW endorsed Walter Mondale, the obvious choice using the criterion of electability. Mondale had already garnered a large number of endorsements from other organizations, especially the unprecedented prenomination backing of the AFL-CIO. He led all the other candidates in the polls and had a well-funded, sophisticated, and experienced campaign staff developing solid position papers on issues of importance to women. Five of the thirty-seven votes cast by NOW's board went to Alan Cranston, the designee of the California State NOW organization. No other candidate received votes, not even Sonia Johnson, a nationally known feminist, who was seeking the nomination of the Citizens party.

The endorsement of NOW was highly coveted, and all agreed that Walter Mondale had gained an edge in the race for it. Its effect will be revealed only later in the campaign, both with respect to the effort put forth by women on Mondale's behalf and with respect to the gains for women in the Democratic platform and, if he wins, in the Mondale administration. Given the identification of the Democratic party both with feminist goals and with social programs, and the character of the gender gap, which is at least as much an economic phenomenon as a sex-based one, it is unlikely that the evidence will be conclusive. However, the political events of 1983 suggest that the presence of women on the political scene has in fact assumed an unprecedented importance, and the gender gap, whatever its "true cause," must be credited with that outcome. In 1983, women's issues achieved a new degree of salience.

In the small November election, women made strong showings. Martha Collins became governor of Kentucky, the only woman governor in the nation. A Republican woman, Donna Owens, was elected mayor of Toledo, and Dianne Feinstein and Kathy Whitmire won reelection as mayor of San Francisco and Houston, respectively. The returns suggested that women enhanced political party success, as feminists had argued they would.

Conclusion

In October, a gala at the Kennedy Center in Washington, D.C., commemorated the twentieth anniversary of the report of the President's Commission on the Status of Women. Appointed by John F. Kennedy in 1961, and chaired by Eleanor Roosevelt, the commission outlined in its report, for the first time, a national agenda for women's equality. It included equal opportunity for women in public and private work places, access to educational programs at all stages of life, constitutional protection against sex discrimination in the law, provision of community services for women, including federally funded day care, and an array of other goals. The modest plan acknowledged differences between men and women, and women's primary responsibility for family welfare; it proposed only a few pieces of federal legislation and a number of changes motivated largely by good will. Although it did not encompass the breadth and depth of the fundamental alterations generated and accomplished by the women's movement that caught fire in the late sixties, the commission broke new ground. Looking back after twenty years, one could see that a remarkable number of the commission's agenda items had been addressed. The appearance of an effective gender gap gives hope that the program may yet be achieved in its entirety, despite the efforts of the Reagan administration to turn back the clock on women's rights.

The gender gap, which shed its light on the political scene in 1983, reflects the fact that women, more than men, are affected by downturns in the economy and by cutbacks in social programs. Women's individual economic disabilities derive from institutional arrangements, like the practice of paying less for women's work, that can be changed. As the recognition of such facts gains greater currency, the gender gap may ultimately become the lever to effect some long-sought and fundamental changes in many public arenas.

References

CHISHOLM, C., and A.W. STEWART. 1983. *The ERA since 1978: A bibliographic review*. Public administration series, P-1196. Monticello, Ill.: Vance Bibliographies.

Coalition on Women and the Budget. 1983. *Inequality of sacrifice: The impact of the Reagan budget on women*. Washington, D.C.: Coalition.

GOLDSMITH, J. 1983. *Gender gap '84—women reject Reagan*. Speech presented to the National Press Club. Washington, D.C.: National Organization for Women.

HONEGGER, B. 1983. Reagan has not fulfilled his promise. *Washington Post*, 2 August.

HORST, J.D. 1983. The application of Title VII to law firm partnership decisions: Women struggle to join the club. *Ohio State Law Journal* 44, no. 3:841–90.

New budget, old story: Federal budget cuts hurt women. 1983. *National NOW Times* 16 (April):3, 5.

O'CONNOR, K., and L. EPSTEIN. 1983a. Beyond legislative lobbying: Women's rights groups and the Supreme Court. *Judicature* 67 (September):134–43.

O'CONNOR, K., and L. EPSTEIN. 1983b. Sex and the Supreme Court: An analysis of judicial support for gender-based claims. *Social Science Quarterly* 64 (June):327–31.

PATERSON, J., and L. EDMUNDS. 1983. An agenda for the new (and slightly improved) Congress. *Ms.* 11, no. 2:83–86.

President Reagan's 50 States Project "Status of the States" 1982 year-end report. 1983. Washington: [Executive Office of the President].

ST. GEORGE, D. 1983. Administration may have to shelve its relaxed minority hiring rules. *National Journal*, 22 October, pp. 2170–73.

TYBOR, J.R. 1983. What "up or out" means to women lawyers. *American Bar Association Journal* 69 (June):756–59.

U.S. Commission on Civil Rights. 1983. *Equal opportunity in presidential appointments*. Washington, D.C.: U.S. Commission on Civil Rights.

U.S. Department of Justice. 1983. *The third quarterly report of the attorney general to the president and the cabinet council on legal policy as required by executive order no. 12336*. Washington, D.C.: U.S. Department of Justice.

WILSON, K. 1983. Reagan is shortchanging women, says G.O.P feminist Kathy Wilson, and he may pay for it next year at the polls. *People Weekly*, 1 August, pp. 93–94.

WWR: WEAL Washington Report. 1983. Issue for April-May and many others outline the components and progress of the Women's Economic Equity Act legislative package.

Selected Congressional Hearings

U.S. Congress. House Committee on Education and Labor. Subcommittee on Employment Opportunities. *Oversight hearings on the OFCCP's proposed affirmative action regulations*. Washington, D.C.: GPO, 1983.

U.S. Congress. House Committee on Education and Labor. Subcommittee on Labor-Management Relations. *Legislative hearing on pension issues*. Washington, D.C.: GPO, 1983.

U.S. Congress. House Committee on Energy and Commerce. Subcommittee on Commerce, Transportation, and Tourism. *Nondiscrimination in Insurance Act of 1983*. Washington, D.C.: GPO, 1983.

U.S. Congress. House Committee on Post Office and Civil Service. Subcommittee on Human Resources. *Pay equity: Equal pay for work of comparable value*. 2 vols. Washington, D.C.: GPO, 1983.

U.S. Congress. House Select Committee on Aging. *Women's pension equity*. Washington, D.C.: GPO, 1983.

U.S. Congress. House Select Committee on Aging. Subcommittee on Retirement Income and Employment. *The impact of Reagan economics on aging women: Oregon*. Washington, D.C.: GPO, 1983.

U.S. Congress. House Select Committee on Aging. Task Force on Social Security and Women. *Inequities toward women in the Social Security system*. Washington, D.C.: GPO, 1983.

U.S. Congress. Senate Committee on Commerce, Science, and Transportation. *Fair Insurance Practices Act*. Washington, D.C.: GPO, 1983.

U.S. Congress. Senate Committee on Finance. *Potential inequities affecting women*. 3 vols. Washington, D.C.: GPO, 1983.

U.S. Congress. Senate Committee on Finance. Subcommittee on Social Security and Income Maintenance Programs. *Women's career choice equity legislation.* Washington, D.C.: GPO, 1983.

U.S. Congress. Senate Committee on the Judiciary. Subcommittee on the Constitution. *Constitutional amendments relating to abortion.* Washington, D.C.: GPO, 1983.

Bibliography

ABZUG, BELLA, with MIM KELBER. *Gender Gap: Bela Abzug's Guide to Political Power for American Women.* New York: Houghton Mifflin, 1984. Noted feminist politician gives detailed interpretation of women's voting behavior and strategies for increased political clout. Includes useful appendices with names of organizations and resources for women in politics.

BAER, JUDITH A. *Equality under the Constitution: Reclaiming the Fourteenth Amendment.* Ithaca, N.Y.: Cornell University Press, 1983. Argues that true equality of civil rights has yet to be achieved, and that the judicial process has not extended the Fourteenth Amendment as far as the Constitution urges.

BAXTER, SANDRA. *Women and Politics: The Visible Majority.* Ann Arbor: University of Michigan Press, 1983. Revised edition of her earlier work, with a significant change in the subtitle (formerly "invisible").

BONEPARTH, ELLEN, ed. *Women, Power and Policy.* New York: Pergamon Press, 1982. Review of the impact on women of government policies in areas such as housing, employment, child care, and crime; women's involvement in policymaking and in new arenas such as foreign policy and militarism.

BUHLE, MARI JO. *Women and the American Left: A Guide to Sources.* Boston, Mass.: G.K. Hall, 1983. Historical and contemporary bibliography.

BURNETT, BARBARA A. *EveryWoman's Legal Guide: Protecting Your Rights at Home, in the Workplace, and in the Marketplace.* New York: Doubleday, 1983. Very clear, well-documented guide to legal problems, such as contracts, consumer complaints, real estate, family law, employment discrimination, and crime. Includes state-by-state guide to further sources of information.

CONOVER, PAMELA JOHNSTON, and VIRGINIA GRAY. *Feminism and the New Right: Conflict over the American Family.* New York: Praeger, 1983. Reviews political ideologies and organizing strategies of each side, evaluates successes in affecting public behavior and decisions.

DIAMOND, IRENE, ed. *Families, Politics, and Public Policy: A Feminist Dialogue on Women and the State.* New York: Longman, 1983. Includes theoretical articles on political issues, and analyses of specific areas of social and family policy; concludes with feminist proposals for change and comparisons with other societies.

FLANZ, GISBERT H. *Comparative Women's Rights and Political Participation in Europe.* Dobbs Ferry, N.Y.: Transnational Publishers, 1983.

14th National Conference on Women and the Law. *1983 Sourcebook.* Washington, D.C.: Georgetown University Law Center. Extensively documented list of conference sessions, panelists, resources. Major annual event.

GELB, JOYCE, and MARIAN LIEF PALLEY. *Women and Public Policies*. Princeton, N.J.: Princeton University Press, 1982. Presents four case studies of credit rights, pregnancy benefits, Title IX, and abortion rights.

McGLEN, NANCY E., and KAREN O'CONNOR. *Women's Rights: The Struggle for Equality in the Nineteenth and Twentieth Centuries*. Combines history with current political analysis, using social movement theory to assess the accomplishments of feminists at different times. Heavily documented.

NELSON, BARBARA J. *American Women and Politics: A Selected Bibliography and Resource Guide*. New York: Garland, 1983. Thorough, covering all aspects of politics, women's rights, feminist movements, specific topics such as economics.

PETCHESKY, ROSALIND POLLACK. *Abortion and Woman's Choice: The State, Sexuality, and Reproductive Freedom*. New York: Longman, 1983. Review of legal, moral, and political battles surrounding abortion; places the practice and control of abortion in historical and ideological contexts.

SAPIRO, VIRGINIA. *The Political Integration of Women: Roles, Socialization, and Politics*. Urbana: University of Illinois Press, 1983. An analysis of the joint effects of marriage, motherhood, homemaking, and gender ideology on the political behavior of women who came of age during the late 1960s.

SEALANDER, JUDITH. *As Minority Becomes Majority: Federal Reaction to the Phenomenon of Women in the Work Force, 1920–1963*. Wesport, Conn.: Greenwood Press, 1983. Government policy toward women workers, especially as affected by wartime.

SMEAL, ELEANOR. *Why and How Women Will Elect the Next President*. New York: Harper & Row, 1984. Smeal, former president of NOW, offers analyses similar to Abzug's (above) with extensive practical information on political action committees and running for elective office.

TINKER, IRENE, ed. *Women in Washington: Advocates for Public Policy*. Beverly Hills, Calif.: Sage Publications, 1983. General policies and case studies as in Boneparth, and Diamond and Gelb, but outstanding for presenting articles by noted long-time women leaders Marguerite Rawalt, Catherine East, Arvonne Fraser, and Esther Peterson, and activist experts such as Jane Roberts Chapman, Marcia Greenberger, and Nancy Russo.

TONG, ROSEMARIE. *Women, Sex, and the Law*. Totowa, N.J.: Rowman & Allanheld, 1983.

WEISBERG, D. KELLY, ed. *Women and the Law: A Social Historical Perspective*. Cambridge, Mass.: Schenkman, 1982. Scholarly essays on the history and sociology of women's situation under criminal, property, and family law.

Resources

Organizations

Center for the American Woman and Politics, Eagleton Institute of Politics, Rutgers University, New Brunswick, NJ 08901. Coordinates current research, maintains extensive files of data, produces reports; excellent source.

League of Women Voters of the United States, 1730 M St. NW, Washington, DC 20036. Nonpartisan activist and educational organization with a long history of involvement with women and politics.

National Center on Women and Family Law, 799 Broadway, Room 402, New York, NY 10003. Provides a number of reports and information packets to assist attorneys and activists in reforming child custody laws, battered women's laws, and the like.

National Conference of Black Lawyers, Section on Women's Rights, 126 W. 119th St., New York, NY 10026. First organized in 1983, this section sponsors conferences for lawyers and community organizers, serves as advocate on relevant issues, monitors the legal profession, and so on.

National Organization for Women, 425 13th St. NW, Washington, DC 20004. The *National NOW Times* is one of the single best sources for tracking women's issues at the national level and also reports on the activities of NOW chapters around the country. NOW maintains a separate Legal Defense and Education Fund, 132 W. 43d St., New York, NY 10036.

National Women's Education Fund, 1410 Que St. NW, Washington, DC 20009. Devoted to aiding women to become effective candidates for political office; sponsors seminars, writes training materials.

National Women's Political Caucus, 1411 K St. NW, Washington, DC 20005. Works with politicians and activists from both major parties; undertakes fund raising; serves in coalitions to promote women's appointment to government posts and to encourage women to register to vote.

Women's Campaign Fund, 1725 Eye St. NW, Washington, DC 20006. Supports political campaigns of women in both parties.

Women's Equity Action League, 805 15th St. NW, Washington, DC 20005. *WEAL Washington Report* and *WEAL Informed* (a fast legislative alert service) provide quick yet comprehensive details on the status of legislation and judicial action related to women's economic issues, education rights, pensions and Social Security, women in the military. Known for good analyses of the impact of budget cuts, WEAL is one of the most persistent and effective lobbyists for women's issues.

Women's Legal Defense Fund, 2000 P St. NW, Washington, DC 20036. Helps women to challenge discriminatory laws, provides educational materials and manuals for both consumers and lawyers on topics such as name changes, divorce, pregnancy rights, child custody, pay equity.

Women's Research and Education Institute, 204 Fourth St. SE, Washington, DC 20003. Research arm of the Congressional Caucus for Women's Issues, WREI monitors ongoing research in all areas of policy relating to women, commissions special reports, sponsors briefings, provides data and analyses to legislators.

Journals

Law and Inequality: A Journal of Theory and Practice. Minneapolis, Minn.: University of Minnesota Law School. Considers a wide range of issues of jurisprudence and social policy from a gender perspective, and from those of race, ethnicity, and class.

Women & Politics: A Quarterly Journal of Research and Policy Studies. New York: Haworth Press. Interdisciplinary approach, with articles from historical, sociological, economic, and legal angles.

Women and the Law Report. Washington, D.C.: published by Newsletter Services, Inc., under the direction of Goldfarb, Singer & Austern. Newsletter highlighting judicial, legislative, and administrative developments in abortion, child care, domestic violence, employment, ERA, health, and so on.

Pyschology

Sarah Barbara Watstein

"Woman. I understand the word itself, in
that sense, has gone out of the
language. Where we talk of woman . . .
you talk of women, and all the difference
lies therein."

Isak Dinesen, "The Old Chevalier," in Seven Gothic Tales (1934).

By any conventional standard, the amount of literature on the psychology of women published in 1983 was massive. The degree of scholarly and public interest in the area has been, and remains, high. Examination of the recent literature on the topic reveals a number of themes weaving through the year, six of which are pursued in this review. These include women's identity, women's bonds and bonding, the profession and practice of psychology, therapy and counseling issues, feminist critiques of existing theory and research, and teaching the psychology of women.

Women's Identity

Gender and Sex Roles and Sex-Related Differences

The ads for Sydney Pollack's *Tootsie* read: "What do you get when you cross a hopelessly straight, starving actor with a dynamic red-sequined dress?" "America's hottest new actress!" is the answer, and indeed, if the breakaway success of this movie is any evidence, interest in understanding what it is like to be a woman, what it means to be masculine or feminine has reached a new height. As Teri Garr, the female lead surmises, "I guess you can't say enough about role reversal . . . everybody seems to be interested in it" (Dworkin 1983).

An appreciation and understanding of women's identity involves awareness of gender roles; the acquisition and development of sex roles and sex-role orientation (masculinity, femininity, and androgyny); and the effects of sex-related differences on expectancy, aspiration and performance, ability and activity, self-esteem and self-confidence. A plethora of concepts, with varied and sometimes vague meanings, surround the issue of gender role. An overview of many of these concepts, and of the varied directions for research, is contained in the work *Sex Role Research* (Richardson and Wirtenberg 1983). The essays integrate historical and cultural perspectives on the development of sex roles with studies of the methodological issues apparent in this field.

Sherif (1982) offers a valuable contribution toward understanding the psychology of women in a social context by clarifying what she determines are "needed concepts" in the study of gender identity: self-system and reference persons, groups and categories, social power, status, and role relationship. By thus reducing the number of concepts surrounding the issue of gender roles, Sherif makes an important beginning toward our understanding of women. Cahill (1983) outlines a theoretical framework of sex-role development which he calls social interactionism. Within this framework, the most appropriate strategy for studying issues of gender development is observation of naturally occurring interactions. Though a departure from previous strategies, which hinged on constructed tests and artificial interactional situations, it integrates the insights of existing theories of sex-role development, such as social learning, into a coherent theoretical framework that stresses the centrality of social experience to the gender development process. It is useful in understanding the continuous process of gender development over the entire life span.

As the acquisition and development of sex roles were assessed and reassessed in 1983, so too the acquisition of sex-role attitudes were systematically studied. Explorations of contemporary women's perception of parenthood (Knaub, Eversoll, and Voss 1983; Hare-Mustin, Bennett, and Broderick 1983) raised questions concerning what is or is not a desirable adult role, and what accounts for the components of these complex attitudes. Knaub's findings included: (1) the expectation that parenthood will be among the subjects' adult roles, but will be delayed; (2) a rejection of the idea that motherhood is a prerequisite to women's happiness and fulfillment; (3) a confused perception of the effect of parenthood on men's lives; and (4) a suggestion that although the majority of women indicate that they will parent, most felt inadequately prepared for this role. Hare-Mustin examined images of motherhood as the core component of gender-role definition, thereby contributing to our knowledge of the components of the attitude toward motherhood and how it varies with different groups.

Sex-role attitude structure and change were also examined by Dworkin and Dworkin (1983), whose study demonstrated that sex-role attitude structure and change are affected by gender conflict. Specifically, the authors noted that initially multidimensional sex-role attitude structures, change, coalesce, or become more unified in reaction to gender conflict, and that sex-role attitudes tend to become more modern or liberal in reaction to such conflict. The Dworkins' concern with preconditions for the emergence of unified sex-role attitudes is an important departure from the sex-role literature in both sociology and psychology with its emphasis on whether sex-role attitudes are multidimensional or unidimensional.

Some interesting and tentative hypotheses about the processes leading to the acquisition of sex roles, gender identity, and sexual orientation are provided by Fleishman (1983a, 1983b). Challenging existing theories, Fleishman claims that sexual orientation is acquired during a sensitive period from birth to three years through physical interaction with significant others. By isolating physical contact as the factor contributing to sexual orientation and distinguishing it from processes leading to the establishment of gender identity and the acquisition of sex roles, this hypothesis accounts for the existence of male and female homosexuals who are stereotypically masculine and feminine, respectively. It also accounts for the development of sexual orientation of infants raised in single-parent families, and for the finding that many individuals have experienced sexual attraction to the same or opposite sex long before puberty or before engaging in actual sexual acts (Whitam 1977). A longitudinal study of parent-infant physical and social interaction as it bears on the child's eventual sexual orientation will provide empirical evidence for Fleishman's hypothesis.

Any discussion of the acquisition of sex-role identity and orientation involves consideration of masculinity, femininity, and androgyny. Since it was touted in 1973 as a construct whose time had come (Heilbrun 1973), the androgyny concept has appealed to psychologists, historians, scholars of literature, proselytized researchers, and clinicians. The concept has a checkered career and even Sandra Bem, the progenitor of psychological androgyny, appears to have shifted her focus to sex typing in her recently formulated gender schema theory (1981).

A study by Lubinski, Tellegen, and Butcher (1983) was designed to investigate the implications for mental health of masculinity and femininity and to illumine further Bem's contention (1974) that androgynous individuals are mentally healthier than sex-typed individuals. Results provided only partial support for masculinity and femininity as measures of psychological well-being and challenged Bem's theory (1974, 1979a) that androgyny epitomizes psychological health. The most relevant and provocative findings are the strong relation of positively valued masculinity to indicators of psychological well-being and the fact that the strength of the relation is the same in men and women. A finding of equal interest is the fact that

masculinity and femininity do not temper or mitigate one another to enhance an individual's overall subjective well-being.

Pursuing the implications of Bem's earlier theorizing relevant to androgyny (1976, 1979b), Pyke and Graham (1983) attempt to refine and integrate gender schema and androgyny theory. The authors note that the integration of the two appears problematic, in that the relationship between
"being sex-typed" and the "process of sex-typing" requires clarification and
elaboration, as does the issue of sex-typing and self-esteem.

Of special interest is the political perspective provided by the authors.
Pyke and Graham note that, from its inception in psychology, androgyny
has been a "political issue characterized by polemics." They question
whether it is possible to disassociate the political/ideological overtones from
the scientific investigation of androgyny and hypothesize that the value
judgments that permeate this literature have contributed to the very undo-
ing of the construct.

The hypothesis derived from Bem's work that androgynous and sex-
typed individuals are differentiated by the presence or absence of beliefs in
"gender polarity" was called into question by others. McPherson and Spetrino (1983) found that women are less likely than men to use implicit personality schema based on traditional sex stereotypes. This lends support to
the argument that being classified as either androgynous or sex-typed does
not necessarily mean the same thing for women and men (e.g., Jones, Chernovits, and Hanssen 1978), and that sex differences are perhaps more important than androgyny researchers have realized.

Another study that challenges psychological androgyny theory looked
at the relationship between psychological androgyny and interpersonal and
situational adaptability (Lee and Scheurer 1983). The study supported the
view that, insofar as instrumental or masculine personality characteristics
are culturally valued, it is advantageous for women and men to possess the
positive qualities typically termed masculine. The findings question to
what extent psychological androgyny is a feminist view of the ideal, and
suggest that androgyny may be defined in a way congenial to the values of
researchers who are sensitive to the changing roles of women and men.

Also, several major steps for research in the psychological characteristics of bisexual, heterosexual, and homosexual women were made through
the year. These include the validation of a psychometric instrument intended to measure masculine gender identity in females (Blanchard and
Freund 1983), the measurement of masculinity, femininity, body cathexis,
and self-esteem among bisexual, heterosexual, and homosexual women
(LaTorre and Wendenburg 1983), and an assessment of both male and female homosexual stereotypes (Taylor 1983). Finally, and also related to sex-
role identity, the effect of sex-related differences on expectancy, attribution
and achievement, performance and aspiration, and self-esteem received
considerable attention in the past year.

The hypothesis that sex differences in perceptions of achievement are a function of stereotypical sex-role orientation was explored (Erkut 1983). Erkut's findings are consistent with currently popular models of women's achievement: women's lower expectancy for success and their tendency to be less likely than men to attribute their performance to ability. What is equally interesting is his observation that it appears that a feminine sex-role orientation is the critical variable vis-à-vis expectancy, attribution, and achievement.

Danziger examines the factors affecting the educational and occupational aspirations of male and female high school students, and notes that perceived opportunities affect aspirations (Danziger 1983). Other research (Monahan 1983) indicates that sex differences exist in high school students along the dimensions of debilitation in performance and aspiration for future performance, depending on different degrees of evaluative stress and past performance.

Related to performance, the relation between sex-related differences and spatial ability was noted (Newcombe, Bandura, and Taylor 1983). Their research involved development of a scale to measure the spatial experience of adolescents and adults. Their data show that, indeed, more spatial activities tend to be masculine rather than feminine sex-typed. Future research on performance will no doubt explore whether sex differences in spatial activity coincide with the augmentation of sex differences in spatial ability: does activity affect ability, as required by an experiential account of sex differences in spatial ability, or does ability affect activity?

Studies of the relationship between psychological growth and well-being and sex-role type continue to flourish. A review of these studies indicates that the conceptualization and measurement of the construct of self-esteem is as problematic as attempts to define the complex construct of sex role. Significant emerging trends include attempts to (1) expand the study of relationships between sex-role type and self-esteem into the area of personal values (Dorgan, Goebel, and House 1983); (2) assess the suggestions that women display lower self-confidence than men in almost all achievement settings (Lenney, Gold, and Browning 1983); (3) test the adequacy of models that have guided research on the relation between sex-role orientation and psychological well-being (Whitley 1983); and (4) investigate the effect of women's studies courses on both self-esteem and career goals (Zuckerman 1983), and on assertiveness, self-actualization, and locus of control (McVicar and Herman 1983).

Sexuality

Dr. Ruth Westheimer's call-in radio program "Sexually Speaking" on WYNY, *Psychology Today*'s regular feature, "The Sexes: Crosstalk," and the Scholar and Feminist IX Conference, "Towards the Politics of Sexuality," held at Barnard College in 1982 are all evidence of a growing interest in recent years in the examination of women's relationships to sexuality. The construction of all sexualities and a quest to understand sexuality as a political and personal goal emerged as the focus of considerable discussion and writing in 1983.

One of the most profound and profoundly important contributions in this area is *Powers of Desire: The Politics of Sexuality* (Snitow, Stansell, and Thompson 1983). The essays in this anthology raise an array of new issues and questions. How and why does a culture determine what it considers to be sexual? What are the consequences of the fact that in our era people can experience basic shifts in sexual mores within one lifetime? Is sexual variety evidence of the social malleability of sexuality? How can we understand the processes by which movements of sexual "freedom" have so often ended by constricting homosexuality, female sexuality, and sexual excitement?

Reading through the essays, one becomes conscious of the trend to categorize sexualities. How have these definitions of sexuality and sexual community served people? What has it cost them? What contradictions arise inside communities defined by sexual practice? What forces hold the institution of heterosexuality in place, and how deep and enduring are women's ties to it? One also becomes aware of assumptions about the erotic expression of power and about the relation of erotic roles to gender, affirming the basic feminist insight that sex is a political issue.

The emergence of a lesbian-feminist s/m movement within the tradition of women's and gay liberation has become the locus for this insight. The rise of s/m among lesbians is chronicled in *Coming to Power: Writing and Graphics on Lesbian S/M* (Samois 1982), an anthology of erotica, theory, and personal testimony. It is countered by *Against Sadomasochism* (Linden, Russell, and Leigh 1982), which contributes a radical feminist perspective to the debate (this subject is treated more fully in the chapter on lesbians). A more conventional approach to sexuality is demonstrated by British feminist Sheila Kitzinger in *Woman's Experience of Sex* (1983). She reasserts the view that sexual liberation has not necessarily meant women's liberation, but slips into a somewhat biologically determinist stereotype with her notion that women's sexuality is based on a greater need for "love," "feeling," and erotic culmination in the experience of birth. Her book also examines such topics as sexual harassment, homosexuality, and grieving.

Educators have long struggled with the problem of teaching about sexuality at the secondary and undergraduate levels. *Changing Boundaries* (Allgeier and McCormick 1983) is a very readable text, aimed at both men and women, which presents psychological and sociological discussions of the development of sexuality and sex roles. Informed by recent feminist work, chapters examine the impact of sexuality on our lives through such topics as family violence, sexual harassment, lesbian/gay life-styles, rape, and pornography.

Women's Bonds and Bonding

We live in an age hungry for information about women's relationships to one another and to men. Indeed, much of what might be loosely classified as "must reads," "must sees," or "most talked abouts" in 1983 concerned women's relationships to one another, specifically in their roles as mothers and daughters, friends and sisters.

Mothers and Daughters

Returning to the site of women's first experiences, the family, and specifically, to women's positions as daughters in the family, Gilbert and Webster (1982) hypothesize that it is the experience and the institution of daughterhood that prepares women to know themselves as women and as victims. Their examination and analysis of the process that socializes women to accept victimization is reported in *Bound by Love: The Sweet Trap of Daughterhood*. Here they argue that this process begins at birth and continues through adulthood and that, although intentional, it is not necessarily conscious and functions to reproduce the two-gender system in which men are powerful and women are powerless.

One of the most deeply probing examinations of the mother-daughter relationship is Marsha Norman's play, *'night, Mother*, which won the 1983 Pulitzer Prize for drama. The play makes disturbing statements about responsibility and courage, as it looks at a daughter's determination to hold on to the recently gained control of her mind and body even to the point of suicide. It is Norman's understanding of her characters that the relationship between mother and daughter is crucial and predictive of how the daughter will experience herself, not only in relation to her mother, but in relation to the world. Norman suggests that mothers and daughters have been betrayed by a false promise. Mothers believe they were promised some reward for their labors, and daughters want something, but not necessarily the something that mothers can give. *'night, Mother* gives voice to the anger over these false promises, attesting to the pain of the mother-daughter relationship as it is best understood in the context of a love affair, where the daughter is the irreplaceable loved one.

The mother-daughter knot is also examined in James L. Brock's *Terms of Endearment*, a film in which a mother focuses on struggling to be "good" as she participates in the successive treacheries of her daughter coming of age, marrying, becoming a mother, and dying. As in *'night, Mother*, the mother-daughter relationship is illumined as one of the most complicated, most ambivalent, and most fascinating relationships of all.

Friendship and Sisterhood

The theme of friendship in women's lives is explored in Diane Kurys's film, *Entre Nous*. Kurys focuses on two women who ache to escape from their bourgeois married life. The friends want to open a shop, drive cars, go to Paris. Although they were women loving men, they ultimately leave their husbands because of each other's influence, and we are left with the sense of their friendship as something very strong in their lives.

The dual themes of friendship and sisterhood, both literal and spiritual, are used to explore the divided side of modern Germany and the dark side of feminism in Margarethe von Trotta's *Heller Wahn*, or *Sheer Madness*. Like *Entre Nous*, this film focuses on the developing friendship between two women and the kind of transference that occurs that causes the fragile balance of sexual power in their lives to shift and shatter. Von Trotta provokes us to ask questions. Have friends the right to imply that other women's lives are wrong, half-lived? Is it possible to expect to combine commitment to self and career with an equal relationship? Or is the "we" of marriage, as it has evolved through the years, in some profound way a contradiction of the "I" of self-realization?

John Sayles's *Lianna* also focuses on several aspects of women's friendships, including the little-noted but crucial aspect of coming out, the lesbian's relationships with her straight women friends, women's tendencies to loneliness and friendships, and men's inability to have women friends because such a relationship may imply they have been turned down sexually.

The concept of sisterhood has been an important unifying force in the contemporary women's movement. By stressing the economic, ideological, and experiential similarities among women, this concept has been an important influence in the study of the psychology of women. Dill (1983) offers a critique of sisterhood as a binding force for all women, and an examination of the limitations of the concept for both theory and practice when applied to women who are neither white nor middle class. Dill recognizes and accepts the objective differences among women (race and class) and argues for allowing these differences to enrich women's political and social action rather than divide it. The psychological relevance of this discussion cannot be ignored: it is through first seeking to understand struggles that are not particularly shaped by one's own immediate personal priorities that we will begin to understand the psychology—the needs and priorities—of all women.

Partners

Various kinds of couple configuration—heterosexual, gay male, and lesbian cohabiters—are described in Blumstein and Schwartz's sociological study *American Couples: Money, Work, Sex* (1983). The findings of this exhaustive study help women in all kinds of couple configurations to identify roles and to develop an understanding of how to make gender work for the possibility of a lifetime relationship. Two questions raised by the study that cannot be ignored by women in their roles at partners are (1) how do gender requirements set the stage for how individuals will interact as a couple and (2) what is there about men's and women's roles that enhances relationships and what is there about these roles that undermines them?

It is interesting that the first systematic, longitudinal look at the male couple was also published in 1983. David McWhirter and Andrew Mattison's *The Male Couple: How Relationships Develop* serves as a tentative formulation, derived from 156 couples, of the developmental stages through which male couple relationships move, and clearly has relevance for heterosexual couples and lesbian cohabiters. McWhirter and Mattison contend that "gays balance a relationship better"; because of this, it can be reasoned, partners in a heterosexual configuration, and presumably lesbian cohabiters, can learn from gays how to live by societal gender rules—and how to do it well.

The Profession and Practice of Psychology

The most important development in the profession and practice of psychology with regard to women is the increasing visibility and growing status of women in the profession. In the past forty years, psychology has moved from a minor academic discipline to an accepted science and a firmly established profession. Psychology has done well—and so, in the main, have its women. That women are now beginning to flex their muscles and finally to obtain power within psychology is evident by (1) their representation, since the postwar period, in high-status activities (i.e., in experimental psychology and the field of psychometrics); (2) the fact that they have successfully overcome the prejudicial image of them as merely service-oriented do-gooders; (3) their acceptance as staff members; (4) the emergence of a number of organizations for female psychologists; and (5) their need to separate and to develop institutions within the discipline designed to combat the deeply entrenched "old boy" system that continues to plague psychology.

The accomplishments of women psychologists are well documented in two recent works (O'Connell and Russo 1983; Stevens and Gardner 1982) that are the first to give a broad context to the work of these women and that will stand as essential biographical and bibliographical sources.

In addition, the fact that women in psychology today have something close to equal status for the first time in history is reflected in the existence of a few psychological journals specifically concerned with issues and questions related to the psychology of women.

Required reading in this latter category includes *Psychology of Women Quarterly*, which began in 1976, and *Women & Therapy*, which began in 1982. A welcome contribution to the understanding of the psychology of women and to the ongoing work for social change is *Women & Therapy*'s volume 2, numbers 2–3, entitled "Women Changing Therapy: New Assessments, Values & Strategies in Feminist Therapy." Content highlights include assessments of conflict, women and anger in psychotherapy, women and weakness, lowering the barriers between women, experiences in male-dominated professions, and the consequences of abortion legislation. Also included are reviews of change and creativity at mid-life and discussions of stress and mental health issues for Hispanic women, the self-reliant strength of black women, and the lesbian perspective. Finally, the volume is concerned with new strategies in feminist therapy around the issue of sexual bias in relationship counseling, problems in long-term marriages, the role of politics in feminist counseling, women in interracial relationships, therapists coping with sexual assault, the reality of incest, and lesbian mothers' custody fears.

That America is psychology oriented and that women are today among the most productive, most influential, and most eminent contributors to the field of psychology are partial clues to the success of one of the best sellers of 1983, *August* (Rossner 1983). The story concerns attachments and one woman's experience of psychoanalysis over five years. It is about women's experience of intimacy—what happens when love turns to hate or when we are abandoned. It is about women's experience of their self-image and the components of their well-being. It is, finally, about women and connectedness, and their particular need to find the past's place in the present and thereby make it useful. *August* is a compelling novel. As we become intensely absorbed in the characters' separate and connected lives, we learn much about them and about the emerging identity and voice of women in psychology.

Therapy and Counseling Issues

Depression, anger, eating disorders, the disrepair of the family, child and wife abuse, and incest surfaced as some of the major issues therapists and counselors have confronted in their work with women.

Depression and depressive symptomatology in women continue to be a focus of research and of *New Yorker* cartoons.

In the past year, trends in research interest are noted in work on psychosocial correlates of depressive symptomatology in adult women (Warren and McEachren 1983), postpartum adjustment (Cutrona 1983; Livingood, Daen, and Smith 1983), premenstrual syndrome (Eagan 1983), and women's experience of stress (Davis 1983). The damaging aspects of women's traditional sphere, the home, are revealed by studies on agoraphobia (Seidenberg and DeCrow 1983) and housewives' depression (M. Morgan 1983). This interest in depression is reflected in the popularity of several notable films and plays, including *Frances*, *Sophie's Choice*, and *'night, Mother*, as well as the novel *August*.

In her important book on anger, Tavris (1983) asks not merely "Why do people become angry?" but more significantly, why they do *not* become angry. She explores our capacity and need to behave as if the world were just and the defenses we construct against admitting the injustices experienced throughout our lives. These defenses include denigrating the victim, denying the evidence, or reinterpreting the event entirely. The book has special significance for women: as the traditionally more powerless sex, they are more likely to be the victims of injustice than men. Tavris's work stands against the psychologically bankrupt and politically self-defeating arguments concerning women and anger. She homes in on the line between blame and responsibility, discriminating between the sources of anger that we can do something about and those we cannot address.

Concern with chaotic eating behavior in contemporary American life remains high. Women's cultural obsession with weight has blurred and, in many cases, erased the line between simple eating and having an eating disorder—a distorted pattern of thinking about and behaving around food. Psychiatrists tell us that the range of eating behaviors and attitudes form an eating arc. This arc consists of people with anorexia nervosa, bulimics, chronic dieters, occasional dieters, and finally, normal eaters who oppose the anorexics at the other end of the arc. In addition to describing disorders, more recent literature (Neuman and Halverson 1983) has sought to answer such questions as how counselors and therapists get those who need help to seek it out, what counselors and therapists do when those who need help request it, and what can be done that is preventive in nature. It is likely that increasing attention will be paid to the front-line professionals who work with those with eating disorders in the coming years.

The frazzling of love and family connections is another ongoing national issue. Few would deny that the family as we know it is in a state of change. *The Hearts of Men: American Dreams and the Flight from Commitment* (Ehrenreich 1983) challenges observers who attribute the "demise" of the family to economic changes that sent women into the work place in the past forty years, and argues that men have played a central role in this process. The nuclear family system, unstable to begin with, started coming unstuck before this wave of feminism, when the breadwinner ethic and the ideology supporting it "collapsed as a persuasive set of expectations." This witty and intelligent book says something that has rarely been said and that has profound implications for the psychology of women: men have not acted in response to feminism, but, rather, they have as always done what they wanted to do.

Researchers and clinicians in different fields are increasingly concerned about family violence, specifically both with wife and child abuse and incest. In a review of the literature on family violence, Breines and Gordon (1983) point to the differences among the three types. Issuing from a feminist perspective (seeing family violence as produced within a gendered society in which male power dominates), this study makes two arguments relevant to all three types of family violence: (1) to be accurately viewed, violence must be placed in an entire social context, and (2) with the family as the locus of struggle and support, gender and age structuring is a source of power differences and personal tensions. *I Never Told Anyone* (Bass and Thornton 1983) brings together painful personal accounts by survivors of child sexual abuse. With its introductory analysis, bibliography, and lists of treatment centers, it will be useful as a tool for education and counseling.

The relationship between sex-role socialization and the mental health of women continues to be explored. Several essays in *The Second X and Women's Health* (Fooden 1983) contribute to our understanding of the many factors in this relationship as do those included in *The Stereotyping of Women* (Franks and Rothblum 1983), both wide-ranging works based on conference papers. Feminists in psychology and psychiatry are still pushing for less sexist approaches to treatment, as demonstrated by Miriam Greenspan's proposals and critiques in *A New Approach to Women and Therapy* (1983).

Feminist Critiques

Key feminist critiques of the traditional psychological view of female development have been made by Gilligan, Eichenbaum and Orbach, and Bassin. Also of significance this year were studies by Sayers and by Morgan, each of which explored the question "is the personal political?"

In a Different Voice (Gilligan 1982) is one of the most influential feminist critiques of psychology written to date, so much so, indeed, that the very name *Gilligan* has become a buzzword in both academic and feminist circles. Gilligan argues that psychology has persistently and systematically misunderstood women—their motives, their moral commitments, the course of their psychological growth, and their special view of what is important in life. In an attempt to correct such misinterpretations and to refocus psychology's view of female personality several complex questions are asked. If male development is mainly a matter of increasing separation from others to achieve autonomy and independence, does that mean that women have failed to grow into mature adults if their development involves a continuous struggle to balance their responsibilities to others with their commitment to themselves? If men see morality chiefly as a matter of impartial justice, are women less moral if they see morality more as a matter of care? If men are willing to sacrifice relationships with others in pursuit of achievement, are women willing to sacrifice achievements to preserve relationships?

Contrary to the belief that when women fail to develop in the way men do, something must be wrong with women, the author concludes that it is more likely the case that something must be wrong with psychological theory. Predicated on the finding that men in this culture tend to see the world in terms of their autonomy (and are overthreatened by intimacy), whereas women tend to see the world in terms of connectedness (and are overthreatened by isolation), her book has created a new appreciation for a previously uncataloged female sensibility as well as possibilities for new understanding between the genders. In an article in *Ms.* heralding Gilligan as Woman of the Year (1983), Lindsay Van Gelder comments, "Post-Gilligan, it will be much harder for researchers to equate 'human' with male and to see female experience as simply an aberrant substratum" (Van Gelder 1984). Gilligan's theories "speak about the differential access of the genders to certain kinds of understanding, not the superiority of one gender over the other." Without blaming men, she calls on women to find their own different voices and use them. She provides a vocabulary and context for women and men to envision new worlds: when Gilligan is first read it is difficult to stifle an "aha!"

What Do Women Want (Eichenbaum and Orbach 1983) is another book that was written to raise questions, and it also contributes to the remapping of the whole domain of human development. Focusing on the thread of dependency that runs through all relationships, Eichenbaum and Orbach explode the myth of dependency and propose a radically new way to view both women's and men's emotional dependency. Arguing that dependency is a basic human need and that achieving autonomy and independence rests on the gratification of this need, the authors distinguish between economic and emotional dependency relationships. They hypothesize that women are fearful of independence and success because, while they have traditionally been dependent economically, they have been raised to be depended upon emotionally. The authors investigate the way the patriarchal system shapes our sense of gender, influences the sex-role personalities and behaviors that women and men develop in order to be at home in the world, and consequently shapes our emotional lives in damaging ways.

Specifically, they confront the forbidden feelings concerning women and dependency, the great taboo of men's dependency, dependency dynamics in couples, sex and dependency, the effect of pregnancy on the dependency dynamic, and friendship between women, attempting to answer the question, "what do women want?" Their description of the way dependency operates in women's friendships and intimate relationships contributes to a new understanding of the dependency needs women experience.

The fact that the traditional psychoanalytic view of female development is incomplete has been of increasing concern among the feminist revisionists within the psychoanalytic framework. An example of an attempt to loosen the hold that existing psychoanalytic theory has on clinical observation is Bassin's paper on women's images of inner space (Bassin 1982). Focusing on women's interiority, not their inferiority, she advocates a psychoanalytic interpretive environment that will allow and encourage the development of what is biologically present and active in women, rather than looking exclusively at what is missing. It is suggested that the potential for increased female development is latent under the limited interpretive categories for women's affective/cognitive experiences such as castration anxiety and penis envy. A proactive manifestation of women's psychobiological development is advocated, one that is sensitive to images of inner space in female analysands' productions and that contains language categories for the feminine experiences that draw on women's own composition for their foundation.

The primacy of personal experience, including "feelings," and an understanding of the political and social structure of personal experience and feelings form the basis of feminist praxis. The question "is the personal political?" lies at the heart of challenges to the assumptions underlying this principle. Of special note, as concerns psychoanalysis and feminism, are two direct challenges to this ideological separation of public and private raised during the year under review (Sayers 1983; Morgan 1983).

Sayers examines two psychoanalytically based accounts of sexual divisions in society—those of Juliet Mitchell and Nancy Chodorow. She argues that a major source of the appeal of these accounts is the links they make between the personal and the political. At the same time, she notes that the very priority these accounts give to personal experience results in their implying that existing sexual divisions are constant and immutable. Freud's account of psychology is also considered, and a contrast is made between his attention to our ignorance about, and the contradictions that exist within, personal experience and consciousness and the lack of such attention in Mitchell's account on patriarchy and Chodorow's on mothering. In this, Freud's work serves to underline the point Sayers makes, that "personal consciousness is not the firm foundation that we have sometimes taken it to be in developing the theory and practice of feminism."

Morgan further demonstrates the tenacity of the gender-biased assumptions and frameworks of the dominant social scientific tradition. She challenges theories that dichotomize forms of experience: thought and feeling, objectivity and subjectivity, rationality and emotion. Her aim is toward the construction of a theoretical framework that recognizes the centrality of feelings in human experience and that seeks to understand the articulation of thought, feeling, and action in political and social life.

Teaching the Psychology of Women

A crucial debate is underway that will shape the development of women's studies throughout and beyond the 1980s: is women's studies a discipline in its own right, inclusive of and for all women, or shall feminist scholarship be incorporated into the disciplines and mainstreamed into curricula across disciplines? The assumptions and differences between these two approaches—autonomy versus integration—the points where their arguments meet, and the strategies of each are of interest to scholars in the traditional disciplines and those in women's studies.

Of interest here is the fact that this debate has been continued at the discipline level in psychology. Increasing research, teaching, and interest in the psychology of women have established that this area is supported by a separate body of knowledge and literature. Scholars have recently begun to debate whether the psychology of women should be developed as a discipline in its own right or whether courses in this area should be mainstreamed into psychology curricula. The fall 1982 issue of *Psychology of Women Quarterly* was devoted to the teaching of the psychology of women. Guest editor Marilyn Johnson asked, "Is there any longer a need for psychology of women courses or should we focus on courses in sex differences? Should we work to put ourselves out of a job by integrating content from psychology of women into most of our courses?" The issue examined advocacy versus scholarship in the psychology of women and analyzed the faculty and courses of this emerging field as well as the clash of values between the traditional academic setting and the revolutionary, nontraditional curriculum area. It also considered other factors unique to the teaching of psychology of women, such as the emotional effect of the content on students, the role of the teacher vis-à-vis the students, the impact of feminism on education, and pedagogic principles essential for use in teaching the psychology of women.

This move toward some theoretical exploration of issues in teaching the psychology of women is continued in "Mainstreaming the Psychology of Women into the Core Curriculum" (Freedman, Golub, and Krauss 1982). The theme of this essay is that women's courses have served as a catalyst, and the content should now be phased into traditional courses. The authors suggest that much of the material relating to women, as well as new approaches to traditional topics, belong to the core curriculum which is the only way the majority of students may be reached. They conclude with the following emphasis: "A psychology for women and men must involve a coherent body of knowledge that falls within the mainstream of psychology, with potential application of this knowledge to improve people's lives."

This sort of discussion and the continuing research, teaching, and interest in the psychology of women attest to the fact that the jury is still out in regard to the question of autonomy versus integration. Nonetheless, the traditional approach is being challenged. The assumptions and stereotypes comprising the androcentric bias that has characterized much of the history of psychology are being questioned, and basic theoretical issues are being viewed from a new perspective.

References

ALLGEIER, E.R., and N.B. McCORMICK. 1983. *Changing boundaries: Gender roles and sexual behavior.* Palo Alto, Calif.: Mayfield Publishing Co.

BASS, E., and L. THORNTON, eds. 1983. *I never told anyone: Writings by women survivors of child sexual abuse.* New York: Harper & Row.

BASSIN, D. 1982. Woman's images of inner space: Data towards expanded interpretive categories. *International Review of Psycho-Analysis* 9:191–203.

BAUCOM, D.H. 1983. Sex role identity and the decision to regain control among women: A learned helplessness investigation. *Journal of Personality & Social Psychology* 44, no. 2:334–53.

BEM, S.L. 1974. The measurement of psychological androgyny. *Journal of Consulting and Clinical Psychology* 42:155–62.

──────. 1976. Probing the promise of androgyny. In *Beyond sex-role stereotypes*, edited by A.G. Kaplan and J.R. Bean, 48–62. Boston: Little, Brown.

──────. 1979a. Beyond androgyny: Some presumptuous prescriptions for a liberated sexual identity. In *Psychology of women: Issues in psychology*, edited by J. Sherman and F. Denmark. New York: Psychological Dimensions.

──────. 1979b. Theory and measurement of androgyny: A reply to the Pedhauzer-Tetenbaum and Locksley-Colten critiques. *Journal of Personality and Social Psychology* 37:1047–54.

──────. 1981. Gender schema theory: A cognitive account of sex-typing. *Psychological Review* 66, no. 88:354–64.

BERMAN, E.M., and H.I. LIEF. 1975. Marital intimacy from a psychiatric perspective: An overview. *American Journal of Psychiatry* 132:583–92.

BILLINGHAM, K.A. 1982. Building a course on psychology of women: Method and resources. *Psychology of Women Quarterly* 7, no. 1:32–44.

BLANCHARD, R., and K. FREUND. 1983. Measuring masculine gender identity in females. *Journal of Consulting and Clinical Psychology* 51, no. 2:205–14.

BLUMSTEIN, P., and P. SCHWARTZ. 1983. *American couples.* New York: William Morrow & Co.

BORGES, M.A., J.R. LEVINE, and P.A. NAYLOR. 1982. Self-ratings and projected ratings of sex role attitude. *Psychology of Women Quarterly* 6, no. 4:406–13.

BREINES, W., and L. GORDON. 1983. The new scholarship on family violence. *Signs* 8, no. 3:490–531.

CAHILL, S.E. 1983. Reexamining the acquisition of sex roles: A social interactionist approach. *Sex Roles* 9, no. 1:1–15.

CARMEN, E., and F. DRIVER. 1982. Teaching women's studies: Values in conflict. *Psychology of Women Quarterly* 7, no. 1:81–95.

CUTRONA, C.E. 1983. Causal attributions and prenatal depression. *Journal of Abnormal Psychology* 92, no. 2:161–72.

DANZIGER, N. 1983. Sex-related differences in the aspirations of high school students. *Sex Roles* 9, no. 6:638–95.

DAVIS, D.L. 1983. Woman the worrier: Confronting feminist and biomedical archetypes of stress. *Women's Studies* 10, no. 2:135–46.

DILL, B.T. 1983. Race, class, and gender: Prospects for an all-inclusive sisterhood. *Feminist Studies* 9, no. 1:131–50.

DORGAN, M., B.L. GOEBEL, and A.E. HOUSE. 1983. Generalizing about sex role and self-esteem: Results or effects. *Sex Roles* 9, no. 6:719–24.

DWORKIN, R.J., and A.G. DWORKIN. 1983. The effect of integender conflict on sex-role attitudes. *Sex Roles* 9, no. 1:49–57.

DWORKIN, S. 1983. Teri Garr: Her real role in "Tootsie" *Ms.* 11:39–43.

EAGAN, A. 1983. The selling of premenstrual syndrome. *Ms.* 12, no. 4:26–31.

EHRENREICH, B. 1983. *The hearts of men: American dreams and the flight from commitment.* New York: Anchor/Doubleday.

EICHENBAUM, L., and S. ORBACH. 1983. *What do women want: Exploding the myth of dependency.* New York: Coward-McCann.

ERKUT, S. 1983. Exploring sex differences in expectancy, attribution, and academic achievement. *Sex Roles* 9, no. 2:217–31.

ETAUGH, C., and E. FORESMAN. 1983. Evaluations of competence as a function of sex and marital status. *Sex Roles* 9, no. 7:759–65.

FISHER, B. 1982. Professing feminism: Feminist academics and the women's movement. *Psychology of Women Quarterly* 7, no. 1:55–69.

FLEISHMAN, E.G. 1983a. Sex-role acquisition, parental behavior, and sexual orientation: some tentative hypotheses. *Sex Roles* 9, no. 10:1051–1059.

————. 1983b. Sex-role acquisition, parental behavior, and sexual orientation: Some tentative hypotheses—a rejoinder. *Sex Roles* 9, no. 10:1063–65.

FLEMING, J. 1982. Fear of success in black male and female graduate students: A pilot study. *Psychology of Women Quarterly* 6, no. 3:327–41.

FOODEN, M., ed. 1983. *The second X and women's health.* New York: Gordian Press.

FRANKS, V., and E.D. ROTHBLUM. 1983. *The stereotyping of women: Its effects on mental health.* New York: Springer.

FREEDMAN, R.J., S. Golub, and B. KRAUSS. 1982. Mainstreaming the psychology of women into the core curriculum. *Teaching of Psychology* 9, no. 3:165–68.

GILBERT, L., and P. WEBSTER. 1982. *Bound by love: The sweet trap of daughterhood.* Boston: Beacon Press.

GILLIGAN, C. 1982. *In a different voice: Psychological theory and women's development.* Cambridge, Mass.: Harvard University Press.

GRAVENKEMPER, S.A., and M.A. PALUDI. 1983. Fear of success revisited: Introducing an ambiguous cue. *Sex Roles* 9, no. 8:897–900.

GREENSPAN, M. 1983. *A new approach to women and therapy.* New York: McGraw Hill.

HARE-MUSTIN, R.T., S.K. BENNETT, and P.C. BRODERICK. 1983. Attitude toward motherhood: Gender, generational, and religious comparisons. *Sex Roles* 9, no. 5:643–61.

HASKELL, M. 1983. Women's friendships: Two films move beyond the clichés. *Ms.* 12, no. 6:23–27.

HEILBRUN, C.G. 1973. *Toward a recognition of androgyny*. New York: Alfred A. Knopf.

JOHNSON, M. 1982. Research on teaching the psychology of women. *Psychology of Women Quarterly* 7, no. 1:96–104.

JONES, W., M. CHERNOVITS, and R. HANSSEN. 1978. The enigma of androgyny: Differential implications for males and females? *Journal of Consulting and Clinical Psychology* 46:298–313.

KAHN, A.S., and P.J. JEAN. 1983. Integration and elimination or separation and redefinition: The future of the psychology of women. *Signs* 8, no. 4:659–71.

KIMLICKA, T., H. CROSS, and J. TARNAI. 1983. A comparison of androgynous, feminine, masculine, and undifferentiated women on self-esteem, body satisfaction, and sexual satisfaction. *Psychology of Women Quarterly* 7, no. 3:291–93.

KITZINGER, S. 1983. *Woman's experience of sex*. New York: Putnam.

KNAUB, P.K., D.B. EVERSOLL, and J.H. VOSS. 1983. Is parenthood a desirable adult role? An assessment of attitudes held by contemporary women. *Sex Roles* 9, no. 3:355–62.

LaTORRE, R.A., and K. WENDENBURG. 1983. Psychological characteristics of bisexual and homosexual women. *Journal of Homosexuality* 9, no. 1:87–97.

LEE, A.G., and V.L. SCHEURER. 1983. Psychological androgyny and aspects of self-image in women and men. *Sex Roles* 9, no. 3:289–306.

LENNEY, E., J. GOLD, and C. BROWNING. 1983. Sex differences in self-confidence: The influence of comparison to others' ability level. *Sex Roles* 9, no. 9:925–42.

LINDEN, R., D.E.H. RUSSELL, and S. LEIGH. 1982. *Against sadomasochism: A radical feminist analysis*. East Palo Alto, Calif.: Frog in the Well.

LIVINGOOD, A.B., P. DAEN, and B.D. SMITH. 1983. The depressed mother as a source of stimulation for her infant. *Journal of Clinical Psychology* 39, no. 3:368–75.

LORD, S.B. 1982. Teaching the psychology of women: Examination of a teaching-learning model. *Psychology of Women Quarterly* 7, no. 1:70–80.

LUBINSKI, D., A. TELLEGEN, and J.N. BUTCHER. 1983. Masculinity, femininity, and androgyny viewed and assessed as distinct concepts. *Journal of Personality and Social Psychology* 44, no. 2:428–39.

McPHERSON, K.S., and S.K. SPETRINO. 1983. Androgyny and sex-typing: Differences in beliefs regarding gender polarity in ratings of ideal men and women. *Sex Roles* 9, no. 4:441–51.

McVICAR, P., and A. HERMAN. 1983. Assertiveness, self-actualization, and locus of control in women. *Sex Roles* 9, no. 4:555–61.

McWHIRTER, D., and A. MATTISON. 1983. *The male couple*. Englewood Cliffs, N.J.: Prentice-Hall.

MONAHAN, L. 1983. The effects of sex differences and evaluation on task performance and aspiration. *Sex Roles* 9, no. 2:205–15.

MORGAN, M. 1983. *Breaking through, how to overcome housewives' depression.* Minneapolis: Winston Press.

MORGAN, S. 1983. Towards a politics of "feelings": Beyond the dialectic of thought and action. *Women's Studies,* 10:203–23.

NEUMAN, P.A., and P.A. HALVERSON. 1983. *Anorexia nervosa and bulimia: A handbook for counselors and therapists.* New York: Van Nostrand Reinhold.

NEWCOMBE, N., M.M. BANDURA, and D.G. TAYLOR. 1983. Sex differences in spatial ability and spatial activities. *Sex Roles* 9, no. 3:377–86.

NOSBACK, J., and P. WEITZ. 1983. *The sourcebook of sex therapy, counseling and family planning.* New York: Van Nostrand Reinhold.

O'CONNELL, A.N., and N.F. RUSSO, eds. 1983. *Models of achievement: Reflections of eminent women in psychology.* New York: Columbia University Press.

PYKE, S.W., and J.M. GRAHAM. 1983. Gender schema theory and androgyny: A critique and elaboration. *International Journal of Women's Studies* 6, no. 1:3–17.

RICHARDSON, B., and J. WIRTENBERG. 1983. *Sex role research: Measuring social change.* New York: Praeger.

RICHARDSON, M.S. 1982. Sources of tension in teaching the psychology of women. *Psychology of Women Quarterly* 7, no. 1:45–54.

RIS, M.D., and D.J. WOODS. 1983. Learned helplessness and "fear of success" in college women. *Sex Roles* 9, no. 10:1067–72.

ROBBINS, J.H., and R.J. SIEGEL. 1983. *Women changing therapy: New assessments, values & strategies in feminist therapy.* New York: Haworth Press.

ROSSNER, J. 1983. *August.* Boston: Houghton Mifflin.

RUSSO, N.F. 1982. Psychology of women: Analysis of faculty and courses of an emerging field. *Psychology of Women Quarterly* 7, no. 1:18–31.

SAMOIS. 1982. *Coming to power: Writings and graphics on lesbian s/m.* Boston: Alyson Publications.

SAYERS, J. 1983. Is the personal political? Psychoanalysis and feminism revisited. *International Journal of Women's Studies* 6, no. 1:71–86.

SEIDENBERG, R., and K. DeCROW. 1983. *Women who marry houses: Panic and protest in agoraphobia.* New York: McGraw Hill.

SHERIF, C.W. 1982. Needed concepts in the study of gender identity. *Psychology of Women Quarterly* 6, no. 4:375–95.

SIMARI, C.G., and D. BASKIN. 1983. Sex-role acquisition, parental behavior, and sexual orientation: Some tentative hypotheses—a critique. *Sex Roles* 9, no. 10:1061–62.

SMITH, E.J. 1982. The black female adolescent: A review of the educational, career and psychological literature. *Psychology of Women Quarterly* 6, no. 3:261–88.

SNITOW, A., C. STANSELL, and S. THOMPSON, eds. 1983. *Powers of desire: The politics of sexuality.* New York: Monthly Review Press.

SPENCE, J.T. 1983. Comment on Lubinski, Tellegen, and Butcher's: Masculinity, femininity, and androgyny viewed and assessed as distinct concepts. *Journal of Personality and Social Psychology* 44, no. 2:440–46.

SPENCE, J.T., and R.L. HELMREICH. 1978. *Masculinity and femininity: Their psychological dimensions, correlates and antecedents*. Austin: University of Texas Press.

SQUIRE, S. 1983. *The slender balance*. New York: G.P. Putnam's Sons.

STEVENS, G., and S. GARDNER. 1982. *The women of psychology*. Cambridge, Mass.: Schenkman Publishing Co.

STONE, E. 1983. Playwright Marsha Norman: An optimist writes about suicide, confinement and despair. *Ms.* 12, no. 4:56–59.

TAVRIS, C. 1983. *Anger: The misunderstood emotion*. New York: Simon & Schuster.

TAYLOR, A. 1983. Conceptions of masculinity and femininity as a basis for stereotypes of male and female homosexuals. *Journal of Homosexuality* 9, no. 1:37–53.

TELLEGAN, A., and D. LUBINSKI. 1983. Some methodological comments on labels, traits, interaction, and types in the study of "femininity" and "masculinity": Reply to Spence. *Journal of Personality and Social Psychology* 44, no. 2:447–55.

UNGER, R.K. 1982. Advocacy versus scholarship revisited: Issues in the psychology of women. *Psychology of Women Quarterly* 7, no. 1:5–17.

VAN GELDER, L. 1984. Carol Gilligan: A leader for a different kind of future. *Ms.* 12, no. 7:37–40, 101.

WARREN, L.W., and L. McEACHREN. 1983. Psychosocial correlates of depressive symptomatology in adult women. *Journal of Abnormal Psychology* 92, no. 2:151–60.

WHITAM, F.L. 1977. The homosexual role: A reconsideration. *Journal of Sex Research* 13, no. 1:1–11.

WHITLEY, B.E. 1983. Sex role orientation and self-esteem: A critical meta-analytic review. *Journal of Personality & Social Psychology* 44, no. 4:765–78.

Women & therapy 1, no. 1 (Spring). 1982. New York: Haworth Press.

ZUCKERMAN, D.M. 1983. Women's studies, self-esteem, and college women's plans for the future. *Sex Roles* 9, no. 5:633–41.

Women of Color in the United States

Jacquelyn Marie and Elaine Bell Kaplan

More and more women, in 1982–83, were researching, writing, and discussing stories related to the relationship of women of color to other women, to men, to the family, and to their jobs, as well as to the world of art and literature. We have picked "the story" as the theme of our review of these issues because these women—black, Asian American, Hispanic, and American Indian, come from traditions in which storytelling conveys the personal in all its bitter and sweet glory.

Although these women have been affected by government policies that have cut back on support for them and their families, the most important event has been the positive changes they are making in their lives and in the way people write about them. (We have to point out, however, that we need stories from other ethnic groups such as Arab American women.) Within this context, then, the story is viewed as an art form, a way of communicating in fiction and in research. We will present stories of gender, visibility, role models, and marginality issues, and then discuss women of color's critique on these issues.

Gender Issues: Stereotypes

Women of color are recognizing and writing about the tendency to stereotype them as black matriarchs, as perfect mothers/wives, passive nurturers, and followers. Wendy Law-Yone, a Burmese American, writes in her novel *The Coffin Tree* (1983) about a female protagonist who takes on the role of protector-nurturer of her sick, dependent brother because they are poverty-stricken aliens in America and he is her only link to the Old World. American Indian women, although often pictured as walking ten paces behind their men, have also been leaders in their own tribal communities. American Indian women of the Ohoyo Resource Center are trying to tap that tradition by producing videos and newsletter articles about their leadership conferences. Still, Beatrice Medicine (1983) reminds us that we must not lose sight of the sexism in the American Indian community as "traditional views of Indian women are still strongly ingrained in the socialization of both sexes in all tribes" (63).

Black women, on the other hand, are responding to the matriarchal stereotype by moving beyond it to their own interpretation of history. Dorothy Burnham (1983) talks about the unique situation of women caught in a slavery system that determined their productive lives by their reproductive lives (see also Lebsock 1982). These same slave women had power as healers although the limited formal power was held by black men (Jones 1982).

Recently, women of color have been actively working, through the use of film and literature, to change these stereotypical concepts. In a series of 16mm. films made for schools and communities, women are depicted as breaking away from traditional values (*Black Girl* 1982; Chase, 1983). *Chile Pequin* (1982) is about a Chicana who leaves her small-town, closely knit family and traditional father to attend a university.

The images of mothers and daughters are also changing. In a film produced by the Asian American community, *Okazaki* (1983) shows Genny Lim, a playwright, confronting her mother, a first-generation Chinese American. Her mother wishes her to work in an office, not as an author, because "You no work so hard and you make more money." A mother in Paula Gunn Allen's "Indian Mother Poem" (1982) reiterates, "No you can't use me / but you can share / me with me as though / I were a two-necked wedding jar / they make, over in Santa Clara— / some for each of us / enough" (120).

Authors and researchers are now focusing on women's stories as workers. In *Mammies to Militants* (1982), Harris finds that authors have presented domestic workers slowly evolving from despair to recognizing their self-worth and power. Lea Ybarra (1982), in focusing on working Chicana wives, reports that women are dropping the notion that family life is the focus of their identity. Chalsa Loo and Paul Ong's study (1982) of Chinatown's sewing women presents the other side of the women's story when they conclude that Chinatown women work in "highly isolated labor markets, and have very limited opportunities for upward mobility" (82).

Visibility

While women of color are writing about their struggles and empowerment, their lives have been affected by the continuing ideology and policies of the Reagan administration. For example, Reagan's antipathy to civil rights and affirmative action is emphasized by his attempt to eliminate the Civil Rights Commission or, in lieu of that, to change its focus from enforcing affirmative action policies to undercutting what the commission sees as special interest groups (5 of 8 members . . . 1983). Ironically, the former commission published a report stating that President Reagan has never appointed a woman of color to a federal post (U.S. Commission on Civil Rights 1983).

Along with women of color's invisibility in major federal positions, there is an overwhelming problem of visibility in terms of statistical information. Often statistics on women of color are lumped into categories labeled "women" and "minorities." Most important, recent research suggests that women of color have not experienced the same kind of work and family experience (Simmons 1983; Glenn 1983; Loo and Ong 1982) as have white women (Palmer 1983b). Housing problems, home health care, child care, and employment are a few of the problems facing not only black women but, as Rosemary Cooney and Vilma Ortiz's study (1983) indicates, Puerto Rican and Mexican American women as well.

In addition, we have culled statistical data on employment, health, and family that are not reassuring for women of color. Historically, black women have not fared well in the labor market, and this trend continues to influence their employment rate: in 1983, 34 percent were unemployed (U.S. Bureau of Labor Statistics 1983). Over half of employed black women are still found in technical, clerical, sales, and service occupations. We know very little about Asian American women's employment rates. However, Elaine Kim and J. Otani (1983) report that although their level of education is higher than white women's, their wages are lower. In fact, many Asian American women work in low-profile, low-status, and low-paying occupations.

In 1982, 56 percent of black female householders and 55 percent of all Hispanic female householders were impoverished. These figures are high when compared to 28 percent of white female, 15 percent of black male, and 17 percent of Hispanic male householders, or 16 percent of black and Hispanic husband-wife families (U.S. Bureau of the Census, 1982, 20). The National Advisory Council on Economic Opportunity (1980) warns us that if this rate continues to climb, "the poverty population would be composed solely of women and their children by about the year 2000" (19). We suspect that, unless conditions radically change, the majority of that poverty population will be women and children of color. In fact, as the media take up the catch phrase, "feminization of poverty," Phyllis Palmer (1983a) points out that it might be more truthful to call it the "racial feminization of poverty" (5).

Black women themselves are telling stories about their economic hardships and broken dreams, as well as their desires to offer their children a better life (Cummings 1983). Some women, in response to the stereotype of the welfare mother, are taking on two jobs, child raising and working full-time. According to Howard University sociologist Harriet McAdoo

(Manuel 1983), "The women we've been talking to [are] doing everything possible to remain independent" (36).

This image of the "superwoman" takes a terrific toll on the health of women of color. Elaine Copeland (1982) points to the societal pressures that restrict many black women's ability to function more positively and that may affect their mental health. Unfortunately, there are also significant obstacles to health care, including cost, language, and cultural barriers (Lopez 1983; Rosenhouse-Persson and Sabagh 1983). A primary source for health care is also needed. Most of these women often have no health care services at all (U.S. Commission on Civil Rights 1982).

While these stories reflect the hardship many women of color endure, women are beginning to change their situation. Some women are starting to operate their own health care clinics. Moreover, a group of black women presented the first National Conference on Black Women's Health along with an exhibit on women healers for 1,500 women at Spelman College in June 1983. In taking action into their own hands, these women are echoing Fannie Lou Hamer's words, "I'm sick and tired of being sick and tired" (Royster 1983).

Lesbians of color are also concerned with becoming more visible. In struggling to get their stories out, they are publishing newsletters and autobiographies through their own small presses. Tsunami Press of Seattle (Chumu 1982) and Kitchen Table Press of New York (Gomez, Moraga, and Romo-Carmona 1983) are publishing essays and newsletters. *Onyx*, a new black lesbian newsletter printed in Berkeley, California, reported on a Lesbians of Color Conference held at the Cottontail Ranch in Malibu on 8–11 September 1983.

Lesbians of color are renaming and rethinking themselves, not only through newsletters and conferences, but also through autobiographical poems and novels (Tsui 1983; Allen 1982). Audre Lorde in *Zami* (1982) recalls her early years in New York. She discovers her identity through the process of breaking away from her traditional Grenadian mother's restraints, working out relationships with her women lovers, and eventually realizing her debt to her island foremothers. We expect to hear more stories about lesbian women of color's struggle to grow and to fit into their own ethnic culture as well as the lesbian community.

In 1983, stories from women of color began to reach a wider audience. Not only did the large publishing companies print their stories, but also these women became more visible when their work won major awards. Alice Walker won the Pulitzer Prize for *The Color Purple* (1982). She wrote Celie's story with startling knowledge and compassion for the overwhelming economic and emotional deprivation of a poor southern black woman, who slowly gains a sense of her power and self-worth through the loving support of her woman friend and lover. For Alice Walker, purple is a "womanist" color—a sign of strength.

Cathy Song became the first Asian American to win the Yale Younger Poets award for her book of poems of Asian American women, *Picture Bride*

(1983). The title alludes both to the exploitation of Asian women through "mail-order" marriages and to the poetic images of women as strangers in an alien culture, discovering their voices through Song. The American Book Award winners of 1983 included Gloria Naylor for her first novel, *Women of Brewster Place* (1982) and Alice Walker for her novel, *The Color Purple* (1982).

Oral history has become an exciting new source for stories about the everyday lives of women in their family and community activities (Tsuchida 1982). *Shandaa in My Lifetime* (Herbert 1982) relates the reminiscences of Belle, a Gwich'in woman in her hundreds who has lived through most of Alaska's recorded history. Her words in Gwich'in and English accompanied by wonderful photographs of her and her family tell of her rugged rural life. As Belle puts it, "Ah Grandchild, the poor women had the kids while the men just went out hunting" (140).

Role Models

Women of color are finally getting their chance to act as role models. Through such media as oral history, interviews, films, videos, and articles, they are relating their experiences in music, art, science, and other fields. The lively and honest film on women gospel singers, *Say Amen Somebody* (1982); the oral histories of Bessie Jones (Stewart 1983), a Georgia Sea Island singer/collector/preserver of slave-time ring games and play-party songs; and the International Sweethearts of Rhythm (Handy 1983), a 1940s Mississippi women's jazz band—all are examples of the songs, stories, and lives of black women singers and musicians being brought to light.

Artists have not been overlooked either, although more research, interviews, and critical studies should be done to give women of color their place in art (Gouma-Peterson 1983; Lichtenstein 1983).

For Hispanic women college students deciding on nontraditional careers, the *Intercambios Femeniles Newsletter* (1983) lists the latest statistics, networks and organizations, and employment opportunities in technology; most important, it presents Hispanic women doctors, chemists, and engineers relating their own experiences. In a video produced by Loni Ding, *With Silk Wings* (1983), Asian American women talk about their nontraditional work in such areas as television, bartending, law, and welding. Women role models are much more visible on public television; we expect to see more positive images of women of color in the future.

Marginality

At the end of 1982, Bettina Aptheker (1982) was hardly alone in wishing "white women to . . . steep our selves in the literature, the history, and the lives of women of color" (15). Angela Davis (1982) joined Aptheker in calling for women who teach women's studies to move beyond the traditional white middle-class perspective. In 1983, other women began to assess what they saw as racism in the women's studies programs (Butler 1982; al-Hibri 1983). These articles and essays represent a trend toward placing women of color, along with white women, at the center of scholarship.

In turn, this central placement of the issues raised by women of color is attracting further attention from scholars. For instance, Vicky Spelman (1982) worries about the "dynamics of marginality in women's studies classes" when "old pedagogical rules," "class room etiquette," and "the materials" reflect the values of white women. She proposes that course material must speak to *all* women and that students should be encouraged to speak up and challenge one another, which might engender conflict but may also lead to better communication. She calls for a dialogue between women's studies and black studies. Spelman College has taken note of the need for black colleges to communicate with women's studies programs. It is the first black college to offer a women's studies minor that will integrate black women's studies into an analysis of women's experiences (*Women's Research . . .* 1983).

Women of color's growing concern with placing themselves within the developing scholarship about women culminated in a debate about their exclusion from women's studies, black studies, ethnic studies, and the major social science literature (Sanchez 1983). Are they to do research on sexism in their own communities or should racism and sexism in the white community be their top priority? Should they affiliate themselves with black studies or with women's studies (Hull 1982)? Although a number of women of color have chosen to focus on women's issues, they have had to address the racism of white women at the same time that they have had to defend themselves from accusations in their community that they are abandoning the cause for a "white, middle-class woman's thing" (Simmons 1983, 15).

We gather from their writings and research that some women are growing more and more concerned about what support they will receive if they continue their feminist scholarship or if they address what one author calls their "twoness" (Simmons 1983). Eleanor Smith (1983) writes that "the historical relationships of black and white women clearly show that very little, if anything, has been achieved for black women from so-called alliances" (15).

Other women are adding their voices to the debate by exploring the historical reasons for the estrangement between women of color and white women. Bonnie Thornton Dill (1983), in her essay on relationships between white and black women, limits the concept of sisterhood to middle-class white women. Palmer (1983b) suggests another reason for the lack of solidarity between women of color and white women by noting this society's two opposing images of these women. Palmer suggests that white women benefit from their class and race status, and Dill wants white women to move beyond their limited focus on "women's issues to ally with groups of women and men who are addressing other aspects of race and class oppression" (147).

Some women of color did raise the gender issue at the 1983 Summer Institute on Teaching, Researching, and Writing about Women of Color at Memphis State University's Center for Research on Women. Forty-eight women of color faculty, students, and staff from all parts of the United States focused on such topics as women's work and women's participation in organizations (*Memphis State . . .* 1983, 1). While women's relations with men were discussed to some degree in a small group, the issue of women's powerlessness was not addressed at the larger seminars, which led many women to wonder what kind of research they could produce in an environment that supports a code of silence in regard to such issues as wife battering and child abuse by men of color. In response, a group of women formed their own workshop in which to discuss patriarchy.

Another example of the conflict for women of color was the inability of the 1983 National Women's Studies Association "to produce a sufficient number of women of color panelists" for a conference, although many of them participated in cultural events. This problem resulted, according to the conference evaluation, in more explicit accusations of racism than in any other year except 1981 when racism was the conference theme (B. Davis 1983, 11).

A growing number of women of color, however, are making the message clear. They will continue to do feminist scholarship by responding to the racism in the white community and to the sexism in their own community. Members of Mujeres en Marcha organized a panel discussion at the 1982 National Association of Chicano Studies conference in order to address their concerns about their colleagues' sexism. One speaker, Gloria Holquin Cuadrez, wanted to know why "the attempt to assert issues around sexism is often met with resistance and scorn" (Mujeres en Marcha 1983, 17). In Teresa Cordova's closing remarks, she raised the issue of "whether there is room for a feminist movement within the Chicana community" (29). At another conference, Maria Matute-Bianchi (1982) addressed this issue—if sexism in their own communities does not change, women of color will be barred from doing important research and from having collegial networks that could enhance their professional careers and give "the psychological and emotional support" they need to survive in academe (16).

Critique on New Scholarship

The seventies saw the emergence of new critical thought by white feminists. Now in the eighties, we have another body of criticism by women of color. Maxine Baca Zinn's (1982a) and Lea Ybarra's (1982) work reflects a body of studies that replaces the cultural determinist theory with an examination of Chicanas in the larger structural dimensions of social organization. Zinn's study suggests that high fertility of Chicanas has to be explained by economic considerations, availability of birth control services, and attitudes and behaviors toward these women. She notes that although "an impressive body of social science literature on Chicanas is unfolding," Chicano scholars need to address themselves to overcoming inequalities by producing research that will be the "lever for social change" (1982b, 7).

In 1983, undergraduate and graduate students at the University of California, Berkeley, formed the Berkeley Women of Color Collective in order to critique the scholarship in their own disciplines of history and sociology. In their newsletter, they wrote they were "disappointed, frustrated and angered by the absence of women of color in all the relevant literature used in courses taught on this and other university campuses" (*Berkeley Women* . . . 1983, 1). Elaine Bell Kaplan focused on the need for feminist scholars to develop a theory of gender that raises questions about black matriarch ideology, about the New Right's attempt to use that ideology, and how black women have survived by building female support groups (Kaplan 1983).

In another article, Sandra Uyeunten (1983) critiques American labor history for not providing "critical information" and "analysis of the experiences of Nisei" (Japanese American) women (9). All these women—black, Japanese, Chinese, Filipino, Southeast Asian—rejected the popular definition of them as "minorities."

Women of color are also beginning to critique literature. The theory behind this criticism is best exemplified in Barbara Smith's essay in the landmark book, *All the Women Are White* . . . (1982). Criticism by women of color differs from feminist or ethnic criticism as it looks at racial, cultural, class, and sexual orientations as well as the sex of the author. In Barbara Smith's words, "Until a Black feminist criticism exists, we will not even know what these writers mean" (159). She explains further that the black feminist critic "would think and write out of her own identity and not try to graft the idea and methodology of white/male literary thought" (64). Thus, Smith interprets Toni Morrison's novel *Sula* as lesbian literature "not only because of the passionate friendship between Sula and Nel but because of Morrison's consistently critical stance toward the heterosexual institutions of male/female relationships, marriage, and the family" (165). One of the passages Smith uses as an example is the adult Nel grieving when Sula, her childhood friend, leaves: " 'We was girls together,' she said as though explaining something" (170).

As black feminist criticism seems to arise from a black feminist movement, so a critical essay on Chicana poetry is firmly rooted in the Chicana author's understanding of the Chicano movement. Elizabeth Ordonez, in "Sexual Politics and the Theme of Sexuality in Chicana Poetry" (1983), states unequivocally that "Chicana feminism has been a natural consequence of the overall Chicano struggle for justice, equality, and freedom

. . . Chicana activists were indeed allowed full freedom to go out into the streets provided the frijoles were on the table in time for supper" (317). This theme of sexual oppression within the *movimiento* affects Chicana poetry and informs Ordonez's essay.

American Indian women, another group seldom heard, have their stories to tell. They too are discovering their strengths as leaders, their oral traditions of spider woman and Mother Earth, their grandmothers' storytelling, and their culture's strong sense of family (Allen 1983b). *Studies in American Indian Literature* (Allen 1983a) contains several critical essays on American Indian women's literature. "Ain't Seen You Since" is a thoughtful essay comparing white and American Indian mother-daughter relationships in women's poetry (P. Smith 1983). As Marnie Walsh puts it briefly but graphically in her poem, "Bessie Dreaming Bear: Rosebud, South Dakota, 1969," "We all went to town one day / went to a store / bought you new shoes / red high heels / ain't seen you since" (115).

We also find Asian American women authors discussing mother-daughter relationships. Elaine Kim in her book, *Asian American Literature* (1982), critiques Hisaye Yamamoto's tale, "Yoneko's Earthquake," written in 1951 as the story of an Issei immigrant mother told through the "oblique vision" of her Nisei daughter (158). Kim, a Korean American is examining these Asian American stories from their "sociohistorical and cultural contexts" (xv).

Oral communication, through interviews of women of color by women of color, is another source for discovering their experiences. Claudia Tate in her book, *Black Women Writers at Work* (1983), has taken on this task and performed it well. In her foreword, she continues the critical stance begun by Barbara Christian in her definitive historical study, *Black Women Novelists* (1980). Tate writes, "Black women writers usually project their vision from the point of view of female characters" (5). Christian expands on this view: "Black contemporary women writers are challenging the very definition of women and are beginning to project their own definitions of themselves as a means of transforming the content of their own communities' views on the nature of women and therefore on the nature of life" (252).

Our extensive review of the literature indicates that all women of color—writers, researchers, and critics—are redefining themselves and transforming that literature.

Conclusion: Getting the Story Out

We still need stories of and by women of color. Too many women have already disappeared and "countless others have never been permitted to sing in public" (Stetson 1982). Although we discovered a new bibliography on American Indian women that at last cites articles on contemporary women (Green 1983), there is still a scarcity of other bibliographies, primary materials, and critical studies and research. If allowed to emerge, scholarship on women of color should generate controversial, yet exciting and original stories.

References

ALLEN, P.G. 1982. *Shadow country*. Los Angeles: American Indian Studies Center, University of California.

ALLEN, P.G., ed. 1983a. *Studies in American Indian literature: Critical essays and course designs*. New York: Modern Language Association of America.

ALLEN, P.G. 1983b. *The woman who owned the shadows*. San Francisco: Spinsters Ink.

APTHEKER, BETTINA. 1982. Race and class: Patriarchal politics and women's experience. *Women's Studies Quarterly* 10, no. 4:10–15.

BACA ZINN, MAXINE. 1982a. Mexican-American women in the social sciences. *Signs* 8, no. 2:259–72.

————. 1982b. Social research on Chicanos: Its development and direction. *Social Science Journal* 19, no. 2:1–8.

Berkeley Women of Color Newsletter. 1983. Institute for Social Change, University of California at Berkeley, 1 no. 1:1.

Black girl. 1982. Planning Ahead Series. Berkeley, Calif.: Extension Media Center. 16 mm., 30 min., color.

BURNHAM, DOROTHY. 1983. Black women as producers and reproducers for profit. In *Woman's Nature*, edited by Mariam Lowe and Ruth Hubbard, p. 29–38. New York: Pergamon Press.

BUTLER, JOHNNELLA A. 1982. Toward a plural and equitable society. *Women's Studies Quarterly* 10, no. 2:10–11.

CASTILLO, S. 1983. *Intercambios Femeniles* Stanford University, 1, no. 8 (Winter).

CHASE, DORIS. 1983. *Mask*. Los Angeles: Concepts. Videocassette, 30 min., color.

Chile pequin. 1982. Planning Ahead Series. Berkeley, Calif.: Extension Media Center. 16 mm., 30 min., color.

CHRISTIAN, B. 1980. *Black women novelists: The development of a tradition, 1892–1976*. Westport, Conn.: Greenwood Press.

CHUMU, M. 1982. *Coming out colored: Salir a la luz como lesbianas de color*. Seattle, Wash.: Tsunami Press.

COONEY, ROSEMARY S., and VILMA ORTIZ. 1983. Nativity, national origin, and hispanic female participation in the labor market. *Social Science Quarterly* 64, no. 3:510–23.

COPELAND, ELAINE J. 1982. Oppressed conditions and the mental health needs of low-income black women: Barriers to services, strategies for change. *Women and Therapy* 1, no. 1:13–26.

CORDOVA, TERESA. 1983. Closing remarks. In *Chicanas in the 80's: Unsettled issues*, 29–31. Berkeley: Chicano Studies Library Publication Unit, University of California.

CUADREZ, GLORIA HOLQUIN. 1983. Whether subtle or blatant, sexism is our reality: It is also yours. In *Chicanas in the 80's: Unsettled issues*, 6–7. Berkeley: Chicano Studies Library Publication Unit, University of California.

CUMMINGS, J. 1983. Heading a family: Stories of 7 black women. *New York Times*, 21 November.

DAVIS, ANGELA. 1982. Women, race and class: An activist perspective. *Women's Studies Quarterly* 10, no. 4:5–9.

DAVIS, BARBARA H. 1983. NWSA diversity: Comments and complaints from the conference. *Women's Studies Quarterly* 12, no. 1:8–11.

DILL, BONNIE THORNTON. 1983. Race, class, and gender: Prospects for an all-inclusive sisterhood. *Feminist Studies* 9, no. 1:131–50.

DING, L. 1983. *With silk wings: On new ground*. San Francisco: Asian Women United of California. Videocassette, 60 min., color.

GLENN, EVELYN NAKANO. 1983. Split households, small producers and dual wage earner: An analysis of Chinese-American family strategies. *Journal of Marriage and the Family*, February, pp. 35–45.

5 of 8 members of new civil rights panel seen sympathetic to Reagan policies. 1983. *Chronicle of Higher Education*, 14 December.

GOMEZ, A., C. MORAGA, and M. ROMO-CARMONA, eds. 1983. *Cuentos: Stories by Latinas*. New York: Kitchen Table Press.

GOUMA-PETERSON, T. 1983. Elizabeth Catlett: The power of human feeling and of art. *Woman's Art Journal* 4, no. 1:48–56.

GREEN, R. 1983. *Native American women: A contextual bibliography*. Bloomington: Indiana University Press.

HANDY, D.A. 1983. *The international sweethearts of rhythm*. Metuchen, N.J.: Scarecrow Press.

HARRIS, T. 1982. *From mammies to militants: Domestics in Black American literature*. Philadelphia: Temple University Press.

HERBERT, B. 1982. *Shandaa in my lifetime*. Fairbanks: University of Alaska, Alaska Native Language Center.

al-HIBRI, A. 1983. Unveiling the hidden face of racism: The plight of Arab American women. *Women's Studies Quarterly* 11, no. 3:10–11.

HULL, GLORIA T. 1982. The bridge between black studies and women studies. *Women's Studies Quarterly* 10, no. 2:12–13.

JONES, JACQUELINE. 1982. My mother was much of a woman: Black women, work, and the family under slavery. *Feminist Studies* 8, no. 2:235–69.

KAPLAN, ELAINE. 1983. Some notes on black women. *Berkeley Women of Color Newsletter* 1, no. 1:4–6.

KIM, E.H. 1982. *Asian American literature: An introduction to the writings and their social context*. Philadelphia: Temple University Press.

KIM, E.H., and J. OTANI. 1983. *With silk wings: Asian American women at work.* San Francisco: Asian Women United of California.

LAW-YONE, W. 1983. *The coffin tree.* New York: Alfred A. Knopf.

LEBSOCK, SUZANNE. 1982. Free black women and the question of matriarchy: Petersburg, Va., 1784–1820. *Feminist Studies* 8, no. 2:270–92.

Lesbian of color conference in LA. 1983. *Onyx: Black lesbian newsletter*, 11, no. 5 (October-November):3.

LICHTENSTEIN, G. 1983. Naranjo women—the evolution of a craft tradition. *Ms.* 11 (April):58–60.

LOO, CHALSA, and PAUL ONG. 1982. Slaying demons with a sewing needle: Feminist issues for Chinatown's women. *Berkeley Journal of Sociology* 27:77–88.

LOPEZ, IRIS. 1983. Extended views: Social coercion and sterilization among Puerto Rican women. *Sage Race Relations Abstracts* 8, no. 3:27–40.

LORDE, A. 1982. *Zami, a new spelling of my name.* Watertown, Mass.: Persephone Press.

MANUEL, J.C. 1983. Identifying the special strengths—and needs—of the black family. *Christian Science Monitor*, 14 November.

MATUTE-BIANCHI, MARIA. 1982. A Chicana in academe. *Women's Studies Quarterly* 10, no. 1:14–16.

MEDICINE, BEATRICE. 1983. Indian women: Tribal identity as status quo. In *Woman's Nature, Rationalizations of inequality*, edited by Marian Lowe and Ruth Hubbard, 63–74. New York: Pergamon Press.

Memphis State University Center for Research on Women Newsletter. 1983. 2, no. 1:1.

Mujeres en Marcha. 1983. *Chicanas in the 80's: Unsettled issues.* Berkeley: Chicao Studies Library Publication Unit, University of California.

National Advisory Council on Economic Opportunity. 1980. *Critical choices for the 80's.* Twelfth Report. Washington, D.C.: GPO.

NAYLOR, G. 1982. *The women of Brewster Place.* New York: Viking Press.

OKAZAKI, S. 1983. *The only language she knows.* San Francisco: Mouchette Films. 16 mm., 19 min., color.

ORDÓÑEZ, E. 1983. Sexual politics and the theme of sexuality in Chicana poetry. In *Women in Hispanic literature: Icons and fallen idols*, edited by Beth Miller. Berkeley: University of California Press.

PALMER, PHYLLIS. 1983a. The racial feminization of poverty: Women of color as portents of the future for all women. *Women's Studies Quarterly* 11, no. 3:4–6.

————. 1983b. White women/black women: The dualism of female identity and experience in the United States. *Feminist Studies* 9, no. 1:151–70.

ROSENHOUSE-PERSSON, SANDRA, and GEORGES SABAGH. 1983. Attitudes toward abortion among Catholic Mexican-American women: The effects of religiosity and education. *Demography* 20, no. 1:87–98.

ROYSTER, J.J. 1983. The first national conference on black women's health issues. *Women's Resource Center Newsletter* 2, no. 2 (December).

SANCHEZ, CAROL LEE. 1983. Racism: Power, profit, product—and patriarchy. *Women's Studies Quarterly* 11, no. 3:14–16.

Say amen somebody. 1982. George Nierenberg, director. New York: United Artists Classics.

SIMMONS, ALTHEA T.L. 1983. The black woman—overcoming the odds. *Crisis: A Record of the Darker Races* 90, no. 6:253–312.

SMITH, B. 1982. Toward a black feminist criticism. In *All the women are white, all the blacks are men, but some of us are brave: Black women's studies*, edited by Gloria T. Hull, Patricia Bell Scott, and Barbara Smith, 157–74. Old Westbury, N.Y.: Feminist Press.

SMITH, ELEANOR. 1983. Historical relationships between black and white women. *National Women's Studies Association Newsletter* 2, no. 1:15–18.

SMITH, P.C. 1983. Ain't seen you since: Dissent among female relatives in American Indian women's poetry. In *Studies in American Indian literature—critical essays and course designs*, edited by Paula Gunn Allen, 108–20. New York: Modern Language Association of America.

SONG, C. 1983. *Picture bride.* Yale Series of Younger Poets. New Haven, Conn.: Yale University Press.

SPELMAN, VICKY. 1982. Combating the marginalization of black women in the classroom. *Women's Studies Quarterly* 10, no. 2:15–16.

STETSON, E. 1982. Black women in and out of print. In *Women in print I: Opportunities for women's studies research in language and literature*, edited by Joan E. Hartman and Ellen Messer-Davidow, 87–106. New York: Modern Language Association.

STEWART, J., ed. 1983. *Bessie Jones, for the ancestors.* Urbana: University of Illinois Press.

TATE, C., ed. 1983. *Black women writers at work.* New York: Continuum.

TSUCHIDA, N., ed. 1982. *Asian and Pacific American experiences: Women's perspectives.* Minneapolis: Asian/Pacific American Learning Resource Center, University of Minnesota.

TSUI, K. 1983. *The words of a woman who breathes fire.* San Francisco: Spinsters Ink.

U.S. Bureau of the Census. 1982. *Money income and poverty status of families and persons in the United States*, series P-60, no. 140. Washington, D.C.: GPO.

U.S. Commission on Civil Rights. 1982. *Health insurance: Coverage and employment opportunities for minorities and women.* Washington, D.C.: GPO.

U.S. Commission on Civil Rights. 1983. *Equal opportunity in presidential appointments.* June. Washington, D.C.: GPO.

U.S. Bureau of Labor Statistics. 1983. *Employment and earnings* 30, no. 11 (November). Washington, D.C.: GPO.

UYEUNTEN, SANDRA. 1983. Filling the gap in the labor history of Japanese-American women. *Berkeley Women of Color Newsletter* 1, no. 1:8–9.

WALKER, A. 1982. *The color purple.* New York: Simon & Schuster.

Women's Research and Resource Center Newsletter. Spelman College, 1983. 2, no. 2:1.

YBARRA, LEA. 1982. When wives work: The impact on the Chicano Family. *Journal of Marriage and the Family* 44, no. 1:169–178.

Bibliography

ALBERS, PATRICIA, and BEATRICE MEDICINE, eds. *The Hidden Half: Studies of Plains Indian Women.* Washington, D.C.: University Press of America, 1983.

"Asian Women." *Bridge* 8, no. 3 (Summer 1983). An issue on Asian American women that discusses sexism and racism with a "focus on women's strength." Includes stories on Hiroshima survivors, artist Mayumi Oda's goddess visions, and a film on a sewing woman in Chinatown.

BRANT, B. 1983. A Gathering of Spirit: North American Indian Women's Issue. *Sinister Wisdom*, no. 22–23. Letters, stories, and poems from American Indian women.

CARRERA, ANGIE. Women of color: Struggling together for the future. *off our backs* 13, no. 10:14–15. Covers the National Strategies Conference for Women of Color held in Washington, D.C. in October, 1983.

CAZENOV, NOEL A. A Women's Place: The Attitudes of Middle-Class Black Men. *Phylon* 44, no. 1 (1983):12–32. This study found that low-income black men with traditional values are more likely to disapprove of women's liberation issues than are middle-income black men.

Chicana. Hollywood: Interamerican Pictures, 1979. Sylvia Morales narrates a film based on Ana Nieto-Gomez's research on Chicanas and Mexicanas from pre-Colombian society to present-day farmworkers.

CORNWELL, ANITA. *Black Lesbian in White America.* Tallahassee, Florida: Naiad Press, 1983. A new book of essays by and on black lesbians.

CUMMINGS, J. Breakup of Black Families Imperils Gains of Decades. *New York Times*, 20 November 1983. Part one of a two-part series on the black family.

DAVIS, MARIANNA W., ed. *Contributions of black women to America.* Columbia, S.C.: Kenday Press, 1982. 2 volumes of essays covering film, art, science, medicine, music, government.

MARSHALL, PAULE. *Praisesong for the Widow.* New York: G.P. Putnam's Sons, 1983. A novel about a black American woman who finds her roots in Grenada.

NIVENS, BEATRYCE. *The Black Woman's Career Guide.* Garden City, N.Y.: Anchor Press/Doubleday, 1982. Specific information on "steering your own ship" in the business world.

Ohoyo: Indian Women Speak. Wichita Falls, Texas: Ohoyo Resource Center, 1983. A videotape of the 1982 northwest Ohoyo regional conference.

SMITH, BARBARA. *Home Girls: A Black Feminist Anthology.* New York: Kitchen Table Press, 1983. An anthology of stories and essays by black women.

SWERDLOW, AMY, and HANNAH LESSINGER. *Class, Race and Sex: The Dynamics of Control.* Boston: G.K. Hall, 1983. Essays from the seventh and eighth Scholar and Feminist conferences at Barnard College in New York, 1980–81.

TSUCHIDA, NOBUYA, ed. *Asian and Pacific American Experiences: Women's Perspectives*. Minneapolis: Asian/Pacific American Learning Resource Center, University of Minnesota, 1982. Essays and historical overview of Asian American women.

WALKER, ALICE. *In Search of Our Mothers' Gardens: Womanist Prose*. New York: Harcourt Brace Jovanovich, 1983. A collection of poems, stories, and essays written by Alice Walker between 1966 and 1982.

WILSON, HARRIET E. *Our Nig; or Sketches from the Life of a Free Black*. Introduction and notes by Henry Louis Gates, Jr. New York: Vintage Books, 1983. A reprint of the first Afro-American novel published in the United States (1859). Wilson wrote of the trials she endured in the North as a servant.

WINEGARTEN, RUTHE. *I Am Annie Mae*. Austin: Rosegarden Press, 1983. A case study of a seventy-four-year-old woman's journey from domestic work to a business career; she is also active in community and political work.

WILSON, EMILY. *Hope and Dignity: Older Black Women of the South*. Philadelphia: Temple University Press, 1983. Oral histories and photographs of 20 black women from North Carolina.

Work

Sara E. Rix and Anne J. Stone

Nineteen eighty-three was a year of considerable progress for women workers. Some of the gains were more symbolic than anything else, but others involved tangible benefits for substantial numbers of workers. Dominating the media for several days, for example, was physicist Sally Ride, the first American female astronaut and the most visible proof to date that women can succeed in occupations traditionally closed to them. Nontraditional workers demonstrated further progress, if on a less newsworthy scale, when over twenty women in New York City were granted full firefighter status at the end of their probationary period. And finding "extraordinary evidence of intentional discrimination," a federal judge ruled in favor of two other firefighters who had been dismissed from their jobs; reinstatement with back pay was ordered (Shenon 1983).

Working women scored a few other points as well. The Associated Press, in settling a ten-year-old sex and race discrimination case, will pay over $1 million to current and former female and minority employees and establish a five-year affirmative action program for women and minorities. In October, the Equal Employment Opportunity Commission, General Motors Corporation, and the United Auto Workers agreed to the largest nonlitigated settlement in the commission's history. Under the terms of this five-year agreement, General Motors will provide in excess of $42 million to resolve several hundred claims of employment discrimination against minorities and women. GM women at all levels clearly stand to benefit from provisions to train women for supervisory positions in manufacturing operations, to provide career development workshops for clerical workers, to establish a special training program for white-collar women and minorities, to set up an executive development program for minority and female placements, and to set aside $15 million for endowments to colleges and technical schools that will give preference to women and minorities in the distribution of those funds.

The development with the most potential significance was probably a U.S. district court finding that the State of Washington was guilty of pervasive sex-based wage discrimination. In that case, which highlighted what may be a growing role for unions in fighting for equity for women workers, the court ruled that Washington State must compensate government employees who were being paid less than other employees in jobs that required similar effort, knowledge, and abilities. Though some men were employed in these lower paid positions, they were, for the most part, women's jobs. The American Federation of State, County and Municipal Employees (AFSCME), which brought this class-action suit to court, was able to demonstrate the consequences of job segregation: for every percentile increase in the number of women in a particular job, the monthly wage decreased by $4.52. A conclusion from this and other wage comparisons is that jobs dominated by women pay less than jobs dominated by men simply because they are women's jobs and not because of inherent differences in the merit of the work.

Women's employment issues also received well-publicized attention on Capitol Hill in 1983. To ensure that women's need for employment would not be overlooked by emergency jobs legislation, the Congress agreed to a substantial raise in the proportion of Community Development Block Grant funds that states could use to create the types of jobs that women would be likely to fill. The Social Security Amendments of 1983 went a long way toward guaranteeing universal Social Security coverage, an important asset for job changers, persons with sporadic work patterns, and those in marginal jobs. Women predominate among the latter two groups.

Day care was of prime concern to the drafters of the 1983 Economic Equity Act, a major legislative reform package with bipartisan support. In this vein, a small but important step was the U.S. Senate's decision to establish a day care center for the children of Senate staff.

Overview of the 1983 Labor Force

The female labor force continued to grow in 1983, albeit at a slower rate than in the past. During the year, some 48.5 million women were working or looking for work; their civilian labor force participation rate of 52.9 percent was up from 52.6 percent a year before (U.S. Department of Labor 1984).

While these figures translate into an additional 748,000 women who found or sought paid employment in 1983, at least 1 million women, and often considerably more, had joined the ranks of the labor force in each of the past ten years. Even in 1982, when unemployment rates were at their highest level since 1941, the number of women in the labor force increased by nearly 1.1 million. Between 1970 and 1982, the female labor force grew at an annual rate of 3.5 percent (Fullerton and Tschetter 1983); in contrast, the 1982–83 increase was only 1.6 percent.

Women are expected to account for nearly two-thirds of the growth in the labor force through the 1990s (Marshall 1983). According to the most recent Bureau of Labor Statistics (BLS) projections for 1995 (Fullerton and Tschetter 1983), the largest projected increase for any group will be for women between the ages of twenty-five and thirty-four. Currently, 69 percent of the women in this age group are in the labor force; by 1995, that figure may approach 82 percent. Since these women have, and will undoubtedly continue to have, most of their children before age thirty-five (if they are going to have any), their increased labor force participation can be expected to further demands—seen in 1983 and discussed below—for public- and private-sector policies that will enable women more effectively to manage both family and employment responsibilities.

Women and the Economic Recovery

Among the most heartening news in 1983 was the steady and sharp drop in the unemployment rate, from 10.3 percent in January to 8.1 percent in December, an improvement benefiting both women and men. Traditionally, women's unemployment rates have been higher than those of men, but in 1982, that pattern reversed itself, in part because women tended to be employed in jobs that were, at least at the time, relatively recession proof (e.g., in clerical work and service industries). This reversal continued throughout 1983, resulting in an average annual unemployment rate of 9.2 percent for women and 9.9 percent for men.

As these figures might suggest, women fared rather well when it came to new employment, accounting, as they did, for 60 percent of the increase in employed persons in 1983. Nevertheless, the picture was by no means entirely rosy: the number of women working part time for economic reasons (i.e., because they could not find full-time employment) grew by nearly 5 percent (to 3.2 million). Close to 1 million additional women could be classified as discouraged workers who might enter the labor force if they felt their chances of finding a job were more favorable. These women are not technically unemployed, since they are not looking for work, but if all of them were, the unemployment rate for women would have been almost two percentage points higher in 1983.

Unemployment as a Women's Problem

Old myths die hard, and few have taken as long to expire as the one that minimizes the financial contribution that working women make to the family coffers.

But because men support the family and women's pin money is hardly the mainstay, or so the myth goes, unemployment among women has generated neither the concern of public officials nor the scholarly attention that has been accorded to their male counterparts. Consequently, the existing literature provides few insights into how women are affected by, and cope with, the unemployment experience (Rayman 1983; Kempers 1983).

Yet, in 1983, nearly 5.8 million women in the labor force were maintaining families, another 4.9 million were living alone, and 1.6 million had unemployed husbands (U.S. Department of Labor 1984). Even if it were the case that all other women were working solely for little extras or self-satisfaction, that would leave over 12 million women for whom unemployment could spell economic disaster.

The extent to which women are left at least as vulnerable as men when unemployment hits—and often more so—has been documented in a recent study of a plant closing in an economically depressed Pennsylvania community (Snyder and Nowak 1983; Nowak and Snyder 1983). The increasing prevalence of multi-earner families often serves to cushion the impact of unemployment of one of the partners (Klein 1983), but, as Snyder and Nowak discovered, unemployed women did not necessarily have the support of a wage-earning husband to fall back on: two-thirds of the women in their study were never married, or were widowed, separated, or divorced, and many of these had the additional burden of caring for children and/or parents.

Job skidding, or slipping down the occupational hierarchy after unemployment, has been the focus of some attention in the literature on male unemployment; women are apparently not immune to this problem. If the Pennsylvania women managed to secure employment at all, they were, according to Nowak and Snyder, more likely to "skid into low-wage, low-status occupations" (e.g., service and sales, often only part time), experiencing in the process a wage drop of 38 percent, which was more than twice that of the reemployed men in the sample.

These women's experience with unemployment and its aftershocks may have been all the more traumatic in view of the fact that they had succeeded in making inroads into nontraditional jobs that were typically more highly paid than "women's" jobs; comparable employment in the depressed economy of Pennsylvania was not available.

Deaux and Ullman (1983) also stress the negative impact that the recent recession has had on women in nontraditional employment. In their study of women in the steel industry, these authors comment on the apparent effectiveness of affirmative action and equal opportunity policies in broadening opportunities for women in the steel industry in the late 1970s, but, they point out, the "current economic climate has effectively eliminated all gains made by women" (165). As noted, steel is not an expanding industry, and it is unlikely that women, so recently hired and consequently first fired, will ever recover their hard-won positions.

Former secretary of labor Ray Marshall strikes a similarly pessimistic note in his assessment of jobs and job opportunities for women in the 1980s (Marshall 1983). Noting that it is tight labor markets that facilitate the employment of women in nontraditional jobs, as well as their advancement, he points out that the demand for work is—and it might be added, will continue to be—such that it has been necessary to create two or three jobs simply to reduce unemployment by one.

Women's Work

Dramatic breakthroughs in the status of working women are not to be expected over a one-year period; however, the persistence of job segregation and a widening of the male-female wage gap over the past twenty-five years (Blau 1983) remain a cause for concern among women's activists and advocates.

Comparisons of published data for 1983 with those for earlier years have been made more difficult by the introduction of a new classification system for occupational data collected in the Current Population Survey. Hence, clerical workers—easily identified as such in BLS publications—are now subsumed in the category "administrative support, including clerical," a category with substantially more subclassifications than previously. (Although the new system's refinement is more informative, the process of identifying changes and trends has become more time consuming.) Whatever the work, persons employed in administrative support jobs were overwhelmingly female—80 percent—in 1983, as they were in 1982 and before. In fact, four out of every five women work in just twenty-five of the more than four hundred occupations listed by the U.S. Department of Labor (*Pay equity* . . . 1983).

Were it not for the fact that job categories dominated by women pay so much less than those dominated by men, sex segregation in the work force would not be especially troublesome. That a large male-female wage gap exists is beyond dispute: the ratio most commonly reported is that year-round, full-time working women earn 60 cents for every dollar earned by men so employed, a discrepancy that has not changed appreciably over the past thirty years. Rytina (1983) confirmed this disparity in an assessment of earnings ratios derived from both weekly and annual wage data, although weekly wage comparisons revealed a somewhat more favorable ratio of 65 cents to the dollar. Wide variations, however, are found within specific occupational classifications. Among sales workers, for example, women's wages were only about 52 percent of men's wages, whereas among health workers (a category that does not include physicians and dentists), the differences disappeared. The latter example, though encouraging, was relatively rare.

The earnings ratio may widen or narrow, depending on a number of other factors. Full-time working women work, on the average, fewer hours per week than full-time working men, although these differences alone cannot explain a 35 to 40 percent wage gap.

Assessment of data for twenty-five-to-thirty-four-year-old white women and men in the National Longitudinal Survey (NLS) found an earnings gap of about 34 percent (Boyer 1983), but this difference narrowed to 12 percent after taking into consideration such factors as job tenure, education, and differences in work experience. It might even have been narrower if other as yet unmeasured and/or hard-to-measure variables as motivation, effort, and quality of vocational training were entered into the assessment.

While some would challenge the inference that lower motivation and less effort explain some of the wage gap, there is a continuing controversy over whether women "voluntarily" opt for jobs that make fewer demands on them and where the penalty for labor force withdrawal (e.g., to care for children) is minimal (Polachek 1979; Bohen 1983). Goldberg (1983, 63) on the other hand, has argued that the *nature* of typical women's jobs discourages continuity: "there is no particular reason to make a lifetime commitment to unpleasant unrewarding work, if one can avoid it."

In an evaluation of ten-year data for middle-aged women in the National Longitudinal Surveys (i.e., women who were thirty to forty-four at the beginning of the period), Daymont and Statham (1983) were unable to support the hypothesis that differences in labor force commitment were responsible for occupational segregation. Employment in atypical or male-dominated occupations was only slightly more common among white women with a strong labor force commitment than among those with a weak one, and blacks with a strong labor force commitment were actually more likely than less committed blacks to work in typical female occupations.

Although labor force commitment did not explain occupational choice, it did affect earnings, leading the researchers to conclude that "taken together, variation in family responsibilities, human-capital accumulation, and labor-market commitment explained a substantial portion of the variation in earnings." However, these factors did not explain all the variance, "implying that other factors, such as labor-market discrimination are also at work" (Daymont and Statham 1983, 73). Blau (1983) has contended that about 50 percent of the existing male-female wage gap can be traced to discrimination.

Missing from many discussions of occupational segregation, commitment, and unemployment is the type of class-based analysis found in a recent collection of British research papers (Gamarnikow et al. 1983). Placing gender and social class at the center of the study of work and work processes, these essays look at women's participation in labor unions and in such areas as banking, hairdressing, and factory work.

Comparable Worth

Some economists maintain that the path to earnings parity lies in removing barriers to atypical jobs, and while this may be true, at least in individual cases, it assumes that atypical jobs—those dominated by men—pay more because they are worth more. Women's advocates have increasingly rejected this notion, and the push for comparable worth, or equal pay for work of equal value, superseded interest in job desegregation in 1983.

Although one might conclude that virtually everything that could be said about comparable worth was published in a two-volume report of hearings before the subcommittees on Human Resources, Civil Service, and Compensation and Employee Benefits of the House Committee on Post Office and Civil Service (*Pay equity* . . . 1983) and in an elaboration of both sides of the issue (Gold 1983), the last word is hardly in.

At the heart of the debate are some key questions. Is it really possible to develop acceptable measures of the worth of disparate jobs? And who will compensate victims of an inequitable wage history? Marshall (1983) has argued that the difficulties of measuring pay equity and applying it precisely in specific situations are not unique to the comparable-worth controversy; they are true of most pay problems. In the Washington State case, comparable worth *had* been established, although many observers might not have agreed with the state's job evaluation.

Officials in Washington have warned that this decision might "break the bank," as it were, and force program cutbacks, layoffs, or tax increases. However, other states and local jurisdictions are apparently managing to support comparable-worth initiatives.

Another unanswered question involves the impact that the implementation of comparable-worth policies will have on labor costs and the market economy. Comparable-worth opponents have argued that the market efficiently establishes wage scales based on labor supply and demand and that a national policy of comparable worth would "not only drive up costs, but also shatter the free-market system of pricing jobs" (Price 1983, 58). Proponents, in contrast, vocally reject this contention. In any case, "the battle lines have been drawn" (Price 1983, 58), and comparable worth, with all its complexities, is likely to dominate employment considerations well into the future.

Technology

Relatively little is known with certainty about the impact of technological developments on employment opportunities for women. On the one hand, technological advances have lessened the requirement for those abilities or attributes, such as brute strength, that have justified excluding women from so many jobs. Other impediments aside, women should be able to increase their numbers in male-dominated industries as a result of many of the new technologies (Deaux and Ullman 1983).

On the other hand, rapid technological change is also characterizing female-dominated occupations, such as clerical work, and concern exists not only about the potential replacement of people with machines, but also about deskilling, a loss of autonomy, and the possible misuse and abuse of electronic monitoring of output.

Although large-scale job loss is not an inevitable consequence of office automation, especially over the short run, it may preclude the need for additional workers and reduce the rate of growth in this area. Over the long run, Gutek (1983) predicts that offices will probably contain fewer workers than they now contain. When completed, a study by the Office of Technology Assessment, begun in 1983, on the impact of office automation should shed considerable light on these issues of concern to women.

"The potential for job change due to technology cuts across all job categories" (Wider Opportunities for Women 1983), and middle managers may also have some reason to fear the application of new technologies if *Business Week*'s assessment is any guide (A new era . . . 1983). According to this article, the raison d'être of middle managers has been the gathering and processing of information, functions that are being taken over by computers. Since it has been at this level that women had been making some inroads into management, any shrinking of opportunities will set women back.

In view of the fact that further technological change in the work place is all but inevitable, it would help to know how women accept and adapt to the changes. Aside from a recent analysis of fairly old data (Form and McMillen 1983), insights into this relationship are somewhat speculative. Form and McMillen conclude that most employees—including women—who experience automation "accept it as normal and adjust to it, especially if *their control over work is preserved as it generally appears to be*" (174; emphasis added).

Unfortunately, the degree to which one can generalize from this observation is limited by the age of the data, which were collected well before the "paperless office" became a reality. Control over work may have been enhanced by the technological developments of the late 1960s, but it is threatened by those of the present.

The jury is still out on the impact of many technological developments, particularly video display terminals (VDTs), on the health of the users. The National Research Council (1983) found no evidence that the use of VDTs, per se, causes harm to the visual system. Rather, the differences in reported symptoms between workers in VDT and non-VDT jobs may be more directly related to characteristics of the work situation than to characteristics inherent in VDTs. Not everyone, however, would agree with this conclusion (e.g., Frank 1983; Stanley 1983).

The Balancing Act

While the surge of married women into the work force and the increasing likelihood that women will continue to work after marriage are not new developments, married women were working in record numbers in 1983.

More than 24 million wives were employed in 1983, up nearly half a million from 1982. The vast majority (86 percent) were in dual-earner marriages. Five percent had unemployed husbands. A substantial majority (70 percent) worked full time, averaging just over forty hours a week on the job.

Wives' earnings contributed substantially to the financial well-being of married-couple families. The median income of families with a wife in the paid labor force in 1982 was $30,342—42 percent higher than the median income of couples without a working wife (U.S. Bureau of the Census 1983b).

Fifty-four percent of working wives had children under eighteen. Of all working women with children under eighteen, about one fifth were single parents.

All working women with husbands and/or children are likely to experience some conflicts in attempting to balance their responsibilities on the paid job with the primary responsibility they usually bear for household and child care. The conflicts are most severe, however, and have the most disturbing implications for employment prospects in the case of working mothers, whatever their marital status.

The discouraging news in 1983 was that, despite the presence of millions of mothers as well as fathers in the work force, little progress is being made to help working parents cope. The evidence reported in 1983 suggests that employers get involved in helping employees to combine work and family responsibilities only if the bottom line seems to require them to do so. For example, employers tend to concern themselves with child care only if it is vital in order for them to hire and retain young mothers. Hospitals, one of the few industries in which employer involvement in child care is widespread, are a case in point. "In terms of significant national trends, the movement [toward more employer involvement in child care] is virtually imperceptible" (Children's Defense Fund 1983, 8).

Moreover, even if such provisions as liberal leave policies for child care, part-time work, and flexible schedules become much more common than they now are, women will continue to be at a disadvantage in the work place if it is always mothers, rather than fathers, who make use of these offerings. As long as it is women who are the ones to step off the fast track to meet family responsibilities, they will be at a competitive disadvantage in career advancement as it is presently structured. The broader social implications of this are examined by Joan Huber and Glenna Spitze, who conclude that women's labor force participation is the most crucial variable in predicting change in family roles (Huber and Spitze 1983).

As in the past, employed mothers—and those who want to enter the work force—typically try to work out private child care arrangements, relying more often than not on kin to look after small children. Twenty-nine percent turn to grandmothers and other relatives. Only 15 percent (up slightly from 13 percent in 1977) use group child care arrangements. Approximately 17 percent cobble together a combination of arrangements ("multiple arrangements") to ensure that their children are looked after continuously while they work (U.S. Bureau of the Census 1983a).

Fourteen percent of all working mothers (17 percent of those currently married) with children under five depend on the children's fathers (three-fourths of whom are themselves employed) for child care. Many of the parents in these cases may manage by working different shifts so that one parent can care for the children during all, or most, of the time the other parent is at work.

Among all dual-earner couples with children in which both spouses work full time, more than one-third include at least one spouse who works other than a regular day shift (Presser and Cain 1983). Most commonly the father takes an evening shift and the mother works the day shift. Normal family life must be especially difficult to achieve for the 10 percent of full-time dual-earner parent-couples whose work schedules do not overlap at all.

The stresses produced by the difficulties in juggling the demands of a paid job with the needs of household and family have an impact on domestic life. A small study of men who have assumed a substantial degree of responsibility for household management and child care found "tensions [between spouses] because of conflicts over priorities and timing" (Beer 1983, 85). On the other hand, many of the men surveyed in this study reported that they had become more sympathetic to their spouses' "balancing" problems. Some also found that they had begun to define themselves more in terms of their role in the home and less exclusively in terms of their occupations. (Incidentally, to the extent that this pattern becomes widespread among men, they may find unemployment less psychologically disastrous. Rayman [1983] found job loss to be typically more damaging to men than to women because a male's self-esteem tended to be based almost entirely on his occupation. Because most working wives, on the other hand, had two roles with which to identify, if they lost their paid jobs they generally retained a sense of self-esteem based on their "job" at home.)

In addition to creating strains at home, the difficulty of making satisfactory arrangements for the care of children militates against full-time employment for many women who might prefer it (U.S. Bureau of the Census 1983a). Twenty-one percent of mothers employed part time would work more hours if additional child care were available and affordable. Lack of child care resources keeps many other mothers out of the work force altogether. This is especially true for single mothers; whereas 22 percent of currently married mothers of young children who are not in the work force say they would look for work if child care arrangements could be made, the percentage rises to 45 percent for single mothers.

Moreover, family responsibilities appear to cause mothers who are working to make decisions that effectively limit their opportunities for good jobs and for advancement. Bohen asserts that mothers "do not opt for higher levels of [job] responsibility *because* of their parenting responsibilities" (Bohen 1983, 22).

Particularly discouraging in 1983 were reports that the double burden carried by managerial women with young children is hobbling them in their efforts to compete with male colleagues for higher level jobs. Papers from a 1982 conference at Cornell University addressed general problems of women managers, for example, discrimination, career advancement, and organizational behavior, and the impact of specific family difficulties such as dual-career couples, child care, and leaves of absence (Farley 1983).

Such publications as the *Wall Street Journal* (Toman 1983), the *Financier* (Bremner 1983), and *Fortune* (Rowan 1983) gave prominent coverage to the career/family conflicts facing many women in traditionally male-dominated managerial and professional occupations. Since women began to aim for these careers to any measurable degree just about a decade ago, it is probably not accidental that the spotlight was on them in 1983. Nearly one in three "executive, administrative and managerial" jobs was held by a woman in 1983, compared to one in five in 1973 (U.S. Department of Labor 1983). Clearly, women in managerial jobs are much more visible than they used to be, and the ambitious pioneering young women of the early 1970s are now typically in their thirties, keenly aware of the hands on the biological clock. Many of these women are finding that it is a lot harder to "have it all" than they had anticipated.

A 1983 survey of the thirty-four women among the 1973 graduates of the Harvard Business School (the first Harvard Business School class of which women constituted at least 5 percent) found that although these women are doing well by many standards, as a group they seem not to be doing as well as their male classmates. "Part of the answer doubtless lies in [the] statistics on motherhood, which has taken 40 percent of the women out of the office at least temporarily and, perhaps more significantly, has altered their priorities" (Rowan 1983, 60).

The problem is that the years during which women who want children must bear and raise them are the key years in the struggle for career success, and employers have largely failed to anticipate and to adapt their policies to the pressures that working mothers face (Bohen 1983; Bremner 1983; Toman 1983). Employees who are unwilling or unable always to give the job top priority are at a substantial disadvantage in a corporate or professional structure that is based on what could be expected of male employees whose traditional-role marriages allowed fathers consistently to resolve work/family conflicts in favor of the job. This is true of male as well as female employees, but as a practical matter it is still women who are expected to shoulder the major responsibilities for home and family. "Observation confirms the conclusion that as serious career women begin to have children in large numbers, few men are stepping forward to sacrifice their careers [so that] their hard-pressed wives [can] go on being as productive as before in the workplace" (Bremner 1983, 48).

More part-time options for career women whose children are very young, as well as longer childbirth leaves without career penalty, seem particularly important. Because these options are so often lacking, some women are finding that the only solution is to drop out of the work place for a while. As a result, they are likely to lose career momentum that can never be regained.

Although many employers have made a considerable investment in their managerial women, a tight labor market makes it less likely that employers will feel compelled to respond to the concerns of working mothers (Bremner 1983). A corporate manager commented: "The women moving to higher levels in our firm are single or those with grown children" (Bohen 1983, 19).

If even those mothers with well-paid, upwardly mobile jobs and husbands to help share the load face great difficulties in combining work with family responsibilities, the 20 percent of women workers who maintain families containing children under eighteen face a truly daunting task. Yet "labor force participation rates show these single parents had a strong commitment to the labor force" (Johnson and Waldman 1983, 31). Three-quarters of those whose youngest child was between six and seventeen, and more than half of those with preschool-age children, were in the work force. Eighty-three percent of employed female family heads worked full time. No doubt many of those who have only part-time jobs, or who are not now in the labor force, would be working more if they could make satisfactory arrangements for affordable child care. As noted above, 45 percent of single mothers not in the labor force say they would enter it if child care were available.

The difficulty of combining family and job responsibilities is, however, by no means the only impediment confronting working women who head families. "The increased labor force participation of female family heads has not translated into increased economic security because . . . [of] the combination of female family headship (with concomitant lack of other resources, including second earners) and discrimination in job training and employment" (U.S. Commission on Civil Rights 1983a, 1).

Stressing that full-time employment is not necessarily a ticket out of poverty for families headed by women, the Civil Rights Commission pointed out that a year-round full-time job at minimum wage produced an income below the poverty level for a family of three (the average size of families headed by women) in 1980. This was not only still true in 1983, but the gap—$122 in 1980—had widened to an abyss: the difference between the 1983 poverty threshold (estimated by the Bureau of the Census to be $7,940 for a family of three) and year-round full-time earnings at the minimum wage ($6,968) was more than $1,000.

While there are no data available on how many female family heads worked year round full time for the minimum wage, fully employed women in general are considerably more likely than their male counterparts to have earnings at or below the minimum wage (U.S. Bureau of the Census 1983b). It is perhaps worth emphasizing that a married couple family that can send two adults into the work force full time can manage to stay above the poverty level even if neither earns more than the minimum wage.

The Commission on Civil Rights also concluded that the concentration of women workers into a narrow range of low-paying occupations, made worse by racism, is probably the major factor responsible for the high poverty rate among female-headed families, and that education, while important, will not "redress [their] economic disadvantage" (1983a, 62). Indeed, more than one-third of black female family heads with one or more years of college were in poverty in 1982, according to the U.S. Bureau of the Census (1983b). Nevertheless, Johnson and Waldman noted that working female family heads were much more likely than working wives to lack a high school diploma (23 percent versus 15 percent). This may at least partially reflect the fact that currently married women with little education and marketable skills may be under less economic pressure than single mothers. In any case, the majority of women maintaining families are still in the generally lower paying or lesser skilled jobs within a broad occupational category (Johnson and Waldman 1983).

The Job Training Partnership Act (JTPA), the main piece of employment legislation of the 97th Congress and the successor to the Comprehensive Employment and Training Act (CETA), went into effect on 1 October 1983. While it is obviously too early to ascertain its effectiveness, the act is in part intended to reduce welfare dependency. Consequently, one would expect its training programs to target disadvantaged single women with children. To the extent that these women develop marketable skills in JTPA programs, their movement into more highly paid jobs may ensue.

To ensure that the needs of single parents and low-income women are taken into account by the Private Industry Councils (PICs) that help shape and oversee the training programs developed under the act, California enacted legislation requiring that every PIC in that state include at least one welfare recipient and one child care recipient among its members. However, there was reported to be some resistance to this requirement on the part of private-sector PIC members (Hamilton 1983).

Special Groups

Middle-Aged and Older Workers

In 1983, nearly 12 million women (or 10.7 percent of the total labor force) between the ages of forty-five and sixty-four were in the labor force. As the labor force ages along with the "baby boomers," women in their middle years will become an even more significant component of the labor force. Women over sixty-five have never had a very strong attachment to the labor force, and while the number of workers in this age group has been increasing slightly, their labor force participation rates fell further in 1983 and are expected to continue to do so (Fullerton and Tschetter 1983).

Both the scholarly and the popular literatures have tended to focus on the employment *problems* of middle-aged women, although women have not been accorded the same degree of attention as middle-aged men. It is almost certainly true, as Markson (1983, 73) contends, namely, that "sex and age discrimination combine for women in mid-life to exacerbate their employment problems."

Ending on a somewhat more optimistic note were four recent reports or book chapters on women.

Clark (1983), for example, found no evidence of an age-related increase in labor market problems among nonmarried women in the large, longitudinal Retirement History Survey. Specifically, this analysis of earnings data from 1953–74 revealed no decline in women's earnings relative to men's after their middle forties. This is not to say that there wasn't a wage gap, but rather that that gap did not widen over time. (Even gross income data for one year show a wide gap between male and female workers in their middle and later years, but it, too, narrows with advancing age [U.S. Bureau of the Census 1983b]).

Clark's sample was restricted to a population of nonmarried elderly, whose labor force attachment was typically more continuous than married age-mates, and continuity, obviously, has a favorable impact on lifetime earnings. Shaw (1983), however, took a look at middle-aged reentrants who were out of the labor force for at least five years and found, surprisingly, that time away from work had no effect on earnings. Nor did Shaw find that the wages of older women were lower than those of younger ones, suggesting that "any age discrimination within the age range from the midthirties to the midfifties must operate either beyond entry-level jobs or in hiring decisions that make it difficult for older women to find employment" (Shaw 1983, 42).

In a study of an entirely different type, Rosen (1983) referred to fears of job loss expressed by older blue-collar women in the garment, electrical goods, and food processing industries of eastern New England. The problems of a deteriorating labor market would, they worried, be compounded by age discrimination. Age discrimination was apparently not a problem, however, for after six months, older workers on layoff were as likely as their younger counterparts to have been recalled or to have found a new job. Rosen postulates that because older women were so common in these industries and occupations, employers were just as willing to hire experienced older workers as younger ones.

Another explanation, suggested by the research of Johnson, Dickinson, and West (1983) is that displaced older women are more serious job seekers than other unemployed women and persist in their hunt, thus increasing the probability of eventually finding work.

These studies should not be taken to mean that older women do not face problems in the work force; they do, and the fact was even evident in some of the above research. Rosen, for instance, found that older displaced women who secured new jobs after layoff experienced substantial wage cuts. Johnson, Dickinson, and West also noted that older job seekers who turned to the U.S. Employment Service for assistance were far less likely than their younger counterparts to receive job referrals, an unfortunate occurrence for older women because such referrals substantially improved their chances of finding work.

Women in the Military

The most notable development for military women in 1983 involved the Army's decision to reopen thirteen job categories closed to women the previous year because those jobs "might" involve direct combat. Critics of the Army's 1982 policy change had questioned the decision to exclude women from, for example, all carpentry and plumbing jobs. Since a woman's advancement potential in the military, as in the private sector, depends on her career profile, restricting her exposure to job opportunities would hinder prospects for advancement. The Army also agreed to modify a proposed test of physical strength that would have effectively barred women from the majority of Army jobs. The publication of a statistical profile of military women within the Defense Department, together with an outside analysis of the various philosophies governing policy decisions on women soldiers, seem to indicate a more open approach to the issues than in the past year or two (U.S. Office of the Assistant Secretary . . . 1983; Boening 1983).

In September 1983, the Veterans' Administration appointed an Advisory Committee to focus long-overdue attention on the health, educational, and economic needs of women veterans (Willenz 1983a). Awareness of the contributions and special problems of these women was greatly increased with the book *Women Veterans* by June Willenz (1983b), who is one of the new committee members along with journalist Sarah McClendon, Maj. Gen. (Ret.) Jeanne Holm, endocrinologist and feminist Dr. Estelle Ramey, and others.

Women in Science, Engineering, and Technical Fields

Often at a snail's pace, women have increased their representation in the select, and often highly paid, world of science, engineering, and high technology. Over the five years between 1978 and 1982, women's share of computer specialists rose from 23.1 to 28.5 percent; of engineers, from 2.8 to 5.7 percent; and of life and physical scientists, from 17.9 to 20.6 percent (U.S. Department of Labor 1979, 1983). Women aeronautical and astronautical engineers did not even make BLS's 1978 listing of employed persons by detailed occupation. By 1982, 4 percent of these engineers were women.

In 1983, however, progress seemed to have been halted, at least in engineering. One is struck, for example, by a drop of fifteen thousand in the number of female engineers in that year alone. (Also noticeable were a slight drop in mathematical and computer scientists and a very small increase in the number of natural scientists.) While the apparent loss or disappearance of fifteen thousand engineers might be construed as something of a problem, it is not clear that this is the case. The drop may have been due to sampling error and/or the change in the occupational classification system. Whether women and minority men have fair access to employment in burgeoning high-technology industries was the topic of Civil Rights Commission hearings held in California's expanding "Silicon Valley" (U.S. Commission on Civil Rights 1983b).

A brighter picture for the future is suggested by the thousandfold increase since 1972 in the number of women studying engineering full time, with the result that about 15 percent of all undergraduate students are women (Truxal 1983).

Women's exposure to math and science would also increase with the passage of pending proposals to provide monies for education in these fields. In early 1983, the House of Representatives approved H.R. 1310, which, in improving math and science education, would ensure equal education opportunities for women and other underrepresented minorities. A Senate counterpart measure remained in committee at the end of the year.

Conclusion

"More than ever, American women think their place is on the job," according to the results of a *New York Times* poll (Dowd 1983). The events of 1983 would appear to confirm that working women are here to stay, despite the almost insurmountable barriers of combining work and family lives, pervasive and persistent segregation into jobs with few opportunities for advancement, low wages, and a host of other problems. In 1983, legislative proposals and judicial decisions reflected an increasing acceptance of this fact and an awareness of the need to redress the specific grievances of a growing segment of the population.

References

American Federation of State, County and Municipal Employees (AFSCME). 1983. *Pay equity on trial*. Washington, D.C.: AFSCME.

BEER, W.R. 1983. *Househusbands: Men and housework in American families*. New York: Praeger.

BLAU, F. 1983. *The economic status of women in the labor market*. Testimony presented before the Subcommittee on Civil and Constitutional Rights of the Judiciary Committee of the U.S. House of Representatives, 14 September.

BOENING, S. 1983. Woman soldier, quo vadis? *Parameters*, June, pp. 58–64.

BOHEN, H.H. 1983. *Corporate employment policies affecting families and children: The United States and Europe*. New York: Aspen Institute for Humanistic Studies.

BOYER, J. 1983. The male-female pay gap: Will it narrow? *Urban Institute Policy and Research Report* 13, no. 3:15–17.

BREMNER, J.E. 1983. Trouble ahead for career women. *Financier*, October, pp. 48–52.

Children's Defense Fund. 1983. *A corporate reader: Work and family life in the 1980s.* Washington, D.C.: Children's Defense Fund.

CLARK, R.L. 1983. *Sources of labor market problems of older persons who are also women, handicapped, and/or members of minority groups.* Washington, D.C.: National Commission for Employment Policy.

DAYMONT, T., and A. STATHAM. 1983. Occupational atypicality: Changes, causes, and consequences. In *Unplanned careers: The working lives of middle-aged women,* edited by Lois Banfill Shaw, 61–75. Lexington, Mass.: Lexington Books.

DEAUX, K., and J.C. ULLMAN. 1983. *Women of steel: Female blue-collar workers in the basic steel industry.* New York: Praeger.

DOWD, M. 1983. Many women in poll equate values of job and family life. *New York Times,* 4 December.

FARLEY, J. 1983. The woman in management: Career and family issues. Ithaca, N.Y.: ILR Press, Cornell University.

FORM, W., and D.B. McMILLEN. 1983. Women, men, and machines. *Work and Occupations* 10, no. 2:147–75.

FRANK, A.L. 1983. *Effects on health following occupational exposure to video display terminals.* Lexington: University of Kentucky Department of Preventive Medicine and Environmental Health.

FULLERTON, H.N, Jr., and J. TSCHETTER. 1983. The 1995 labor force: A second look. *Monthly Labor Review* 106, no. 11:3–10.

GAMARNIKOW, E., D. MORGAN, J. PURVIS, and D. TAYLORSON. 1983. *Gender, class and work.* Exeter, N.H.: Heinemann.

GOLD, M.E. 1983. *A dialogue on comparable worth.* Ithaca, N.Y.: ILR Press, Cornell University.

GOLDBERG, R. 1983. *Organizing women office workers: Dissatisfaction, consciousness, and action.* New York: Praeger.

GUTEK, B.A. 1983. Women's work in the office of the future. In *The technological woman: Interfacing with tomorrow,* edited by Jan Zimmerman, 159–68. New York: Praeger.

HAMILTON, K. 1983. Remarks presented before the CAWP Forum for Women State Legislators, sponsored by the Center for the American Woman and Politics of Rutgers University, San Diego, 1–4 December.

HUBER, J., and G. SPITZE. 1983. *Sex stratification: Children, housework, and jobs.* New York: Academic Press.

JOHNSON, B.L., and E. WALDMAN. 1983. Most women who head families receive poor job market returns. *Monthly Labor Review* 106, no. 12:30–34.

JOHNSON, T.R., K.P. DICKINSON, and R.W. WEST. 1983. *Older workers' responses to job displacement and the assistance provided by the employment service.* Washington, D.C.: National Commission for Employment Policy.

KEMPERS, M.B. 1983. Remarks presented before the conference, "Women and Structural Transformation: The Crisis of Work and Family Life," sponsored by the Institute for Research on Women, Douglass College, New Brunswick, N.J., 18–19 November.

KLEIN, D.P. 1983. Trends in employment and unemployment in families. *Monthly Labor Review* 106, no. 12:21–25.

MARKSON, E.W. 1983. *Older women: Issues and prospects.* Lexington, Mass.: D.C. Heath and Co.

MARSHALL, RAY. 1983. *Work & women in the 1980s: A perspective on basic trends affecting women's jobs and job opportunities.* Washington, D.C.: Women's Research and Education Institute.

National Research Council. 1983. *Video displays, work, and vision.* Washington, D.C.: National Academy Press.

A new era for management. 1983. *Business Week,* 25 April, pp. 50–86.

NOWAK, T.C., and K.A. SNYDER. 1983. *Women's struggle to survive a plant shutdown.* Revised version of a paper presented at the annual meetings of the Society for the Study of Social Problems. (Forthcoming in the *Journal of Intergroup Relations* 1984.)

Pay equity: Equal pay for work of comparable value, Part I and *Part II.* 1983. Publication of the joint hearings before the Subcommittees on Human Resources, Civil Service, and Compensation and Employee Benefits of the Committee on Post Office and Civil Service of the U.S. House of Representatives. Washington, D.C.: U.S. Government Printing Office.

POLACHEK, S.W. 1979. Occupational segregation among women: Theory, evidence, and a prognosis. In *Women in the labor market,* edited by Cynthia B. Lloyd, Emily S. Andrews, and Curtis L. Gilroy. New York: Columbia University Press.

PRESSER, H.B., and V.S. CAIN. 1983. Shift work among dual-earner couples with children. *Science* 219:876–79.

PRICE, M. 1983. Women rally to a "worthy" cause. *Industry Week,* 28 November, pp. 56–59.

RAYMAN, P. 1983. *The human and social costs of unemployment.* Paper presented at a congressional seminar on Capitol Hill sponsored by the Consortium of Social Science Associations, the American Sociological Association, and U.S. Representatives Augustus Hawkins, Paul Simon, and James Jeffords, 3 August.

ROSEN, E. 1983. Beyond the sweatshops: Older women in blue-collar jobs. In *Older women,* edited by Elizabeth W. Markson, 75–91. Lexington, Mass.: Lexington Books.

ROWAN, R. 1983. How Harvard's women MBAs are managing. *Fortune,* 11 July, pp. 58–72.

RYTINA, N. 1983. Comparing annual and weekly earnings from the Current Population Survey. *Monthly Labor Review* 106, no. 4:32–36.

SHAW, L. 1983. Problems of labor-market reentry. In *Unplanned careers: The working lives of middle-aged women,* edited by Lois Banfill Shaw, 33–44. Lexington, Mass.: Lexington Books.

SHENON, P. 1983. Women win bias suit against fire dept. *New York Times,* 8 December.

SNYDER, K.A., and T.C. NOWAK. 1983. *Sex differences in the impact of a plant shutdown: The case of Robertshaw controls.* Paper prepared for the annual meeting of the American Sociological Association, Detroit, August.

STANLEY, A.D. 1983. High-tech will hurt women. *New York Times*, 19 September.

TOMAN, B. 1983. Parenthood and career overtax some women despite best intentions. *Wall Street Journal*, 7 September.

TRUXAL, C. 1983. The woman engineer. *Woman Engineer* 4, no. 1:71–78.

U.S. Bureau of the Census. 1983a. *Child care arrangements of working mothers: June 1982.* Current Population Reports, Series P-23, no. 129. Washington, D.C.: U.S. Government Printing Office.

U.S. Bureau of the Census, 1983b. *Money income and poverty status of families and persons in the United States: 1982.* Current Population Reports, Series P-60, no. 140. Washington, D.C.: U.S. Government Printing Office.

U.S. Commission on Civil Rights. 1983a. *Disadvantaged women and their children.* Washington, D.C.: U.S. Commission on Civil Rights.

U.S. Commission on Civil Rights. 1983b. *Women and minorities in high technology.* San Jose, Calif.: U.S. Commission on Civil Rights.

U.S. Department of Labor, Bureau of Labor Statistics. 1979. *Employment and earnings*, 26, no. 1. Washington, D.C.: U.S. Government Printing Office.

U.S. Department of Labor, Bureau of Labor Statistics. 1983. *Employment and earnings*, 30, no. 1. Washington, D.C.: U.S. Government Printing Office.

U.S. Department of Labor, Bureau of Labor Statistics. 1984. *Employment and earnings*, 31, no. 1. Washington, D.C.: U.S. Government Printing Office.

U.S. Office of the Assistant Secretary of Defense (Manpower, Reserve Affairs, and Logistics). 1983. *Military women in the Department of Defense.* Washington, D.C.: U.S. Department of Defense.

WALDMAN, E. 1983. Labor force statistics from a family perspective. *Monthly Labor Review* 106, no. 12:16–20.

Wider Opportunities for Women. 1983. *Bridging the skills gap: Women and jobs in a high tech world.* Washington, D.C.: Wider Opportunities for Women.

WILLENZ, J. 1983a. VA's Advisory Committe on Women Veterans is launched. *Minerva: Quarterly report on women and the military* 1, no. 4:11–15.

————. 1983b. *Women veterans: America's forgotten heroines.* New York: Continuum.

Appendix:
Selected Bibliography of Feminist
Theory and General Social Studies

Sarah M. Pritchard

Within each chapter of *The Women's Annual* are works of feminist theory and analysis related to the specific topics under review. However, there are many books that defy easy categorization and cut across even the fluid boundaries of women's studies. This appendix will selectively annotate such works which were published in 1983 and late 1982 in areas of feminist theory, the women's movement, sociology, and women's relationship to science and technology. The reader is encouraged to consult the references and bibliographies at the end of each chapter and in previous editions of *The Women's Annual*, especially Kathleen Barry's essay in *The Women's Annual: 1982*.

ABEL, ELIZABETH, and EMILY K. ABEL, eds. *The Signs Reader: Women, Gender, & Scholarship*. Chicago: University of Chicago Press, 1983. Reprints of essays from the journal *Signs*, including now-classic essays by Joan Kelly, Carroll Smith-Rosenberg, Evelyn Fox Keller, Adrienne Rich, Catherine MacKinnon, and Hélène Cixous. A must, especially if you didn't subscribe.

ANDERSEN, MARGARET L. *Thinking about Women: Sociological and Feminist Perspectives*. New York: Macmillan, 1983. Wide-ranging study of women's lives (sexuality, biology, aging), gender and social institutions (work, housework, the family, health and reproduction, justice and criminology), and feminist theories of social change and the construction of knowledge. Readable, with a good bibliography.

APTHEKER, BETTINA. *Women's Legacy: Essays on Race, Sex and Class in American history*. Amherst: University of Massachusetts Press, 1982. Marked by clarity of argument and rich historical detail; reviews the struggles of blacks and women over the past century. Uses a materialist analysis of history and assigns a central focus to the experiences of women of color.

BOWLES, GLORIA, and RENATE DUELLI-KLEIN, eds. *Theories of Women's Studies*. Boston: Routledge and Kegan Paul, 1983. First published by the women's studies program at UC-Berkeley; examines the nature of women's studies as an academic discipline, feminist research methodologies, and women's studies as a strategy for change. Very helpful bibliographies.

BRUNT, ROSALIND, and CAROLINE ROWAN, eds. *Feminism, Culture, and Politics*. London: Lawrence and Wishart, 1982. British scholars and activists write about the impact of recent historical, psychological, and socioeconomic trends on the women's movement in the United States and Britain. Less theoretical than other works; includes Marxist and lesbian perspectives.

COWARD, ROSALIND. *Patriarchal Precedents: Sexuality and Social Relations*. Boston: Routledge and Kegan Paul, 1983. Deconstructs anthropological debates on kinship to show ideological assumptions: Marxist and Freudian concepts of the family reflect universalist theories of social development, and the idea of patriarchy implies a false dichotomization of individual/family/society. Contemporary male dominance requires an analysis based on sexual identity.

CHARVET, JOHN. *Feminism*. London: J.M. Dent & Sons, 1982. Short collection of source writings divided into now-common ideological categories: individualist, socialist, and radical feminism. Only the last group includes twentieth-century thinkers; not as good as most similar anthologies.

DECKARD, BARBARA SINCLAIR. *The Women's Movement: Political, Socioeconomic, and Psychological Issues*. 3d ed. New York: Harper & Row, 1983. Updated version of a thorough basic text/reference book. Reviews political, social, and psychological status of American women; women's history in early societies, Europe, and the United States; contemporary issues and movements.

DIXON, MARLENE. *The Future of Women*. San Francisco: Synthesis Publications, 1983. Essays, some previously published, from an American Marxist perspective: women in class struggle, the right-wing attack, Chicanas, "bourgeois" bias of socialist and "reactionary" (radical) feminism. Dixon, active in the Democratic Workers' party, gives insight into actual political organizing.

DUNAYEVSKAYA, RAYA. *Rosa Luxemburg, Women's Liberation, and Marx's Philosophy of Revolution*. Sussex, Eng.: Harvester Press, 1982. Carefully documented study of Luxemburg's ideas and activities, with a fresh analysis of Marx's theories of revolution. Discusses Lenin, Hegel; problems of race and class; earlier women's movements.

DWORKIN, ANDREA. *Right-Wing Women*. New York: Coward-McCann, 1983. Strongly worded and perceptive work on the ideology of the ultraright; why and how some women have chosen to adopt these values for protection from male exploitation.

EISENSTEIN, HESTER. *Contemporary Feminist Thought*. Boston: G.K. Hall, 1983. History of ideas, grouped by phases of development from ca. 1970 on. I: Foundation of de Beauvoir and Friedan (e.g., Millett, Firestone, Brownmiller, Rosaldo); II: Development of woman-centered perspective (Lerner, Rich, Chesler, Chodorow, Griffin, etc.); III: Reaction to extremes of phase II, current conflicts in theory (Daly, Griffin, Dworkin, others). Excellent overview and guide to further readings.

FINCH, JANET, and DULCIE GROVES, eds. *A Labour of Love: Women, Work, and Caring*. Boston: Routledge and Kegan Paul, 1983. Essays on the social context of caring. British views of working women with disabled children, single women, caring for the elderly, the economics of work and caring.

FRYE, MARILYN. *The Politics of Reality: Essays in Feminist Theory*. Trumansburg, N.Y.: Crossing Press, 1983. Lesbian-feminist philosopher's world view as it evolved from 1974 to 1981. Important, flowing ideas on oppression, arrogance, love, anger, separatism, racism, all linked with the metaphor of seeing.

GAMARNIKOW, EVA, DAVID MORGAN, JUNE PURVIS, and DAPHNE TAYLORSON. *The Public and the Private.* Exeter, N.H.: Heinemann, 1983. From the 1982 Gender and Society Conference. Challenging the division of society into gendered spheres, papers look at war and violence, caring, the sexual division of labor, ideologies of reproduction, bias in sociological research.

HARTSOCK, NANCY C.M. *Money, Sex, and Power: Toward a Feminist Historical Materialism.* New York: Longman, 1983. Theories of economics, individual behavior, community, and domination as applied to gender roles, the division of labor, sexuality, class, and power. Sophisticated construction interweaving history, economics, anthropology, sociology, and politics.

HESCHEL, SUSANNAH, ed. *On Being a Jewish Feminist.* New York: Schocken Books, 1983. Historical and contemporary directions for women in Judaism: myths and stereotypes, the Jewish family, Jewish lesbians, women rabbis. Posits elements of a feminist theology of Judaism, Jewish-feminist poetics.

JAGGAR, ALISON M. *Feminist Politics and Human Nature.* Totowa, N.J.: Rowman & Allanheld, 1983. A lengthy work analyzing feminist theories of politics and human nature as voiced by the main branches of feminist thought. Noting how feminist theory transforms the central questions and paradigms, the author supports a socialist-feminist view (as distinct from Marxism).

KELLER, EVELYN FOX. *A Feeling for the Organism: The Life and Work of Barbara McClintock.* San Francisco: W.H. Freeman, 1983. Fascinating book on the 1983 Nobel Prize winner. Keller, a noted feminist philosopher of science, beat the Nobel Committee to the punch in seeing the importance of McClintock's work in genetics and the lack of recognition by the scientific establishment.

KEOHANE, NANNERL O., MICHELLE Z. ROSALDO, and BARBARA C. GELPI. *Feminist Theory: A Critique of Ideology.* Chicago: University of Chicago Press, 1982. Another collection from *Signs* (see Abel, above), this includes more works on the impact of feminism and gender studies on politics, literature, history, philosophy, and social institutions. Great insights from MacKinnon, Kristeva, Zillah Eisenstein, Evelyn Keller, Susan Griffin, Jane Marcus, and others.

LESNOFF-CARAVIGLIA, GARI, ed. *The World of the Older Woman.* New York: Human Sciences Press, 1983. An anthology that critically examines attitudes about older women from a multidisciplinary perspective: legal issues, violence, employment, social status, life in institutions, aloneness.

LOWE, MARIAN, and RUTH HUBBARD, eds. *Woman's Nature: Rationalizations of Inequality.* New York: Pergamon Press, 1983. Closely focused essays on aspects of the role of science in creating and reinforcing myths about women; the political and social impact of these myths, especially on black and Native American women; analyses of male dominance, the division of labor, the dialectic of biology and culture, the false assumption of scientific objectivity.

MacKINNON, CATHERINE A. "Feminism, Marxism, Method, and the State: Toward a Feminist Jurisprudence." *Signs: Journal of Women in Culture and Society* 8, no. 4:635–58. Part II of a major theoretical work; part I (*Signs* 7, no. 3) is reprinted in Abel, above; part II is in Keohane, Rosaldo, and Gelpi. Profound, intricate critique of legal institutions and philosophy; epistemology and politics of sexual objectification. Asserts radical feminist methodology for defining and validating women's experiences.

McALLISTER, PAM, ed. *Reweaving the Web of Life: Feminism and Nonviolence.* Philadelphia: New Society Publishers, 1982. Anthology of essays, poetry, narratives. Section on theory discusses war, patriarchy, resistance, spirituality, sexuality; specific examples of struggle include the draft, tax resistance, antinuclear protest, racism, abortion.

McELROY, WENDY, ed. *Freedom, Feminism, and the State: An Overview of Individualist Feminism.* Washington, D.C.: Cato Institute, 1982. Essays examining historical context and current issues of libertarian feminism. Examines oppression and government intrusion in such areas as the institution of marriage, abortion, trade unions, protective legislation, religion, war, voting. How government has hindered women; new directions for strategy.

McMILLAN, CAROL. *Women, Reason, and Nature: Some Philosophical Problems with Feminism.* Princeton, N.J.: Princeton University Press, 1982. Disputes what she claims are feminist assumptions that the sexes are equal; supports the value of traditional role divisions. Does not move away from a dichotomous world view; posits a "liberated sexuality" wherein women enjoy their procreative nature and are valued for it, to end rationality's alienation from nature.

MIDGLEY, MARY, and JUDITH HUGHES. *Women's Choices: Philosophical Problems Facing Feminism.* New York: St. Martin's Press, 1983. A well-written, straightforward analysis of the various ideologies underlying feminist thought; why these conflict and lead to false dichotomies and oversimplification. Outlines choices women face both in theory (e.g., difference vs. equality, individual vs. community) and practice (such as sexual morality, work and family, male violence).

MURRAY, MEG McGAVRAN, ed. *Face to Face: Fathers, Mothers, Masters, Monsters: Essays for a Nonsexist Future.* Westport, Conn.: Greenwood Press, 1983. Articles on the social construct of the father role and its corollary, women as nurturers in public and private. Topics: myth and religion, psychology, sexism in the work place, the "good provider" role, women in foreign service and politics.

POSTOW, BETSY C. *Women, Philosophy, and Sport: A Collection of New Essays.* Metuchen, N.J.: Scarecrow Press, 1983. Covers issues of fairness for women and girls in sports, the nature and role of competition, judicial and legislative aspects of gender equity, impact of the media, psychology of sports, teaching physical education for girls.

RADL, SHIRLEY ROGERS. *The Invisible Woman: Target of the Religious New Right.* Probes connections between big business and religious groups to reveal threats to women's basic economic, political, and social rights.

REINHARZ, SHULAMIT, MARTI BOMBYK, and JANET WRIGHT. "Methodological Issues in Feminist Research: A Bibliography of Literature in Women's Studies, Sociology, and Psychology." *Women's Studies International Forum* 6, no. 4:437–54. Sections on general feminist theory, access to publishing and research, ignored topics and data, racist and sexist biases in research, cognitive styles of men and women, women's experience as researchers.

ROSSITER, MARGARET. *Women Scientists in America: Struggles and Strategies to 1940.* Baltimore, Md.: Johns Hopkins Press, 1982. Well-written account of how the system excludes women and disregards or appropriates their work. Struggles of individual women; critique of the nature of scientific enterprise. Despite cut-off date, most is still applicable to women today.

ROTHSCHILD, JOAN, ed. *Machina ex Dea: Feminist Perspectives on Technology.*

New York: Pergamon Press, 1983. Disparate group of essays in history and social criticism. Covers household technology, reproductive technology, technology and social change. E. Fox Keller writes on the myths that support science as a masculine domain.

SAYERS, JANET. *Biological Politics: Feminist and Anti-feminist Perspectives.* New York: Tavistock, 1982. Reviews nineteenth- and twentieth-century conventional and feminist explanations of sex differences; how social and ideological factors affect understanding of biology. She takes the position that sex differences result neither totally from biology nor totally from socialization.

SPENDER, DALE, ed. *Feminist Theorists: Three Centuries of Key Women Thinkers.* New York: Pantheon, 1983. Original biographies of twenty-one writers on feminism. Includes major writers (Wollstonecraft, M. Fuller, Lucy Stone, Gilman, Beard, de Beauvoir, Woolf) and minor writers (Behn, Astell, O. Schreiner, Brittain, Matilda Gage, Hedwig Dohm), with summarizing chapter on contemporary thinkers.

STANLEY, LIZ, and SUE WISE. *Breaking Out: Feminist Consciousness and Feminist Research.* Boston: Routledge and Kegan Paul, 1983. Critique of social science research theory and methods. Stating need for new approaches, returns to earlier women's movement emphasis on "the personal": validate use of experience, stop downgrading the subjective, remove elitism from the practice of research. Not so much a blueprint as a position piece.

STEINEM, GLORIA. *Outrageous Acts and Everyday Rebellions.* New York: Holt, Rinehart and Winston. 1983. Steinem's first book is mostly reprints from *Ms.* magazine, showing a progression in her attitudes over a twenty-year span. Essays on various personalities, events, the media; witty and stringent critique of social and political institutions.

TREBILCOT, JOYCE, ed. *Mothering: Essays in Feminist Theory.* Totowa, N.J.: Rowman and Allanheld, 1983. Reflecting the nature of feminist theory, the book is organized into (1) aspects of the practical issues of who cares for children and how; (2) theories of patriarchy, feminist values, and a critique of the desirability of motherhood. Many probing questions are asked from a variety of perspectives.

VETTERLING-BRAGGIN, MARY, ed. *"Femininity," "Masculinity," and "Androgyny": A Modern Philosophical Discussion.* Totowa, N.J.: Littlefield, Adams, 1982. Anthology on the nature, origin, and politics of sex roles; concepts of androgyny in philosophy and psychology; sex equality in specific areas such as sports, family, education. Similar to Andersen, Sayers.

WEINBAUM, BATYA. *Pictures of Patriarchy.* Boston: South End Press, 1983. Sees patriarchal kinship structures replicated in social institutions, even within Marxist revolutionary movements. Uses these "kin categories" to develop radical feminist theories about work, sexuality, economic power.

ZAK, MICHELE WENDER. *Women and the Politics of Culture.* New York: Longman, 1983. Focus is on aspects of the "sexual economy": patriarchy and sex roles, women in the marketplace, ideas and origins of feminist movements. Source documents and bibliographies make it useful as a textbook.

ZIMMERMAN, JAN, ed. *The Technological Woman: Interfacing with Tomorrow.* New York: Praeger, 1983. Short diverse articles on technology and culture, women inventors, history of science; household technology, transportation, energy, urban design; computers in the work place, women in high-tech industries; reproductive technology, science fiction, future conflicts.

Contributors

Sarah M. Pritchard is the reference specialist in women's studies at the Library of Congress, where she has worked since 1977. She is responsible for research, bibliography, and collection development in this field, and is also known for her work with the library's computer systems. She is the author of "Library of Congress Resources for the Study of Women," in *Women in Special Collections* (New York: Haworth Press, 1984), "SCORPIO: A Study of Public Users of the Library of Congress Information System" (*Resources in Education*, July 1981), and other similar articles and reviews. She has graduate degrees in French and in library science from the University of Wisconsin, and is active in a number of organizations related to women's studies, librarianship, and feminist politics.

Adriane Fugh-Berman is a member of the *off our backs* collective and has written on health issues for four years. She has worked as a counselor in reproductive health clinics and is currently in medical school.

Cynthia E. Harrison is deputy director of Project '87, a joint effort of the American Historical Association and the American Political Science Association to support educational, scholarly, and public programs about the U.S. Constitution. In addition to compiling two reference books on women, she has published articles on women and politics in the Truman and Kennedy presidencies and is now at work on a manuscript concerning federal policy regarding women in the period between World War II and the beginning of the women's movement. She received a Ph.D. in American history from Columbia University.

Elaine Bell Kaplan, a graduate student in sociology at the University of California, Berkeley, is planning to write her dissertation on the emerging modern black woman's family and work experience. She is cofounder of the Berkeley Women of Color Collective, and assistant editor for *Women's Stud-*

ies International Forum. Her article, "I Want the Same Kind of Respect: A Black Working Woman Talks about Issues of Equality in Her Life," will be published in a forthcoming issue of *Feminist Issues*.

Susan Shurberg Klein has been involved in extensive volunteer activities focusing on women and education as the chair of the American Educational Research Association, Women's Committee; as the chair of the AERA Special Interest Group, Research on Women and Education; as a member of the Executive Council of the Federation of Organizations for Professional Women; and as a representative to the National Coalition for Women and Girls in Education. She is the editor, author, or coauthor of numerous publications, notably the AERA-sponsored *Handbook for Achieving Sex Equity through Education*, an article on equity for the *Encyclopedia of Educational Research*, "What's Left of Federal Funding for Sex Equity in Education," and "Achieving Sex Equity in Education: A Comparison at the Pre and Postsecondary Levels." A senior research associate at the National Institute of Education, NIE, in the U.S. Department of Education, she received her doctorate in educational psychology in 1970 from Temple University.

Jacquelyn Marie works as a reference librarian at University of California, Santa Cruz. She has provided library and research instruction for many students in women's studies classes. She also writes essays and book reviews on women's issues for various women's publications, including *Women Library Workers Journal*. She has a long-standing interest in issues concerning women of color.

Mary O'Callaghan, R.S.C.J., is a researcher and legislative consultant on human rights, peace, U.S. aid policy, and women's issues. She holds a Ph.D. in history and political science from the University of California, Berkeley, and went on to study at Yale and the Union Theological Seminary. She has taught at Xavier University (New Orleans), Maryville College, San Francisco College for Women, and the American University's Institute for Learning in Retirement. She has also taught at St. Joseph's Teacher Training College and Katigondo Seminary in Uganda.

Sara E. Rix, who holds a Ph.D. in sociology from the University of Virginia, is director of research at the Women's Research and Education Institute (WREI) of the Congressional Caucus for Women's Issues. Before coming to WREI, she was a research scientist specializing in national and international aging issues. Her research interests focus on employment and retirement policy.

Judith Schwarz is a co-coordinator of the Lesbian Herstory Archives and the Lesbian Herstory Educational Foundation, as well as cofounder of Lesbian Heritage/D.C. She was consulting editor for the *Frontiers: Journal of Women*

Studies lesbian history issue in Fall 1979. Her continuing research into the lives and political activities of the Heterodoxy Club has resulted in a book and traveling slide show called *Radical Feminists of Heterodoxy: Greenwich Village, 1912–1940* (Lebanon, N.H.: New Victoria Press, 1982). Her research and teaching interests include single women and lesbians from 1800 to the present, the lives of physically challenged women, and long-term lesbian friendships and relationships. Her M.A. in women's studies and social science is from San José State University (1977).

Hilda L. Smith received her doctorate in English history from the University of Chicago in 1975. The author of *Reason's Disciples: Seventeenth-Century English Feminists* (Urbana: University of Illinois Press, 1982), Smith taught at the University of Maryland from 1973 to 1981, served as acting executive director of the Maryland Humanities Council during 1981 and 1982 and is currently the director of the Humanities and Schools Project, Council of Chief State School Officers, Washington, D.C. In addition to *Reason's Disciples*, she has written articles in the area of women's history and has cochaired the Coordinating Committee on Women in the Historical Profession and the Conference Group on Women's History.

Anne J. Stone, a mid-life reentry worker, joined the staff in 1974 of then-U.S. Congresswoman Elizabeth Holtzman, who gave high priority to issues of significance to women and was one of the founders of the Congresswomen's Caucus. Since coming to the Women's Research and Education Institute in 1981 where she is now associate research director, Stone has authored and coauthored policy papers on various subjects, including employment and unemployment issues for women.

Sarah Barbara Watstein is social sciences/documents reference librarian at the Bobst Library, New York University. Educated at Northwestern University and at UCLA, she is active in professional associations related to librarianship and to women's issues. Her free-lance writing covers such areas as materials and methods for educational research, and burn-out in service professions. She is currently completing a master's degree in public administration at NYU with a specialization in human resources. In New York, she has participated in "Take Back the Night" organizing and is currently a crisis counselor with New York Women Against Rape.

Helen R. Wheeler teaches library science at the University of California and women's studies at community colleges; her consulting focuses on gender equity and media in academe. *Womanhood Media* (the title of one of her books) is her nonprofit pathfinder service for researchers. She holds a B.A. from Barnard College, an M.A. in social sciences from University of Chicago, an M.S. in library science from Columbia University, and a doctorate in curriculum and teaching from Teachers College.

Index

Abel, Elizabeth, 64
Affirmative Action and Equal
  Educational Opportunity Plan
  (Philadelphia), 15
Against Sadomasochism (Linden et al.), 113,
  172
Aging Lesbians and Gay Men (Wolf), 115
Aguiar, Neuma, 96
AIDS (acquired immune deficiency
  syndrome), 31, 42–43
Alcott, Louisa May, 64
Aldridge, Sarah, 116
Allen, Paula Gunn, 188
All the Women Are White . . . (Hull et
  al.), 22–23, 194
American Couples (Blumstein and
  Schwartz), 174
American Educational Research
  Association, 18
American Women Composers before 1870
  (Tick), 74
American Women Writers (Duke et al.), 64
Anderson, Laurie, 135
*Annotated Guide to Women's Periodicals in
  the U.S.*, 126
Ashe, Arthur, 91
Asian American women, 110, 111,
  187–201
August (Rossner), 176

Bailey, Adriene Y., 16
Bailey, Susan, 16, 71
Barnes, Djuna, 117
Barnet, Richard, 86
Barr, Marlene, 64
Bauman, Batya, 111
Beach, Sylvia, 117
Beauvoir, Simone de, 73
Beddoe, Deirdre, 70
Belafonte, Harry, 91
Bell, Linda A., 73

Bell, Susan G., 70
Bell, T., 15
Bem, Sandra, 169–70
Bendectin, 36
Bernard, Jessie, 71
Berube, Allen, 117
Best, Raphaela, 19
Between Ourselves (Payne), 71
Beyond Domination (Gould), 72–73
Bibliofem, 130
Biklen, Sari, 16
Birtha, Becky, 110
birth control, 33–38, 43–44
Black Lesbians (Roberts), 116
Blackwell, Antoinette Brown, 69
black women, 44–45, 47, 65, 71, 74, 110,
  187–201
Black Women's Health Conference,
  44–45
Black Women Writers at Work (Tate), 195
Bloch, Alice, 111, 115
Bob Jones University, 11
Boerma, A., 84
Bornstein, Diane, 64, 65
Boserup, Ester, 82
Boston Women's Health Book Collective,
  44
Boulding, Elise, 82, 83
Bound by Love (Gilbert and Webster), 173
Boyd, Lois A., 68, 69
Brackenridge, R.D., 68, 69
Brenzel, Barbara, 68, 69
Brinker, Ann, 116
Brown, Rita Mae, 111, 116
Brown, William Wells, 65
Buhle, Mari Jo, 70
Bunch, Charlotte, 115
Butler, Elizabeth T., 74

Caldicott, Helen, 93–94
Cancer Journals, The (Lorde), 115

Carter, Jimmy, 89, 149
Cassatt, Mary, 74
Cather, Willa, 63, 64, 117
Center for Science in the Public Interest, 47
Central High School for Girls (Philadelphia), 11–12
Chamberlain, Mary, 68, 69
Changing Boundaries (Allgeier and McCormick), 172
Chavez, Linda, 151
Children's Television Workshop, 20
Chodorow, Nancy, 180
Chopin, Kate, 63, 64
Choy, Christine, 133
Christian, Barbara, 195
Churchill, Caryl, 135
City of Hermits, The (Covina), 116
Clarke, Cheryl, 110
Classroom Climate, The (Hall and Sandler), 19
Cleveland Plain Dealer, 125
Coffin Tree, The (Law-Yone), 187
Color Purple, The (Walker), 110, 190–91
Comedy and the Woman Writer (Little), 64, 65
Coming to Power (Samois), 112, 172
Common Lives/Lesbian Lives, 108, 115–16
Concerns, 23
Cooney, Rosemary, 189
Cordova, Teresa, 193
Cornwall, Anita, 110
Covered Wagon Women (Holms), 71
Cowan, Ruth S., 68
Craft, Christine, 125
Cruikshank, Margaret, 116
Cuentos (Gomez et al.), 110
Cunningham, Myrna, 91

Dallenbach-Hellweg, Gisela, 43
Daughters of the State (Brenzel), 68
Davis, Angela, 191–92
Davis, Elizabeth Gould, 130
Decades of Discontent (Scharf and Jensen), 71
Deere, Carmen, 82
Delany, Martin R., 65
Dellums, Ron, 91–92
D'Emilio, John, 117
Depo-Provera, 43–44
Detroit News, 125
Dickinson, Emily, 61, 62, 64
Diehl, Joanne Feit, 62
Dill, Bonnie Thornton, 192

Ding, Loni, 191
Discipline and Punishment (Foucault), 65
Discovering Reality (Harding and Hintikka), 72, 73
Discovering Women's History (Beddoe), 70
Dobson, Joanne A., 62
Dole, Elizabeth, 148
Donovan, Josephine, 64
Dunn, Nell, 135
Dykewomon, Elana, 111

Edel, Deborah, 111
Educational Testing Service, 19
Ehrenreich, Barbara, 86
Eisenstein, Sarah, 71
Eliot, George, 63
Enter, 20
Entre Nous (Kurys), 173–74
Equal Rights Amendment, 11–12, 89, 124, 145–46, 148, 151, 155
Espinoza, Sanchez, 91

Faderman, Lillian, 117
Falk, Joyce Duncan, 71
Family Planning Perspectives, 32, 34, 37
Feinstein, Dianne, 160
Feldman, Maxine, 111
Feminist Critics Read Emily Dickinson (Juhasz), 61, 62
Feminist Periodicals, 125
Feminist Studies, 67, 72
Fenwomen (Chamberlain), 68, 69
Fight Back (Delacoste), 114
Financier, 212
Finger, Anne, 46
First Conference on Midlife and Older Women, 46
Flowers in Salt (Siever), 68, 70
Foat, Ginny, 125, 137
Folbre, Nancy, 67
For Us Women Newsletter, 126
Foster, Jeannette, 109, 116
Foucault, M., 65
Fowler, Mark, 132
Fox-Genovese, Elizabeth, 70
Frances (film), 176
Fraser, Arvonne, 82–83
French Historical Studies, 71
Friedan, Betty, 64
Frye, Marilyn, 115
Fuentes, Annette, 86
Fund for the Improvement of Postsecondary Education, 14

Garr, Teri, 167
Gay American History (Katz), 117
Gay Community News, 46
Gay/Lesbian Almanac (Katz), 117
Gay Task Force (ALA), 108
Gelfand, Elissa, 65
Gilbert, Sandra M., 62
Gilligan, Carol, 16
Gilman, Charlotte Perkins, 67, 73
Give Us Bread But Give Us Roses
  (Eisenstein), 71
Glasgow, Ellen, 63, 64
Glubka, Shirley, 67
Going Public with Our Vision (Bunch), 115
Goldsmith, Judy, 152, 156, 159
Good, Barbara, 83
Gould, Carol C., 73
Grahn, Judy, 111
Green, Harvey, 68
Green, Mildred D., 74
Greenberg, Selma, 22
Griffin, Susan, 64
Grossberg, Michael, 67

Hahn, Carole, 21
Hamer, Fannie Lou, 190
*Handbook for Achieving Sex Equity through
  Education* (Klein), 15
Handy, D. Antoinette, 74
Harding, Sandra, 72, 73
Harjo, Joy, 111
Harrison, Beverly, 37–38
Hartsock, Nancy, 73
Haskell, Molly, 133
Hatch, Orrin, 37, 155
Hatem, Mervet, 96
Havemeyer, L., 74
Hawthorne, Nathaniel, 65
H.D. (Hilda Doolittle), 64
Health and Medicine News, 43
Health Research Group, 33
Hearts of Men, The (Ehrenreich), 177
Heckler, Margaret, 148, 153–54
Hellman, Lillian, 117
Helms, Jesse, 158
Heresies, 112
Her Immaculate Hand (King and Rabil), 71
Herzog, Kristen, 64, 65
Hintikka, Merrill B., 72, 73
Hirsch, M., 64
Hishon, E. A., 157
Hispanic women, 45, 71, 110, 187–201
Hite, Shere, 32
Holladay, Wilhelmina, 134

Holm, Jeanne, 216
Holms, Kenneth, 71
Homans, Margaret, 62
Honegger, Barbara, 151
Hooks, Bell, 95
Hosker, Fran, 85
Hubbard, Ruth, 32
Huber, Joan, 210
Huf, Linda, 63
Hull, Gloria, 110
Hunter College Women's Studies
  Collective, 22

Ikon, 126
Images of Ourselves, 115
Imagination in Confinement, 65
I Never Told Anyone (Bass and Thornton),
  178
Institute for Policy Studies, 86
International Alliance of Women, 93
International Women's Council, 93
Invisible Women (Spender), 16
Isabell, Sharon, 111
I thought People Like That Killed Themselves,
  116

Jackson, Jesse, 159
JAMA, 40, 42, 47
Jane Eyre, 65
Jardine, Lisa, 61, 62–63
JEB (Joan E. Biren), 117, 118
Jensen, Joan M., 71
Job Training Partnership Act, 13–14
Johnson, Marilyn, 181
Johnson, Sonia, 160
Johnston, Jill, 117
Jones, Bessie, 191
Jordan, Barbara, 64
Journal of American History, 66, 71–72
Journal of Family History, 72
Journal of Social History, 66, 67, 72
Journey to Fulfillment (Taylor), 116
Juhasz, Suzanne, 61, 62
Jump Cut, 137

Kahlo, Frida, 117
Kaplan, Deborah, 32
Katz, J., 117
Katzman, M., 68
Kaye, Melanie, 111
Keeper of Accounts (Klepfisz), 111
Keller, Karl, 62
Kelly, Joan, 62
Kennedy, John F., 82, 94, 160

Kim, Elaine, 195
King, M. C., 71
King's Wife in the Early Middle Ages, The
 (Stafford), 68
Kirkpatrick, Jeane, 149
Kitchen Table Press, 110
Kitzinger, Sheila, 172
Kleinbaum, Abby W., 68, 69
Klepfisz, I., 111
Kurys, Diane, 173–74

Lady in the Tower, The (Bornstein), 64, 65
Lancet, 34
Law-Yone, Wendy, 187
League of Women Voters, 132
Learning Our Way (Bunch and Pollack),
 16
Leavitt, Judith, 67
Lesbian Connections, 108
Lesbian Health Matters! (O'Donnell et al.),
 115
Lesbian Herstory Archives, 111
Lesbian Mothers and Their Children
 (Thomas), 114
Lesbian Poetry: An Anthology (Larkin), 117
Lesbian Sex Mafia, 113
Lesbian Studies (Cruikshank), 116
lesbian women, 45, 65, 107–23, 172, 190
Lessing, Doris, 65
Letters of Margaret Fuller, The (Hudspeth),
 64
Levenstein, Harvey, 67
Lianna (Sayles), 174
Lifetime Guarantee (Bloch), 115
Lim, Linda, 96
Little, Judy, 64, 65
Little Women, 65
Lockheed, Marlaine, 19
Loo, Chalsa, 188
Look Me in the Eye (Rich et al.), 115
Lorde, Audre, 110, 115, 190
Lowell, Robert, 63
Lutz, Bertha, 87

Mae West Is Dead (Jones), 116
Male Couple, The (McWhirter and
 Mattison), 175
Malpede, Karen, 135
Manderson, Lenore, 95
Mansfield, Katherine, 62
Marcus, Jane, 61, 62
Marshall, Joan K., 129
Marshall, Ray, 205
Marshall, Rosalind K., 68, 70

Martineau, Harriet, 71
McAdoo, Harriet, 189
McAllister, Pam, 115
McCarthy, Mary, 63
McClendon, Sarah, 125, 216
McDaniel, Judith, 117
Media Report to Women, 128
Medicine, Beatrice, 188
Melville, Herman, 65
Midwifery Litigators Network, 38
Midwives Alliance of North America, 38
Miller, Christine, 62
Mitchell, Juliet, 180
Mondale, Walter, 159–60
Monthly Vital Statistics Report, 45
Moran, Mary, 18
More Work for Mother (Cowan), 68
Morris, Adalaide, 62
Morrison, Toni, 194
Motherbound (Johnston), 117
Mother Jones, 117, 136
Mott, Lucretia, 64
Movement in Black (Parker), 117
Moynihan, Ruth B., 69
Ms., 16, 32, 179
Mujeres en Marcha, 193

National Assessment of Educational
 Progress, 21
National Association for Lesbian and
 Gay Gerontology, 115
National Council for Social Studies, 21
National Family Planning and
 Reproductive Health Association, 38
National Institute of Education, 19
National Organization for Women
 (NOW), 128, 152, 156, 159
National Science Foundation, 14, 20
National Women's Health Network, 35,
 47
National Women's Studies Association,
 96
Native American women, 45, 65, 110,
 111, 187–201
Naylor, Gloria, 191
Nestle, Joan, 111, 113
New Alexandria Lesbian Library, 114
New Directions for News (East), 124
New England Local Color Literature (Barr
 and Smith), 64
New Feminist Essays on Virginia Woolf
 (Marcus), 61–62
New Lesbian Writing (Cruikshank), 116
New Yorker, 176

New York Times, 47, 124, 125, 129, 135, 146, 149, 217
Nice Jewish Girls (Beck), 111
'night, Mother (Norman), 173, 176
Noda, Barbara, 111
Norman, Marsha, 135, 173
Norsigian, Judy, 43
November Woman (McDaniel), 117
Now That You Know (Fairchild and Hayward), 113

Ochs, Carol, 73
O'Connor, Sandra Day, 149, 153, 158
Offer, Karen M., 70
off our backs, 113, 115
O'Keeffe, Georgia, 74
Older Americans Act Nutrition Program, 46
Old Mistresses: Women, Art and Ideology (Parker and Pollock), 74
Oliveros, Pauline, 74
Olympic Committee, U.S., 21
On Being a Jewish Feminist (Heschel), 111
One Teenager in Ten (Heron), 113
O'Neill, Thomas P., 155
Ordonez, Elizabeth, 194–95
Ortiz, Vilma, 189
Ostriker, Alicia, 64
Our Bodies, Ourselves, 124
Our Right to Choose (Harrison), 37–38
Outdoor Woman's Guide, The (Maughan and Collins), 46
Out from Under, 115
Owens, Dona, 160

Papanek, Hanna, 96
Parade, 20
Parents of Gays, 113
Parker, Pat, 110, 117
Parkerson, Michelle, 110, 117
Philosophy of Woman (Mahowald), 73–74
Physicians for Social Responsibility, 93
Picture Bride (Song), 190–91
Plath, Sylvia, 63, 71
Planned Parenthood Federation of North America, 38, 158
Pogrebin, L. C., 32
Politics of Rebirth, The (Frye), 115
Poppe, Terre, 47
Portrait of the Artist as a Young Woman, A (Huf), 63
Powers of Desire (Snitow et al.), 113, 172
Presbyterian Women in America (Boyd and Breckenridge), 68, 69

Psychology of Women Quarterly, 175, 181
Psychology Today, 171

Queens, Concubines and Dowagers (Stafford), 68, 70

Ramey, Estelle, 216
Rankin, Jeanette, 93
Reagan, Ronald, 9–10, 13, 15, 83, 91, 145–47, 148–52, 159, 188–89
Resources for Educational Equity (WEEA), 13
Reuss, Pat, 152
Reweaving the Web of Life (McAllister), 115
Rich, Adrienne, 63, 111
Richardson, Dorothy, 62
Ride, Sally, 202
Rights of Gay People (Boggan), 114
Roark, Paula, 82
Rocking the Cradle (Hanscombe and Forster), 113
Room of One's Own, A (Woolf), 61
Roth, Darlene, 71
Roth, Moira, 135
Rothman, Barbara Katz, 32
Ruckelshaus, Jill, 151
Ruetler, Rosemary R., 73
Russ, Joanna, 63, 66, 127
Ryan, Mary, 69

Sackville-West, Vita, 117
Sadker, David, 19
Sadker, Myra, 19
Saenz de Rodriguez, Carmen, 42
Safa, Helen, 86
SAGE Writings, 115
Sanger, Margaret, 67
Sapphistry (Califia), 112
Say Amen Somebody (Stewart), 191
Scharf, Lois, 71
Schneider, Claudine, 153, 159
Science News, 41
Scotch Verdict (Faderman), 117
Second National Conference on Lesbian and Gay Aging, 46
Seeing and Evaluating People, (Geis et al.), 20
Self Health, 39
Senior Action in a Gay Environment (SAGE), 115
Serving Women, 68
Seven Days a Week (Katzman), 68
Sexism and God-Talk (Ruether), 73

Sex Role Research (Richardson and Wirtenberg), 168
Sex Variant Women in Literature (Foster), 116
Sexual Politics, Sexual Communities (D'Emilio), 117
Sexton, Anne, 63, 64
Shadow on a Tightrope (Schoenfielder and Wieser), 115
Shakespeare, William, 61, 62–63
Shangold, Mona, 46
Sheer Madness (von Trotta), 174
She Had Some Horses (Harjo), 111
Shelley, Martha, 111
Shockley, Ann, 110, 111
SHUN, 114
Siebert, Muriel, 149
Siever, Sharon, 68, 70
Sinister Wisdom, 108, 111
Sinister Women, 112
Silent Knife (Cohen and Estner), 37
Skip Two Periods, 108
Smith, Barbara, 110
Smith, Eleanor, 192
Smith, Mary Louise, 151
Smith, Nicholas, 64
Song, Cathy, 190–91
Sophie's Choice (film), 176
Spark, Muriel, 65
Spender, Dale, 71
Spitze, Glenna, 210
Spivak, Gayatri, 84
Squier, Susan, 62
Stafford, Jean, 65
Stafford, Pauline, 68, 69
Stein, Gertrude, 64
Stephen, Caroline Emelia, 61
Still Harping on Daughters (Jardine), 61, 62–63
Stowe, Harriet Beecher, 64, 65
Sudden Death (Brown), 116
Suga, K., 70
Sula (Morrison), 194
Surpassing the Love of Women (Faderman), 117
Swenson, May, 64

Tate, Claudia, 195
Taylor, Valerie, 116
Terms of Endearment (Brock), 173
There's Always Been a Women's Movement (Spender), 71
13th Moon, 111

This Bridge Called My Back (Moraga and Anzaldua), 110
Thomas, Helen, 125
Tick, Judith, 74
Tinker, Irene, 82
Title IV regulation, 12–13
Title VII regulation, 156–57
Title IX regulation, 10–11, 12, 23, 153
Toothpick House (Lynch), 116
Tootsie (Pollack), 167–68
Trivia, 126
Tsongas, Paul, 155
Tsui, Kitty, 111

Virginia Woolf: A Feminist Slant (Marcus), 61
Virgins and Viragos (Marshall), 68, 70
Vivien, Renee, 116
Vocational Education Act, 13–14
Voices in the Night (McNaron and Morgan), 114
von Gunden, Heidi, 74
Voyage In, The (Abel et al.), 64, 65

Waiting Rooms (Parkerson), 117
Walker, Alice, 110, 190–91
Wall Street Journal, 212
Walsh, Marnie, 195
War Against the Amazons, The (Kleinbaum), 68, 69
Ward, Barbara, 82
Warnicke, Retha, 68, 70
Washington Post, 146
Weddington, Sarah, 89
We Shall Be Heard (Kennedy and O'Shields), 64
Westheimer, Ruth, 171
Westhill Sociology of Education Conference, 16
We've All Got Scars (Best), 19
Wharton, Edith, 64
What Color Is Your Handkerchief? (Samois), 112
What Lesbians Do (Gayle), 112
Whitmire, Kathy, 160
Whittlesey, Faith, 148
Willenz, June, 216
WLW Journal, 131
Wolfe, Sid, 33
Woman Question, The (Helsinger et al.), 70
Woman/Doctor (Patterson and Macdonald), 115
Woman of the Wolf and Other Stories (Vivien), 116

Woman's Experience of Sex (Kitzinger), 172
Woman's Touch (Ceder and Nelly), 112
Woman Who Owned the Shadows, The (Allen), 111
Women Against Pornography, 112, 113
Women and Food Conference, 95
Women and Nature (Griffin), 64
Women & Performance, 135
Women and Spirituality (Ochs), 73
Women and the American Left (Buhle), 70
Women and the British Empire (Bailey), 71
Women & Therapy, 175–76
Women and Utopia (Barr and Smith), 64
Women and Work in the Third World (conference), 96
Women Artists News, 74
Women, Ethnics, and Exotics (Herzog), 64, 65
+ *Women in Libraries*, 131
Women in Theatre (Malpede), 135
Women of Brewster Place (Naylor), 191
Women of the English Renaissance and Reformation (Warnicke), 68, 70
Women, the Family and Freedom (Bell et al.), 70

Women Veterans (Willenz), 216
Women's Action for Nuclear Disarmament, 94
Women's Art Journal, 74
Women's Diaries, 126
Women's Educational Equity Act Program, 12–13
Women's International League for Peace and Freedom, 93
Women's Review of Books, 126
Women's Role in Economic Development (Boserup), 82
Women's Sports Foundation, 21
Women's Yellow Pages, 128
Woo, Merle, 111
Woolf, Virginia, 61–62, 65
Words of a Woman Who Breathes Fire, The (Tsui), 110
Worldwatch Institute, 85
Wright, Frances, 64
Writing Like a Woman (Ostriker), 64

Ybarra, Lea, 188, 193